Curious Journey

KENNETH GRIFFITH
TIMOTHY O'GRADY

CURIOUS JOURNEY

*An Oral History of Ireland's
Unfinished Revolution*

MERCIER PRESS

MERCIER PRESS
PO Box 5, 5 French Church Street, Cork
16 Hume Street, Dublin 2

Trade enquiries to CMD DISTRIBUTION,
55a Spruce Avenue, Stillorgan Industrial Park, Blackrock, Dublin

First published by Hutchinson & Co. (Publishers) Ltd in 1982
This edition published in 1998

© Kenneth Griffith and Timothy O'Grady, 1998

ISBN 185635 212 9

10 9 8 7 6 5 4 3 2 1

ACKNOWLEDGEMENTS

The authors would like to thank the following people for their help, advice or hospitality, as the case may be: Donncha O Murchu, Sean Caffrey, Gerry O'Hare, Marquita Redston (General Sweeney's daughter), Treasa Ni Fhatharta, Jack Bennett, Gery Lawless, Donal Boyle, Philip MacDermot, Marie Kean, Paddy Kuh, Mrs Nora Harling, Pat Harper, Anthony Whittome, Gareth Wynne Jones, Aled Vaughan and the *Curious Journey* film crew, Seamus de Burca, Robert Jagoe, and the O'Sullivan family of Clonakilty, Co. Cork. Warren Forma and John McGuffin, both provided us with additional interview material with Maire Comerford.

Printed in Ireland by Colour Books Ltd.

Contents

Great age held something for me that was awesome. I was much fonder of the old people in the darkness than I was of young people in the daytime. It's at night you're able to get the value of old people. And it was listening to the old people that I got my idea of Irish nationality.

MICHAEL COLLINS

Preface to 1998 Edition

We first interviewed the subjects of this book in the summer of 1976, when the war in the north of Ireland was only a few years old. The book was finally written in 1981, the year of the hunger strikes. These were times of stark political polarity in Ireland.

Now with the book's republication there is a ceasefire and the President of Sinn Féin has met the President of the United States and the Prime Minister of Britain and, most importantly, is in a process of negotiation with the Unionist Party about the future of their island. Perhaps the time of polarity is beginning to pass into the time of synthesis.

All of the subjects of this book are now dead. It was truly a privilege to have known them. Looking at their accounts now it is impossible not to be struck by a strong sense of familiarity – a massive mandate for independence being met alternately with equivocation and repression, Unionists manipulating weak British governments, the terrible cost to everyone involved of living in such close proximity to violence. They believed theirs would be the generation to end the long historical nightmare. But they did not find complete success. They did not find a way either to bring the Unionists with them or to get through the wall of British political self-interest. That is why their revolution can be called 'unfinished', and why they lived with a degree of disappointment and anticlimax and then with a sense of horrified *deja vu* when war again came to their country when they were old. This book is being republished now with the hope by its authors that, among other things, the lessons of their lives may be of value to the present generation and that the efforts of that generation may allow them to rest in peace.

TIMOTHY O'GRADY

Introduction

The first time that I recall hearing about the island of Ireland was when I was nine years old and I heard my grandfather – who was a stonemason – speak about a neighbour named Flynn. My grandfather said, 'He had the roof of his house burnt over his head in Ireland.'

These words marked my memory forcefully. We were in a darkened room and my grandfather's voice carried that tone which is secretive and implies awfulness. Who he was talking to I don't know. Certainly those words about Mr Flynn were not intended to reach my consciousness – but they did!

We were in a little house in the village of Penally in South Pembrokeshire in my country, Wales. Where was Ireland? Why did someone burn a roof over good-hearted Mr Flynn's head? Many years were to go by before I knew the answer, or the approximate answer, to that question. Today, strangely, the man who possibly gave the orders to hustle Mr Flynn off the island of Ireland was, I am proud to claim, a friend of mine: the late Commandant General Thomas Barry. General Tom was in his eighties when he died in 1980, but then, during Mr Flynn's time, towards the beginning of the Anglo-Irish War of 1916–21, he was a twenty-one-year-old guerrilla leader of the Irish Republican Army and the scourge of the British Army in the south of Ireland; particularly around his own patch in County Cork. Mr Flynn, I believe, was associated with the paramilitary, British-paid Royal Irish Constabulary.

In 1952 I travelled to South Africa on the first of many subsequent professional visits. On that occasion I went as an actor to play Oberon in a Tyrone Guthrie production of *A Midsummer Night's Dream* for the Old Vic. While acting in Johannesburg, a friend from my schooldays called me and easily persuaded me to visit him in Ladysmith, Natal. His name was Peter Strong and then he was a remarkable airman who had opened up Basutoland (today's Lesotho) to aircraft penetration. Lesotho is well-nigh totally mountainous.

Peter Strong flew me into Basutoland, which was memorable, but he did me – inadvertently – another good turn: he showed me the defences of Ladysmith which became famous when that little town was besieged during the Second Boer War (1899–1902) and he took me to the battlefields which lie around the place.

It is fascinating to consider – looking back at one's life – what unexpected but deeply significant personal signposts crop up. They may not seem to be life-changing at first sighting; it is only when they *have* changed the course of your life that you realize the momentous junction. 'He had the roof of his house burnt over his head in Ireland,' was one of those signposts for me; later in Natal, with Peter Strong, another was stuck before my eyes. It was an iron cross marking a burial place. The words on it were singularly brief: 'To a brave British soldier.' Well, there wasn't just one iron cross – there were many and, most evocatively, they were scattered across the hills (kopjes they are called in South Africa) and valleys and plains around Ladysmith.

There, in Natal, it was a very significant time for me. Six and a half thousand miles away from his home, somewhere in Britain, were the material remains of an anonymous soldier. All the clichés were there: in a foreign field; under a blazing sun, etc. But I was looking directly at a reality which begged me to answer a very silent question. (Nothing can be more silent than the summit of a dreadful mountain in Natal called Spion Kop. Touch the earth with your boot and you will expose human bones and – to this very day – military ammunition. Most of the bones were bred around Liverpool and the ammunition tended to come from Foreign Secretary Joseph Chamberlain's Birmingham factory or from the Kaiser's Germany.) The silent question was: why did these men have to die, incongruously, here?

Oh, what a question! And though the answer is stark and hideous and shocking and simple, most British people have never even asked for that answer, though it is ever, uncomfortably, under our British noses. That answer is too close and it has been with us for such a long time. And that answer – when it has been given in Britain – has seldom been presented to us as the horrible reality which it is, but instead as an honourable and noble adventure – which it is not. The 'brave British soldier' lies under his iron cross because we wished to extend our British power across other peoples' lands – both 'black' and 'white' lands – in order to increase our national wealth. The soldier died for imperialism.

From that day, in 1952, I began to study the *reality* of Britain – past, present and future. And, of course, all three of these areas of time are inextricably linked together.

As an artist, as a maker of things, I have always seen art as an effective form of communicating a meaningful, comprehensible human statement. And I am not interested in history for history's sake. The past – the glories and crimes of the past – are not going to disturb me particularly, unless they are directly significant and relevant and informative to our present-day questions and problems which, in their turn, point us towards our future.

The dead British soldiers in South Africa have something to say to us today about our hypocritical mouthings towards the Afrikaners of this moment and to the 'black' people of this very moment. Only by considering the *reality* of the roots of all problems can we truly begin to diagnose the disease that is flourishing here and now. Who was the idiot who said, 'Nothing can be learnt from history'? Everything can be learnt from history. Ask a sound doctor who has to diagnose a patient's pain.

But South Africa is not the specific subject of this book. Ireland is the subject of this book. Why have the Irish burnt more than one roof over many people's heads? Well, the answer is precisely the same as in Natal, South Africa: British imperialism. We British began brutalizing our way across the magical island of Ireland eight hundred years ago for imperial, material reasons, and we still have soldiers and civil servants in six of the thirty-two counties of that country to this very day! The reason why the 'brave British soldier' died outside Ladysmith is precisely the same reason why a British soldier will shortly, once again, die outside the city of Derry (and I haven't a direct line to the Provisional IRA). We British are on another people's land and these people *must* object. And they will continue to object. They *must* continue to object.

If there were armed Irish soldiers here in Britain – or German or Russian soldiers for that matter – I would object. Whether I would find the courage to shoot them or put bombs under them I cannot tell. What I do know – what I do suspect (irony upon irony) – is that men like Winston Churchill and Airey Neave and Louis Mountbatten would have found the pugnacity and courage to try to blow the enemy's presence in Britain to kingdom come. And we would regard such men as heroes; we would not call them 'rats' and 'murder gangs'.

Of course the methods of guerrilla fighters against an established army of occupation have always been frightful. They have to be frightful if the guerrillas are to continue fighting the only form of warfare that is open to them. They would prefer to be more evenly matched. The methods of Menachem Begin were different when he led his Irgun Z'vai Le'umi against the British Army in Palestine during the 'mandate' period to the methods his Israeli soldiers employ today. During the forties, Begin hanged British soldiers and blew up the King David Hotel; today his Israeli troops are probably the most ethical and civilized soldiers on the face of this earth.

At this point I would like to reiterate my attitude clearly. When I have met members of the Provisional Irish Republican Army – and I have met them here in Britain, in the Republic of Ireland, in the United States of America and in Canada – I have *always* stated to them at the beginning of our meeting: 'I have reservations about some of your methods,' adding 'of course with all of my capacity for empathy I can never know, wholly, what it must feel like to be an Irishman.' I remember once, in the foyer of Washington (DC) Airport, having uttered those approximate words, an Irishman replying to me: 'Be that as it may, Mr Griffith; where do you want your bags carried to. . . ?'

But I categorically and wholeheartedly support the simple and proper concept of a united Irish republic. There are thirty-two Irish counties on that island and that republic should have thirty-two counties – not an indecent twenty-six!

What about the Protestants of the northeast, personified by the man who has referred to good popes as anti-Christs – my most detested man, Ian Paisley? Well, *what* about the Protestants of the northeast? And I am a Protestant – from Wales.

England – particularly England rather than Britain, because England was the constant seat of imperial avarice – began attempts to destroy the Irish nation a very long time ago; in earnest during the year 1366 with the appalling Statute of Kilkenny. But *our* year, the beginnings of what Ian Paisley, Conor Cruise O'Brien and Enoch Powell apparently stand for, is 1603 – at the end of the Elizabethan conquest of the Irish Province of Ulster. Then began, with terrible determination, the English policy euphemistically called 'the Plantations'. The English imperial concept was simple in essence: it was to annihilate any Irish opposition to England's material ambitions. The native Irish people of Ulster, having been steam-rollered into defeat by a British army – sadly many Welshmen were present as well as Scots – were now disinherited of their land, and then their territory, this Ulster land, was given to the British conquerors – or certainly to the victors – because some supposed Irish traitors who had assisted the British were included amongst the beneficiaries – in today's parlance, the Irish Quislings. But in the main Ulster was given to the British soldiers who had personally ravaged the land and to the English ruling class and to the Lowland Scots (Paisley's forebears) who were to work the land. This was the evil beginning of today's Protestant dominance of six counties in Ulster. It has been estimated that this brutal policy of the English drove something like two million young Irishmen off their small island during the following two hundred years. And I, as a Brit, and therefore answerable for the British in Ireland today, object with all of the energy that I have. And these cruel historical facts, repeated here, are basically the reasons for the formation and indeed the present existence of the Irish Republican Army. This fact is probably indigestible to large sections of our present-day British Establishment – but face and accept that fact they must – and will, in painful due course. And I disrespectfully suggest to our succeeding governments – 'Conservative' or 'Labour' – that the sooner they face this truth in depth, the more peaceful the future will be.

British 'Liberals' personified by William Ewart Gladstone recognized the truth about Britain in Ireland long ago and they determined to remove our presence from the Irish island. In 1886 Gladstone proposed his first Home Rule (for Ireland) Bill and immediately the sinister operation (legal, through the House of Lords – and illegal, through the coercion of Irish people by British material vested interests) began. The English ruling class – well represented in the House of Lords – now owned much of Ireland and therefore much of Ulster.

The great hope of ethical Britain, Gladstone, raised his proper banner for a free Ireland and was immediately countered by the wretched Lord Randolph Churchill, who, though incipiently deranged (by syphilis, it is believed), knew exactly and instinctively where to strike. Randolph Churchill (father of Winston) said, 'I decided some time ago that if the GOM ['Grand Old Man' as Gladstone was called] went for Home Rule [for Ireland], the Orange card [Scottish-Irish Protestantism – imported during the Plantations] would be the one to play.' Randolph Churchill, for the sake of British imperialism, began to rebeat the rallying Orange Protestant drum to create the awful sectarian division between the Protestant and the native Irish Catholics. There was, of course, an immediate pogrom by the Protestants against the Catholics; the 'Orange card' was 'the one to play if you wanted strife in Ulster'. And we are still suffering from Randolph Churchill's evil inclination at this moment. Also his son, Winston, was a fairly constant enemy of the Irish people – and he was no friend to my people, the Welsh, either – except when he undertook his natural role of warlord and led us collectively against the German warlord, Adolf Hitler. I thank him for that; but for nothing else!

The tug of war in Britain for Irish independence was nonstop – between the truly Liberal spirits who wished to right the ancient wrong and the truly Tory/Conservative spirits who wished to perpetuate the colonial status of Ireland.

In 1913 the Liberals were initially victorious: a Home Rule Bill for Ireland was steered through the House of Commons only to be rejected by the retrograde House of Lords. But the Lords could only *delay* freedom for Ireland, and that fact – the legal inevitability of Home Rule – proved to be the cue for the Scottish–Irish landowning class personified by Sir Edward Carson and Captain James Craig (later to become Lord Craigavon) to take illegal, treasonable action to prevent a united 'Home-ruling' Ireland. And illegal, treasonable action which Britain was to allow to succeed without punishing either Carson or Craig; indeed Britain was to honour them.

On 28 September 1912, Carson and Craig had organized what they called Ulster Day and began signing the 'Ulster Covenant' which was inspired by the 'Scots Covenant' of the early seventeenth century – their mentality had sped to where their granite cold roots lay in Scotland. The Ulster Covenant was an oath to oppose the Irish Home Rule Bill which had been passed through the House of Commons. On top of that, Edward Carson began to buy guns from Germany to arm his Scottish–Irish Protestant followers, guns to be used against the democratic legality of the British House of Commons. That is the truth about the quality of the Union flag-waving Scottish–Irish Protestants of the northeast of Ireland – even to this very day.

In answer to this assault on the democratic structure of Britain – by the Scottish–Irish Protestants living mainly in northeastern Ireland – the Irish–Irish gathered in Dublin and formed the Irish Volunteers, the forerunners of the Irish Republican Army. And they in their turn imported into Dublin a small quantity of guns – the importation of which was more forcibly opposed by the British than the British opposed the large-scale arming of the Protestants by Carson and Craig in the northeast. From that time the shrewder Irish–Irish people knew the reality of Britain's quality. They knew that they would have to fight for freedom – as Irish people have regularly done for the past eight hundred years. Constitutional methods were not going to stand much of a chance, any more than fair play!

Then it was rumoured that the Scottish–Irish Protestants in Ulster, led by Carson and Craig, planned to raid the British Army's armouries in that province of Ulster. This was too much even for the greying London administration and they ordered elements of the British Army occupying the 'south' of Ireland to move northward to oppose this act of rebellion by the Scottish–Irish Protestants.

This deadly serious British military order – provoked by Carson and Craig and backed by an easily stimulated Protestant proletariat, who were screaming to play Randolph Churchill's 'Orange card' – was met by a degenerate mutiny of British officers stationed at the old British military centre in Ireland, the Curragh.

This mutiny was organized by Brigadier General Gough – later, in the 1914–18 war to be well known as 'Bloody' Gough because of his habit of throwing battalions of British soldiers into hopeless advances and massive death. The other two leading mutineers were General Henry Wilson (who was later to be executed by the Irish Republican Army) and General Sir John French. All three were Anglo-Irishmen; that is, Englishmen whose families had secured Irish land for past imperial services rendered.

These three senior British officers threatened to resign their commissions if they were ordered to act against their fellow Protestants in the northeast of Ireland, even though they were being ordered by their democratically elected home government. It should be borne in mind that these three reprehensible characters – who had, of course, recruited many other British officers of a similar class – belonged to the Anglo-Irish land-owning 'ascendancy'. Even with senior British military officers, vested material interests overrode the integrity of constitutional behaviour.

Of course, it was the eve of the 1914–18 war; the British government shamefully gave way. None of these guilty men were so much as arrested; indeed none were relieved of their commissions. The overwhelming majority of Britons must face the old chestnut that there is one rule for them and another for us.

The Irish Volunteers could only wait. And they waited till Easter time, 1916. And that year is where our particular story really begins.

A few years ago I was invited by Lord Grade's ATV Network Ltd to make a film on a subject of my own choosing. After seeing that iron cross in memory of 'a brave British soldier' in South Africa, which sight had stimulated me towards inquiring anger, I had begun to alter the course of my professional life. I began to ease away from being an actor towards researching the truth about our British past and then making films for television which would communicate what I had learnt and then felt. For ATV I decided to organize a film which would communicate to the British viewer the truth about our terrible role in Ireland. I decided to do this by relating the life of perhaps the greatest – and certainly the most successful – Irish patriot: Michael Collins.

Michael Collins began to appear on the Irish activist scene during the Easter Rebellion; he was a junior officer inside the famous General Post Office in Dublin which was the rebellion's headquarters. I believed that if I told the story of this man's life from birth to his early death, I would be necessarily *explaining* to the British viewer the *reasons*, the *facts* that had compelled this good, hard-working young boy to become the most brilliant, unshiftable activist leader that Ireland has ever produced.

It was a wise choice on my part. His life was such a magnificently shaped drama. He was beautiful in every respect: physically and spiritually. Heroes have their uses. Michael Collins was highly intelligent, disturbingly brave, and he carried with him towering principles.

I and a group of first-rate colleagues made the film here in Britain and in the Republic of Ireland. It was everything that I hoped that it would be. Although I knew – as I have already emphasized – that the past is the *cause* of the present, I was careful not to speak directly about the contemporary issues that were and are being fought out in the northeast of Ireland today. Even then, those years ago, I was conscious that Britain opposed certain truths being spoken on British television, particularly about Ireland. We ended our film – smartly – with Michael Collins's death in 1922.

But that truth that we told was prohibited.

Initially the date of transmission was postponed. Then I became uneasy and pressed ATV for an explanation. I was finally informed that Sir (as he was then) Lew Grade had decided 'not to offer the film to the Independent Broadcasting Authority'.

Now the lay person should understand that the well-known television companies of Britain do not 'show', transmit, their offerings themselves, as it were. All of their programmes are fed through this curiously British organization, the IBA. Of course this has its decent, protective, democratic purpose. The IBA guarantees a quality for British television – a standard for British television – and yet it is *not* a government department because, if it were, *that* would imply government control of the broadcasting medium, and that would never do in this democratic society, would it?

And it is true to write that the IBA tries very hard to be liberal. It even tries, so I have observed, to move with the times; though, thank God, not completely with the times! Nevertheless, in a situation such as the Anglo-Irish one, the IBA looks carefully at any programme that expresses an argument against our British role in Ireland.

I began to investigate the reason why ATV was not going to offer the Michael Collins film, *Hang Out Your Brightest Colours*, to the IBA, and after two very entertaining meetings with the totally irrepressible Sir Lew Grade, that astonishing man issued a press statement: 'In view of the present delicate military and political situation in Northern Ireland, I have decided that this is not the time for such a film to be shown in the UK and accordingly this company is not offering it for transmission.'

Of course, that conventional British state point-of-view has been addressed to me very often in the lengthy meantime. And I have always replied that if there were no 'delicate military and political situation in Northern Ireland' I would not have committed my energies towards making films about the Irish island. 'The truth is indispensable,' as Mr Benny Green once said to me while discussing the British in Ireland.

After Sir Lew Grade's announcement there was formidable press and public interest in ATV's suppression of the film. And Members of Parliament asked if they could view it. First Conservatives looked at it, and a few days later Labour and Liberal MPs.

Of the many writings and sayings about the film at this period, I remember most of all – in retrospect – the words of Mr Michael Foot which ended a letter to me:

When we saw your wonderful film a month or two ago, I did promise that I was going to take up the matter again with Sir Lew, and I am most apologetic for not having done so yet.

However, I have, with some of the others who saw it and were as interested as myself, been thinking what we could do.

I am now proposing to write to Sir Lew again, but I thought I should check with you first to see whether there have been any particular developments since we saw it, which we should take into account. . . .

And then Mr William Deedes, Conservative Party spokesman on 'Northern Ireland' affairs: 'There is nothing inaccurate in the film, but . . .'

At that time Mr Jeremy Isaacs was programme controller

for Thames Television, and I succeeded in persuading him to allow me to make a film – for Thames – which would investigate the suppression of the Michael Collins film. (Mr Isaacs is certainly one of the most liberal and enlightened programme controllers that British television has ever had and it is a relief, to such as myself, that he is now in charge of Channel Four.) And the film we made was titled *The Public's Right to Know*. In that film I investigated every possible aspect of the suppression of *Hang Out Your Brightest Colours*, including the relationship between ATV and the IBA.

Sir Lew, of course, had already assured me that the decision not to offer the film to the IBA was entirely his own and at the same time the Independent Broadcasting Authority was putting forward its view of its role in the miserable affair. Here is a quote in a letter from the IBA to Mr Raymond Gower, Member of Parliament:

. . . in fact the programme has not been offered to the Authority for transmission. It was commissioned and produced by ATV and I understand that after viewing the finished film, Sir Lew Grade, who is ATV's Chief Executive, decided that it was inappropriate material for broadcasting at the present time. The company did not therefore put it forward for inclusion in the transmission schedules which, as you know, have to be approved by the Authority.

There is no obligation on a production company to offer for transmission every programme it makes, and I cannot see that there is anything at all reprehensible about ATV's decision in this case. . . .

I then moved my energy forward again on behalf of a proper united Irish Republic – in two different ways. One was to try to compel Sir Lew Grade to exploit the film, which might have involved pursuing lengthy and expensive litigation against his company claiming loss of potential income from overseas sales (a share of which would belong to my company, Tempest Films).

My second effort was to make another film for yet another British television company which would again attempt to *explain* the Irish–Irish point of view about its historical relationship with Britain. This film is the inspiration and true content of this book. We called the completed film *Curious Journey* because it was about my travelling to the Republic of Ireland – me, a Welsh Protestant Brit, travelling to his Irish, Catholic, republican brothers and sisters in total sympathy and complete support. Unusual and therefore 'curious'. Now I have to state at this point the strange fact that I have had to give a legal undertaking after completing the film not to mention the name of this latter television company!

My idea for this film, *Curious Journey*, was unadulterated Welsh Machiavellianism. In the Michael Collins film I had told the story of the hero's life directly to the camera; perhaps 85 per cent of that film was in sychronization – that is, I was actually speaking in vision. And, of course, not only was I using my knowledge and feelings for the history of Ireland in the *writing*, but I was also using all of my histrionic ability in the *telling* of the awesome story. Indeed, it was my particular ability to *tell* the story effectively that was often complained about by the eventual enemies of the project. They complained that the dramatic impact was too evocative – indeed, too provocative.

Therefore in this second film, *Curious Journey*, I devised an idea that would communicate the Irish–Irish truth without my even appearing on the screen at all.

I travelled to Ireland with a film crew from this unnamed television company and we interviewed on film nine old people – two women and seven men – who had all been involved in the struggle for Irish emancipation from Britain from the time of the 1916 Easter Rebellion onward.

The idea was that now – in the late 1970s – they were all shining pillars of respectability: a doctor of medicine, a retired major general of the Irish Army, a senior member of the Dail (the Irish Parliament), a retired governor of Mountjoy Prison, the head of the biggest music-publishing house in Ireland, a senior police officer and two philosophers of Irish affairs, and yet during their early days of activism against the British presence in Ireland we British had referred to them – these very people – as 'murder gangs', 'rats', 'vermin' etc. Indeed the same terms of abuse that we have always levelled at guerrilla fighters who have struggled against us for their freedom even to this very day.

The *film* was going to ask the viewer – through the old patriots' quality – if these people *were* members of 'murder gangs' or were they 'rats' or 'vermin', and the film would ask the viewer to judge for himself or herself what was the old people's true quality. Even though they were members of the IRA!

We filmed these nine elderly activists in their own homes or in places of their choosing. I, as the interviewer, asked each one of them the same three basic questions. First: 'Sir,' (or 'Madam,') 'Would you explain to me, as fully as possible, why you felt compelled to take action against the British presence here on your island?' Second: 'What were you able to do personally for the emancipation of your country?' Three: 'Where do you hope all of this blood and suffering will eventually take your ancient island home?'

Well we filmed these old people and we edited the film, and then we duly handed it to the television company which had financed the project.

As with the Michael Collins film, *Hang Out Your Brightest Colours*, there was again a prolonged delay in the television company announcing the date of transmission of *Curious Journey*. Again, as in the Collins film, I became suspicious and began to lean gently on the company. And after much stalling and vacillation, the programme controller of that company informed me that his company would not be offering the film *Curious Journey* to the Independent Broadcasting Authority for transmission.

Now again I must digress briefly to explain the psychological pressures that are placed on many people working in British television. I have known this programme controller since I was much younger than I am today and I know that he is head and shoulders above the average executive of television companies in Britain – both in intelligence and in the liberal spirit – but his career has led him into a highly responsible company executive position. He is answerable to his company and he must know the rules of that particular game. I believe that when he spoke to me and said, 'Kenneth, I have some bad news for you; we are not going to offer *Curious Journey* to the IBA,' I believe that he deeply and sincerely regretted that this was so. No one could dislike censorship more than he does – but it was his job to tell me this decision had been arrived at.

I replied to the programme controller that I was very angry – particularly on behalf of ever-wronged Ireland. I went on to say, 'I am not going to have a row with you – you and I should never be on opposite sides of the table – but I *am* going to give the company and above all this bloody country and what it stands for the worst possible time I can over this matter. I shall appeal to the press, to the critics, and I shall go to America and appeal to the Irish American influence over there!'

He heard me patiently and I suspect not without humour (he has experienced my freelance temperament quite often over the years) and replied, 'All right, Ken, but before you do any of those things, will you please meet with our managing director, and hear what he has to say?' Ever feeling affection and indeed admiration for my friend, (and to be honest I could not write that about *many* television executives), I replied, 'Of course.'

My friend and partner Mr David Swift and I attended that anonymous company's London offices by appointment to hear what the managing director had to say. We were received most courteously but David, who amongst many other talents is a lawyer, was a little angry when we were introduced to two of the company's lawyers who planned to be present throughout the discussion. David felt that it was unethical on the part of the television company not to have forewarned us that this was their intention.

The managing director pushed the boat out by stating how much he admired the film *Curious Journey*, how many times he had viewed it. That if there was no trouble in 'Northern

Ireland' how proud his company would be to offer it to the Independent Broadcasting Authority.

At this point I intervened and explained – as I had once explained to Lew Grade – that I doubted whether I would have used my creative energy for Ireland if there had been no trouble there. That I had only made the film *because* there was trouble there, that I believed that the centuries-old trouble would only cease when the British people looked fearlessly at their history on that island of Ireland and honestly judged *themselves*. I went on to say that I had enough faith in the British people's sense of fair play to believe that if they once knew the truth about their country's role in Ireland that they would feel ashamed – as I feel ashamed – and would insist that the core of British government must give orders to apologize to the Irish people and then withdraw from their island and country with as much decency as would be possible.

And I *do* believe that the British people are capable of hearing the true story and then behaving decently.

The managing director then reminded me – as Lord Grade had once done – how many British soldiers, etc., had died 'in the North', and I then reminded him, in my turn, that suppressior of truths about Ireland did not seem to help the British cause or save lives – indeed – that it was counterproductive.

I said to him that I was certain, of course, that he, the managing director, was sincere in his concern for the lives of British soldiers in the northeastern part of Ireland, and, therefore, it seemed to me that, in view of the understandable interest in the suppression of Irish truths by the British, it was doubly imperative that the generous, wise words of the nine old Irish patriots in *Curious Journey* should in no way be prohibited on British television. That I could not imagine any act on the part of the British Establishment that would confirm the anger of the Provisionals (and once again underline to them their conviction born out of centuries of bitter experience that the gun was the *only* object that would impress the British) more than the censorship of these honourable old Irish patriots. I added that *I* also was concerned about the loss of life in Ireland – and in my case – in no way less for the lives of the young soldiers of the IRA than for the lives of Britishers.

Once I had said this and caused an impasse, the senior of the two company lawyers asked, 'May I say something, Mr Griffith?'

'Of course, sir.'

And this gentleman uttered the disturbing reality: 'Mr Griffith, our company's television franchise comes up for renewal before the Independent Broadcasting Authority next year.'

'Ah, sir!' I said, 'thank you for telling me the truth!'

The lawyer went on to say that if they – the television company – offered *Curious Journey* to the IBA that might influence it to a decision against the renewal of that franchise.

Again I thanked the lawyer and said that I sympathized with his television company's predicament sincerely, that I fully understood their position as businessmen who were answerable to their shareholders, and that it would be irresponsible of them, as businessmen, to put their company's future in jeopardy. And I meant that sincerely. I finished: 'But isn't it disgraceful and disturbing that you sense that you cannot risk offering certain truths about the British in Ireland – on British television?'

'Yes,' said the lawyer, 'it is disturbing; but that is our problem.'

And then the managing director returned to the strange fray. He said, 'Mr Griffith, we have a proposition which might interest you. In the first place, we do not wish you to be a financial loser.' He went on to explain that he knew that I had accepted half my normal salary for making *Curious Journey* (before an inch of film had been shot the programme controller had proposed this, arguing that a film which explained the Irish Republican point of view might be censored in Britain; the idea was that I would receive the other half of my salary if the film was shown anywhere. And this unconventional deal I agreed to). The managing director said that this unpaid half of my money would be given to me immediately and then he asked me if I would like to own the film entirely, that I could buy it for a nominal sum.

'Like a peppercorn, sir?' I asked.

'Yes,' he replied, 'you can buy *Curious Journey* from us for one pound sterling. But on condition that you remove our company's name from all prints and that you never mention the name of this company in connection with the film.'

In due course, this was agreed to and I have fought tenaciously to keep my end of the bargain to the best of my ability. Of course, it is all a bit silly because many people knew exactly which company I had made the film for and finally it was agreed that all of the technical credits, etc., could be retained at the end of the film – including that of the 'Executive Director'.

That is where the story stands today. However, I would like to pay tribute to this television company. They judged themselves to be in a critical situation. They judged that they should get rid of the film. I suppose it was a matter of deciding to give the IBA no problems if the company could avoid it. They (the television company) felt that they should cultivate a warm, friendly relationship with the IBA if they possibly could. Ah! There's the rub: at the expense of Irish republicans! But at the same time some influence in that television company resented or regretted any frustration of my proper passion for decent rights on the small island of Ireland. Anyway, that undefined influence opposed locking up the film – away from me – as Lord Grade at ATV had done with the Michael Collins film. *This* anonymous television company virtually *gave* me the film – which had cost them a fair sum of money. They did their utmost as far as their fear of the IBA would allow. I only hope that this account in no way injures them in the eyes of that Authority.

I went to America and talked about the suppression of *Curious Journey*. Both *Curious Journey* and *The Public's Right to Know* were shown to two enthusiastic audiences at the 1980 London Film Festival, and I spoke. But a print of *Hang Out*

Your Brightest Colours was not made available by ATV. And so the battle continues.

In alphabetical order here are my brief memories of the people who will be addressing you on the following pages of this book:

Thomas Barry. When I first telephoned General Barry from Moore's Hotel in Cork City I was answered by his batman and friend, who immediately knew who I was and what I signified – particularly in relation to the suppressed Michael Collins film. General Barry's friend was enthusiastic and warm and I was much relieved. To me, Thomas Barry was and is a legend, which is the hardest fact. I was asked if I would telephone again at 1 p.m. and '. . . then the General will speak to you himself.'

At 1 p.m. – very sharp – I dialled again and was told, 'Here is the General.' I was in an emotional state; the man had long been one of my few heroes. General Barry said, 'I know all about your interest in my country, Mr Griffith. What do you want?'

'Well, sir, I need your help . . .'

'Do you know where the Victoria Hotel is?'

'Yes, sir!' (I didn't, but this wasn't a moment for negatives.)

'I'll be outside. You can't miss me; I'm an old man – near blind.'

I grabbed a tie and ran from Moore's Hotel towards the centre of Cork. 'Where is the Victoria Hotel?' And there as I ran up was the great leader himself. He pulled down his glasses, peering at me uncompromisingly.

'Mr Griffith, you're early! Now, my wife is ill in hospital and today is our wedding anniversary. Will you help me select some flowers?'

Tom Barry – blind as he was – stepped off onto the main thoroughfare of Cork and I nimbly got onto his traffic side. At the island I hastened to the other side of the old man. I didn't dare take his arm – though later in our relationship, I am proud to inform you, he expected me to do it. And as we reached the pavement I said to the triumphant warrior, 'Well, sir, I never thought that I would have the opportunity of protecting your left flank.' Again he pulled his glasses down before peering and then, pointing a finger at me, 'Ha!' and he smiled.

After he was very personally honoured in the florist's – 'How is Mrs Barry, General?' – he and I walked by the River Lee. Finally we sat on a seat and General Tom said, 'In twenty minutes a car will arrive there [pointing] and I will have to leave you. What do you want from me?' I told him about the Michael Collins film – and of course Tom Barry knew Michael Collins well – and about the suppression of the film. And at the end of my tale he leaned away from me in an attitude of disbelief.

'Do you mean to tell me, Mr Griffith, that you made a film on the life of Mick Collins and. fifty-five years after his death an instrument of the British Establishment has banned it?'

'Yes, sir.'

'And what reasons did they give?'

'They said that it was an incitement to disorder on the subject of Ireland.'

'They said that about your film?'

'Yes, sir.'

And for the first time Tom Barry touched me. He placed one hand on my right shoulder. 'In that case, son, I'll do anything I can to help you!'

And that is how we achieved our invaluable filmed interview. Again it was brave of Tom Barry. The old man was uneasy because he suspected that he was not as strong and agile mentally as he had once been and he knew that he was once again volunteering to face Ireland's ancient and cruel enemy, Britain. The responsibility weighed heavily on him. He was now, also, pretty deaf. But, he talked to me with a camera running, knowing that his old face and his old, constant words on behalf of Ireland's total independence from Britain were being aimed at our wide television public. He may have suspected that Britain would once again try to shut down his spirit, but he never voiced any doubts to me. He said, exactly, what you are about to read. Oh! how I love and admire that now dead old man.

Maire Comerford. Ah! Ms Comerford! What a handful of unshiftable, constant spirit she was. Here, of the whole cast of nine, was the most pugnacious, determined, relentless, open Irish republican spirit of them all.

Maire, as I was allowed to call this ancient, beautiful lady, was the most difficult to film of everyone. Not that she was shy, it was simply that she had an ingrained reluctance to reminisce; she did not wish to waste her time with old, personal stories (which amongst other things I wanted). No, she wanted to state hard, republican facts.

I must confess that I got a bit cross with her. She was undoubtedly stubborn. Indeed, I shouldn't have been surprised; she had been stubborn for an historical sixty-five years – probably for eighty odd.

Mr Gerald O'Hare, the distinguished Irish republican and at that time the editor of the republican newspaper *An Phoblacht*, had organized our introduction to Ms Comerford. We filmed her in her home at Sandyford, Dublin – a house with many republican treasures tucked away here and there.

As we began to set up our film equipment on the actual day of filming I became aware that two unexpected and substantial men were in the house – Mr Jack Bennett and Mr Colman Doyle. After Ms Comerford introduced us all to them they seemed to fade into the background gloom. The filming started and my tussle with Maire was renewed with added tenacity on my part. Now I believe that in filming people one should give the subject as much freedom and room to ruminate as possible. But, on the other hand, film stock is expensive and I hate wasting money – even Lord Grade's! (It wasn't his film stock on this occasion, incidentally!) I had problems in keeping Ms Comerford to the points that were required for our film. And on top of that small trauma, every so often Maire would stop speaking and she would turn to her movingly attentive friends. They would whisper together. (We, of course, had stopped the camera.) Finally the gentlemen came to me and explained that, when they were young, Maire Comerford had been a mentor to their republican ideals and now that she was much older they were there to support her in any way that they could. Both men were very courteous – particularly when they realized that we were treating Maire with great respect.

Sean Harling. Mr Harling, it seemed to me, was quite different from all the rest of our 'cast'. He had been very close to Michael Collins and to Eamon de Valera – but as a relatively simple, trustworthy friend. Of all of our nine Irish people Sean Harling had no deep philosophical opinions about Ireland's destiny. He was Irish; he was on Ireland's side; he was brave and hard-working. And Michael Collins and Eamon de Valera both trusted him – but when the Irish Civil War began, Sean Harling was uncommitted and lost. For this reason he was to pay a heavy price in the midst of that lethal family war.

While we were arranging to film Sean – who is now dead – at his little home in Cabra, Dublin, the telephone rang and there were threats to kill him – for even speaking to us. But simple, brave Sean – who had chosen the 'wrong' side during the Civil War – was fairly immune to such fear and you can therefore read what he told me.

I believe that once, long ago, there was an attempt to assassinate Sean Harling and he drew his own gun. Such is the dark reality and the bloody flood that has its source in imperialism.

Sean Kavanagh. Sean is an old friend. He was introduced to me by another old Irish friend – Bishop Jeremiah Newman – who was, at the time of that valuable introduction, Monsignor Newman, head of Maynooth, the great Roman Catholic teaching college of Ireland.

Sean Kavanagh, again, had been close to Michael Collins, whom – like so many others – he still deeply loved. There is no other word for it. Sean had been, during the Anglo-Irish War, a train raider for the Irish Republican Army, a very secret agent, and, latterly, during the Irish Civil War – and afterwards – a prison governor. His life had been, inevitably (since he was a proud Irish patriot), pitched into a bitterly cruel, complicated conflict. My own impression of my dear friend Sean was that the Civil War had injured his spirit deeply. He never complained or criticized anyone unless I pressed him with painful questions (off camera) and his replies were always gentle and – to me – devastatingly sad. Once we were alone and I asked the unaskable: 'Sean, if Michael Collins had lived, would he have allowed the execution of leading republicans during the Civil War?' Sean sat as if he had not heard me for a long while, and then, so tragically: 'What were we [the "Free Staters"] to do? They had announced that they were going to assassinate the entire government leadership. Indeed, they had started. What were we to do?' That was all Sean said. I did not press further. His weight of awful regret that Irishmen had ever been brought to a point where they killed one another was clearly a monstrous burden. Irish people, I ask you to turn away from blaming each other and refocus any bitterness that you must feel at the master-villain and cause of it all: Britain.

I once asked Sean Kavanagh where he had found the courage to perform the lethal tasks of his active-service youth. I added my own anxious doubt: 'Would I have found the courage to work for Michael Collins against British imperialism?' Sean stopped his motorcar and said, 'Michael gave you the courage. He would ask you to do nothing that he would not do himself. You were so proud that he had chosen you. Rest assured, Kenneth, Michael would have *given* you the courage as he gave it to me.'

We filmed Sean in his house at Rathmines, Dublin. His life has finally created in him a gentle, even saintlike quality. It must have been different once, but I have known nothing else and I care for him very much. His late wife was also special and was also a friend of mine.

David Neligan. Ah! here was the classic Irish bouncing realist. His language is the inspiration of legend. Sean O'Casey, James Joyce, James Stephens, John Millington Synge and the host of them would have recognized the ingenious rhythms and the satirical second-nature choice of words.

David was – and is – a man of action. Old as he is, after talking to us, he would leap onto his bicycle and *speed* towards a swim. David is a humorous patriot. He has delighted me and made me laugh, but I have also witnessed tears on his face. All of these old patriots share a common burden: the horrors of the past (and, God help us, the lousy British present), but their deep grief is embedded primarily in the tragedy of the Irish Civil War.

David is naughty enough to enjoy a police pension from both the British source and from the Irish Government source. If you can't raise an ironical laugh out of the whole awfulness that Britain has inflicted on Ireland, is it bearable?

We filmed David in his home at Booterstown, Dublin.

John L. O'Sullivan. Of our nine persons John is the only professional politician. He is now an elder statesman amongst County Cork people – and that part of Ireland incorporates a special active, weighty significance. Both Michael Collins and Thomas Barry were Cork men.

Only once have I personally felt the pressure of threat in Ireland and that was during the 1980 Cork Film Festival where I was a guest for a screening of *Curious Journey*. After the screening, at a press conference, I was assailed by the remnants of the Anglo-Irish mentality – and on that occasion by a representative of that unpredictable Irish institution: the *Irish Times*. I was verbally and emotionally assaulted by the elements which had travelled from their haven *within* the Pale. Into that crowded room slowly loomed the big figure of John L. O'Sullivan, followed by a few other formidable old men from the days of the Anglo-Irish War. My old friend, John O'Sullivan, and his surviving comrades had heard what was happening to me and had arrived to give me support and advice. And separate from them, representatives of the present republican movement also made their very positive appearance – to offer me anything I needed. Cork, on that day, was suddenly full of a few new enemies and a grand array of new – and old – friends.

On one splendid occasion I was John O'Sullivan's guest for lunch in the Dail. My old friend escorted me from place to place, solemnly introducing me to members of his own party and to members of the other party, describing me simply as 'a friend of Ireland'. A splendid reward and I thank him.

We first met John L. O'Sullivan at Beal na mBlath – the flowered site of Michael Collins's death. We finally filmed John in a private room of a public house at Bandon, County Cork.

Joseph Sweeney. The complete responsible soldier. He was on the spot – the very spot – for the beginnings of this century's rebellion by Ireland against Britain. I have talked to this man who was a protégé of Patrick Pearse himself. Joseph Sweeney was firing a gun from the General Post Office, Dublin, at the attacking British troops. And he personally helped to carry the wounded body of James Connolly during the evacuation of the burning GPO.

I remember him as a friend and as one of those few people down the track of my life with whom I was critically mindful of correctness. If I were slovenly in any way, Joseph would regret it. But always there would be sympathy. But total honesty. I believe that he was incapable of a dishonest reflection. He once saw one of 'my' documentary films on Irish television. It was called *The Man on the Rock*, about the last six years of Napoleon's life on St Helena.

'What did you think of it, General?' (Joseph was a general in the Irish Army.)

'Too dramatic, Kenneth! Too dramatic!'

I hope and believe that undeceivable Joseph Sweeney felt the same about Sean O'Casey's plays.

He was kind and highly intelligent. We who made *Curious*

Journey were always dealing with outstanding human beings. It is only given to a very few – wherever in the world – to volunteer and perform the actual deeds on behalf of the rest of us. These old people were part of that Irish few. The British Establishment seems to be bitterly puzzling today why a minority of young Irish people have been starving themselves to death on an Irish principle. In 1980 the British Establishment was bleating its short-sighted despicable propaganda that not even the Irish–Irish Catholic population in the northeast were supporting the young heroes of 'H Block'. Today – after the 'H Block Elections' – they are puzzling and complaining about the overwhelming support that has been given to the 'H Block' candidates. No, wherever it might be in the whole world – by the nature of humanity – only a small minority of humans *volunteer* to sacrifice their lives for the rest of us in warfare. Our nine old people were of that calibre – in one way or another.

We filmed General Joseph Sweeney in the Old Dublin Brigade Headquarters of the Old IRA.

Brighid Lyons Thornton. Patriot and Doctor of Medicine. A youthful feminine quality still tumbles out of her. Like the rest she has never wavered ever about the importance to her country of the removal of the British.

Though an elderly lady, she – at the time of filming – was still giving several days' service per week to 'state medicine'. One of my favourite memories of Ireland was escorting Brighid all the way from her elegant home in Fitzwilliam Place to the far-away Rotunda Hospital. To my delight she slapped on a bit of lipstick and, taking my arm (she was a little lame), we set off through Stephen's Green. I think that was the last time that I felt like a traditional beau.

Martin Walton. And here again is a classic Irish character. He has made his way in life by practising his birthright charm and creative intelligence. Like all good honest Irishmen he revels in drama and roguery for reasons of personal and public

entertainment. Here is the unique Irish mixture of intellec-
tualism sold – happily – through theatricality; both comedy
and tragedy practised here.

In his astounding isolated house at Ashtown outside of Dublin, with great Irish wolfhounds abounding, I experienced
some of the most atmospheric images that have ever come my
way. If our British institutional theatres were to consider the
drama of Martin Walton's domestic theatre, they would be
returning to the old colourful lines of Edmund Kean and
David Garrick. But with their resentment towards the necessity of living actors, Martin is not the man for them.

I don't think that Martin is going to object if I write that he
has also put fine Irish blarney to a fighting creative purpose.
Like good Irish whiskey, I, as a full-blooded Welsh rogue,
understand and love my Irish brother across the Irish water.

Well, there they all are – all nine human beings who have
heightened and illuminated my life. Thank you! Thank you!
Each one of them was interviewed and filmed and recorded
for many hours on many different occasions. Our misused film
Curious Journey has one hour's 'screen time' duration, which
only allowed for four or five minutes from each of the magical
nine. And what was selected of their words was selected for
the essential *direction* of the film. Many of the best stories and
statements that the old patriots spoke could not be used in the
film for reasons of structure.

So, the book – not only because these precious minutes have
been denied to you, not only on British television but on
Telefís Eireann also, but because on the following pages you
will virtually receive it *all*.

From the time that I first conceived of the film *Curious
Journey*, my young friend and co-author, Timothy O'Grady,
has worked with me. He and I travelled across Ireland on
many occasions, meeting old people and recording our con-
versations with them. We discussed exhaustively the strategy
and meaning of this book and happily we have never had a
word of disagreement about Ireland. My task has been to elicit

the following responses from our old Irish friends and Timothy's has been to assemble them and to write the linking narrative. We are indeed an odd couple – Timothy, a young man from Chicago, and myself (in the prime of life), from Tenby in southwest Wales. Tim is one of the most faithful, true friends that I have ever had. And that is nice between an Old One and a Young One.

PART ONE

Mr Jeremiah O'Mahony's splendid blooms

1897 to 1915

'I became conscious of my national feelings as a schoolboy. . . . My teacher was Jeremiah O'Mahony . . . and from his schoolboys came most of the company of Volunteers that were first formed there. He was not a soldier, and he hadn't a soldier's outlook, but he instilled in the boys something that they hadn't before – that was to improve their homes . . . to love their country . . . to do everything possible in their lives to help their comrades. . . . He had a beautiful garden which at that time was the pride of everybody. I was only four and a half years when I went to school, but you spent your play hours clearing that garden and planting the flowers. People would come along in their side cars and they stopped outside his school garden to look and to enjoy the splendid blooms. . . .'

John L. O'Sullivan

1

A barbarous country must first be broken by war before it will be capable of good government.

Sir John Davies, author of *A Discovery of the True Causes why Ireland was Never Entirely Subdued*, 1612

Aren't they a remarkable people? And the folly of thinking that we can understand, let alone govern them!

Henry Herbert Asquith, British Prime Minister, in exasperation after a meeting with Irish Nationalists and Irish Unionists on 21 July 1914

On 22 June 1897, Victoria, Queen–Empress, an aged and properly grieving figure clad in black, was transported from Buckingham Palace to St Paul's amid a procession which included dukes, duchesses, princesses and Indian potentates, a crown prince, a papal nuncio and the hierarchy of the British civil service and clergy, and 50,000 troops in regimental splendour – including Cypriot Zaptiehs, camel troops from Bikaner, Canadian hussars, carabiniers from Natal and members of the Hong Kong police. It was her Diamond Jubilee: the nineteenth century, Britain's own, was marching triumphantly to a close and with it the Empire, under Victoria's stern eye, had at last revealed a sublime pattern: heathens were being won for Christ, forbidden continents explored and settled and a disparate world made one with such marvels as the railway and telegraphic cables. Britain, the spectators at that parade must have surmised, was the Land of Destiny.

Just around this time, our nine veterans were first coming to light in Britain's nearest and perhaps most fractious colony: Ireland. There the Imperial administrators did their best for their queen. Union Jacks were hoisted along Dublin's wide avenues; a special Irish Honours List was published; and the Third Hussars staged a regimental parade in the Phoenix Park. In St Patrick's Cathedral the Ascendancy convened for a thanksgiving service and in the countryside some of the more paternalistic landlords brought out their red, white and blue bunting and held Jubilee fêtes for their tenants. The *Irish Times*, at that time the voice of the Unionists, contributed with a rather ungainly 'Jubilee Ode':

> Thou rulest supreme, as no other,
> Queen, Empress and Woman, in one –
> Our Sovr'n, our Lady, our Mother,
> Like whom there is none!

But the *Irish Times* also reported that at 'about half-past nine o'clock . . . a slight break was made in the smoothness of the proceedings.' This was in fact a full-scale nationalist riot: windows were smashed, Imperial monuments were defaced and the police were pelted with stones from the roof of the National Club. James Connolly was inside the National Club; he had arranged with city workers to douse the Jubilee illuminations at a specific time so that he could project lantern slides of famine, evictions and Irish patriots onto an enormous screen in Parnell Square. Elsewhere in the city, the beautiful and impassioned Maud Gonne delivered an inflammatory speech from a soapbox and a mock coffin draped in skull-and-crossbone flags was escorted solemnly to Dublin Castle. All over Ireland the jubilees of Daniel O'Connell, St Columba and any number of priests and monsignors were celebrated energetically while Victoria Regina was studiously ignored. James Connolly wrote:

During this glorious reign, Ireland has seen 1,225,000 of her children die of famine, starved to death while the produce of her soil and of their labour was eaten up by a vulture aristocracy – enforcing their rents by the bayonets of a hired assassin army in the pay of the 'best of the English Queens'; the eviction of 3,668,000, a multitude greater than that of the entire population of Switzerland; and the reluctant emigration of 4,186,000 of our kindred, a greater host than the entire people of Greece. At the present moment 78 per cent of our wage-earners receive less than £1 per week, our streets are thronged by starving crowds of the unemployed, cattle graze on our tenantless farms and around the ruins of our battered homesteads, our ports are crowded with departing emigrants, and our workhouses are full of paupers. Such are the constituent elements out of which we are bade to construct a National Festival of Rejoicing.

Understanding between the two countries had obviously not been reached, despite some seven hundred years of perseverance. The first soldiers loyal to the English Crown to appear in Ireland were a small party of Norman adventurers who landed in south-west Wexford in May 1169. They had come at the bidding of Dermot MacMurrough, King of Leinster, who coveted their advanced military technology. These Normans were quickly absorbed into the Irish pattern of life, transforming the country with their passion for civic order just as they were transformed by it: they learned the Irish language, lived by Ireland's laws and even bleached their hair in the Celtic manner. Invasions at that point were still subject to this process of dialectic.

It was not until the Tudors ascended to the throne in the sixteenth century that England attempted a comprehensive conquest of Ireland. Henry VIII and his daughter Elizabeth I were driven by an acquisitiveness for land, an insecurity about the exposure of their western flank, the religious zeal of the Reformation and a wish to extend their evolving concepts of statecraft. The conquest proceeded from them, becoming more formal and complete as time went on. It was military, particularly so in the seventeenth century under the Elizabethan, Cromwellian and Williamite campaigns. It was cultural, in its attempts to eliminate all remnants of Gaelic society. It was religious, for it tried to end through legislation the Catholic religion in Ireland. It was political, in that it withheld the franchise from the native Irish and debarred them from all positions of power. It was divisive, for it disentangled Norman and English from Celt, Catholic from Protestant, and set them against each other. And it was economic: it seized land, imposed debilitating tariff structures and eventually withheld from Ireland the benefits of the Industrial Revolution. By the latter half of the eighteenth century land owned by Catholics – by far the overwhelming majority in the country – had descended to an incredible 5 per cent.

English Victorians would have regarded such stern measures as the necessary precondition for good, civilizing government. But the Irish Victorians who disrupted the Dublin Jubilee celebrations accepted neither the government nor the wisdom of its Imperial strategy. To them, England, whether conciliatory or coercive, could only be a malign presence in Ireland, and they saw their history strictly in terms of the long series of rebellions against that presence. From the Ulster chieftains' bitter resistance to the latter stages of the Elizabethan campaign, these rebellions had been both regular and ill-fated. Perhaps the most imaginative occurred in 1798, when dispossessed Catholics, radically independent Presbyterian settlers and intellectuals inspired by the French Revolution joined forces. Their enterprise came undone through poor organization, bad weather, informers and unprecedented government ruthlessness, but the new doctrine of Republicanism survived and it gave a coherence to all the popular and unpopular insurrections which followed.

The nineteenth century was crowded with such occurrences: Robert Emmet's small and vainglorious uprising in 1803; the Young Irelanders' in that active year for European revolutionaries, 1848; and the Fenians' in 1867. The century also witnessed two great parliamentary movements. The first was led by Daniel O'Connell, and it succeeded in securing limited Catholic emancipation in 1829 but collapsed under tougher British resistance to his campaign for the repeal of the 1800 Act of Union, which had dissolved the short-lived Dublin Parliament.

The second was led by Charles Stewart Parnell. Parnell, a Protestant, a landlord and a Member of Parliament, had succeeded where those before him had failed: he united under his personal banner all the divergent strains of Irish resistance; he engineered a land revolution which eventually restored most of the lands confiscated by the English in the sixteenth and seventeenth centuries; he saw the British Prime Minister Gladstone through his transformation into an Irish Home Ruler; and he raised Irish nationalist feeling to its highest level in nearly a hundred years.

But Parnell too fell, and his end was quintessentially, absurdly Victorian. His affair with a married woman, Kitty O'Shea, was brought to public notice when her politician husband sued for divorce – possibly at the instigation of Tories who saw in the potential salacious gossip an opportunity to rock Parnell's Liberal ally Gladstone out of office. When the news broke, Gladstone's Nonconformist voters were suitably shocked, leading him to renounce Parnell, and when the Irish bishops joined in, most of Parnell's carefully constructed support at home collapsed beneath him. Home Rule, which he and Gladstone had worked so obsessively to effect, became a lost cause and the entire spectrum of Irish resistance lay in tiny, quarrelsome ruins. Parnell died a year later, in 1891.

Ireland did not easily recover from the shock of Parnell's fall and death, and when Victoria was celebrating her Jubilee the famous Irish resistance was still, apart from the demonstrations in Dublin, virtually dormant.

MARTIN WALTON: People don't realize that we had become the most peaceful country in Europe. All our political leaders, particularly since the collapse of the Fenian movement, and right back from O'Connell onwards, Butt, Shaw, Parnell, they had persuaded us that there was no chance of an unarmed little island fighting this big British Empire. But there was an awful lot we could do by constitutional means. Meanwhile, the older greybeards of the Irish Republican Brotherhood thought it was better to give the impression that the movement had died. They just kept one or two men in every town or important sentry post in Ireland, and gave the impression that the whole movement was dead. At the beginning of the century I don't think there would have been more than 300 members of the Fenian Brotherhood in the whole of the country. The country was unarmed.

British rule at last seemed secure. Festooned British troops could parade unmolested through the city streets, Union Jacks flew from classical public buildings which dispensed British law – the only law in the land – and the heroes of the Empire were commemorated in great monuments throughout Ireland's towns and cities. The whole enterprise was presided over by Dublin Castle – headquarters of those colonial figures the Lord Lieutenant and the Chief Secretary, and mecca for the Anglo-Irish Ascendancy. Of it one Lady Fingal remarked, 'I have been told that for magnificence and brilliance only the Indian Viceregal Court, with its mingling colours of East and West, can compare with the Dublin Castle season.' Its image throughout most of Ireland, however, was encapsulated in a popular lyric about the Statue of Justice surmounting the Castle gates:

> Statue of Justice, mark well her station,
> Her face to the Castle, her arse to the Nation.

All of this Imperial bravado disguised an extreme wariness. Castle officials convinced themselves that the Irish had long memories, along with their disposition to insurrection, and they guarded their possession carefully. They equipped themselves with draconian laws and oversaw an intricate network of landlords, police informers and garrisoned troops.

BRIGHID LYONS THORNTON: I lived in the garrison town of Longford and it was a hotspot of British militarism. We had regiments from time to time. They were very grand, and on Sunday morning we used to watch them march up the main street as we went to Mass at the cathedral. And it was the highlight of my life as a small child going in to hear the band playing. They were very colourful, particularly some Scots regiments, with their buttons and kilts and various colours. At times we had – what do you call them? – horse artillery, and that was a great day to see them marching. It was later on that khaki came in and made it all so drab and dreadful. I didn't then realize the significance of it. It was just something that appealed to a little girl.

Anyone growing up in Ireland as the century turned – as our nine veterans did – was constantly reminded of the un-shiftability of the British Empire. It was a garrisoned country, complete with a deliberately fostered garrison mentality.

TOM BARRY: Of course at that time I had no conception of Irish nationality. I was brought up in the period of school-days where I could name every king and queen in Britain, or in England, but I knew nothing of our own past people because it was definitely excluded from all schools – not alone the National Schools but also a Jesuit college that I went to afterwards. In short, the whole country apparently at that period, without I thinking it was in any way extraor-dinary, was an accepted subject race of Britain.

2

[In stories of the highwaymen who] held aristocratic positions in the community of thieves, [anecdotes] of their ferocity and audacity, of their occasional acts of generosity and good nature, of their amours, of their miraculous escapes . . . there is doubtless a large mixture of fable; but they are not on that account unworthy of being recorded; for it is both an authentic and an important fact that such fables, whether true or false, were heard by our ancestors with eagerness and faith.

Macaulay, *History of England*

The legends represent the imagination of the country; they are that kind of history which a nation desires to possess. They betray the ambitions and ideals of the people and, in this respect, have a value far beyond the tale of actual events and duly recorded deeds, which are no more history than a skeleton is a man.

Standish O'Grady

The salient fact about these efforts at conquest is that they did not succeed. Resistance was so regular and singleminded that Britain could only rule precariously by perpetually reconquering. Ireland's economy was shattered, its patriots vanquished and its military campaigns ill-disciplined and futile; but the idea of a free Irish nation nevertheless grew more vivid in the face of such apparent defeats. It was an idea contained in a body of memory which passed according to a ritual of bequest through generations. This memory was a kind of imaginary history – fabled and versified, diverse but always focused on Irish pride and English treachery. It was as graphic to the Irish as it was incomprehensible to the English and in the end

10

it was of vastly more consequence than all the Imperial resources of parliamentary Acts or military reprisals.

JOHN L. O'SULLIVAN: At that time what we heard from our parents, our grandfathers, friends and neighbours, that tradition came down every year, every generation. And Irish history is a tragic history. If you are an Irishman, just like if you are a native of any country, you love your own country. People are prepared to make sacrifices for the right to live and to govern their own country. That was the attitude of all generations.

MARTIN WALTON: From my earliest childhood I had heard both in song and story tales of the brutal oppression to which we were subjected, both religious bigotry and military oppression, and even from the time I was three or four years of age it was my ambition to follow in the footsteps of the insurgents of 1798 and the Fenians.

I was born in 1901, and the Boer War was just over Arthur Griffith had just returned from South Africa and he wrote prolifically on the appalling happenings in that country, about the concentration camps and how the British acted there. And of course that brought out the stories of the Fenian times and the Land War and the terrible Famine, all the abortive uprisings and the slaughter of thousands of Irishmen. That tradition ran very, very strong, and I heard about it from my mother and father. My father was a printer, the manager of a paper belonging to another great patriot, a Member of Parliament, William O'Brien from Cork. My father was also a member of the Irish Republican Brotherhood, the IRB, and though he never spoke about their meetings or what happened there he was always hammering home his principles. And of course we had commemorations every year for some of the great Fenians who had died, or for men like the Manchester Martyrs who were hanged in the wrong. I give credit to these things for keeping Irish nationality alive. I give credit too to our great poet

Thomas Moore, because during that terrible century his songs like 'Let Erin Remember the Days of Old' and many such songs really kept the spirit alive. You couldn't escape it. I remember as a boy, when I was eleven, twelve, thirteen or fourteen, when we started to make explosives, I remember I used to do exercises to harden my neck against the hangman's rope. I never expected anything else.

JOSEPH SWEENEY: I listened all my life to a nationalist point of view from my father and I'd heard my grandfather at the time of the Boer War. He was a great supporter of the Boers. That nationalist spirit ran through our family and I came to the conclusion that I had to adopt a radical view. My father was active in the Land League times and was arrested and sentenced under the Star Chamber courts and taken to Derry. When I was arrested in 1920 and taken there the old warder asked me my name. I said, 'Sweeney.' 'Where are you from?' says he. 'Burtonport,' says I. 'I had your father in here,' he said.

BRIGHID LYONS THORNTON: My father had been a Fenian and had been in jail. He was a very small farmer and he wouldn't have any great influence, but he was a loyal supporter. He went to meetings and we used to see his membership card when he came back, hidden away somewhere very special in the bottom of the clock. It was green and had Wolfe Tone on it and said, 'Who fears to speak of '98?' He used to take me to Mass at Scramoge and he used to meet Barney Dolan, a lanky man with a beard, and every Sunday he'd say, 'He's the decentest man that ever lived,' and I never knew why, he just said it. 'Really a princely man,' he said. He said they were in jail together in Sligo, and he used to talk about the treadmill. Whether he had done that or not I don't know. And I don't know how long he was in for or what for. Would it be boycotting? I never knew, but he said when they were due to be released there were a lot of food and parcels sent in and Barney Dolan came to him and said, 'Well now we're getting out next week or in a few days and we'll leave that food for the next party that comes in,' which he thought was the most genuine and the most generous thought that any man could have. He was an elderly man, he married late in life, but I knew the minute the Volunteers were started he joined, though he was a man of fifty, or very nearly. These are just snippets that I can remember. It is all just a memory to me. My great regret of course is that I never asked him more about it.

3

The modern literature of Ireland, and indeed all that stir of thought which prepared for the Anglo-Irish War, began when Parnell fell from power. . . . A disillusioned and embittered Ireland turned from parliamentary politics; an event was conceived; and the race began, as I think, to be troubled by that event's long gestation.

W. B. Yeats, *Autobiographies*

The opening years of the twentieth century were a time of explosive social and artistic experiment in Europe, and Ireland, perhaps privy to this, expressed its long-standing resistance to British rule not in parliamentary agitation nor in violent insurrection, but in a cultural revolution. Entirely new organizations – some of them shrill, others benign – came into being with the audacious intention of recreating Irish culture. The Gaelic League and the Gaelic Athletic Association promoted a dying language and forgotten sports. Horace Plunkett and the poet George Russell (AE) sought to save the countryside with their cooperative movement. Trade unionism grew in importance and, with visionary rhetoric, offered deliverance to the urban working class. Maud Gonne's women's group, Inghinidhe na hEireann, added nationalism to the suffragette movement. Arthur Griffith, a journalist, sought to unite these emerging, sometimes contentious forces under the self-reliance doctrine of Sinn Fein. There was, too, a literary revival of world significance led by W. B. Yeats; one of the most extraordinary of its many compelling features was the unprecedented confidence felt by poets that they were actually shaping the national destiny with their verse. It was a time of exuberant revivalism, exotic flamboyance and fertile debate.

14

The old grievances and discontent were finding their voice in what would in other times be eccentric places, and the visionary was becoming more representative than the parliamentarian.

It was not understood in England at the time, but this was the tentative beginning of a new Irish revolution. Parliament had passed a number of conciliatory reforms – most notably the Wyndham Act of 1903, which virtually guaranteed the retransference of land back to peasant ownership – and there was generally more prosperity about. The government believed that this would pacify Ireland, as coercion had not done so. But, as the French traveller and political philosopher Alexis de Tocqueville observed about the immediate preliminaries to the French Revolution, a bad government is most in danger when it begins to reform, when it begins to lift a long-standing burden.

MARTIN WALTON: At that time you had the Gaelic Renaissance and the Gaelic League. I joined the Gaelic League when I was eight years of age. The Gaelic League was primarily to re-establish the Irish language, but it also took in other subjects – Irish literature, dancing and history generally. They gave lectures and talks in these subjects and all that helped. There was an upsurge of everything Irish. We unfortunately haven't given credit to the Irish Parliamentary Party. I would have shot John Redmond at the time, but I've learned a lot since. Their policy with England seemed to decrease the bitterness between the two countries. The old slogan 'No Irish need apply' had gone by the board. And of course when a little bit more liberty and education and all that came along, it meant that more people took up the study of Irish, and Irish ideas. I don't like that horrible expression 'Stand up and be counted', but they were standing up anyway and getting more independent in thought and deed.

BRIGHID LYONS THORNTON: There was a teacher came

15

named O'Dowd and he brought in a teacher of Irish. I remember once we were told that seniors were to stay back but all the juniors were to go home. Well I hid in the back desk in the school, I wanted to see what the teacher of Irish was like. He was Mr Heavey from Athlone, a well-known Athlone family and a very fine-looking man as I recollect. Well he came in and I appeared and the teacher said, 'My God, look who's here,' or something to that effect now, because I was so small, I was only six or seven if I was that. I learned the Irish for herring – *scadán* – and a few words that appealed to me, and then Master O'Dowd took up the Irish and I kept learning Irish with him. He used to take me into the boys' school, which was a great treat in those days. And then there was a *feis* in Strokestown with Irish dancing and the Irish language and everything, and my father brought me up. Canon Malachi Brennan – he died a few years ago – he was the curate and he organized the *feis*. We were brought up to the convent and the nuns tied red handkerchiefs round our heads and we all went in a parade into the town. I went up and I was asked a few questions by some man sitting at a table and eventually I got second prize in Irish. So there I was, a patriot and a hero.

Later on I went to Longford to go to the convent school there, and my uncle brought me in. He was a businessman there, Frank MacGuinness. He was the brother of Joe Mac-Guinness, the republican, and Frank was a nationalist, a Redmondite staunch and strong, and he used to take me cattle-driving. It was a very aggressive thing to do then. You see, there were ranchers around the country who had big farms and who had a lot of cattle, and the others were the peasants, the poor people who had a few acres, like my father. It was the place to go on a Sunday. We'd go to the meeting, stand at the crossroads, and they'd pass resolutions. Then we'd run on the ranches and put the cattle out on the road. Our slogan was 'The road for the bullocks and the land for the people!'

JOHN L. O'SULLIVAN: I became conscious of my national feelings as a schoolboy. I came to the school where Michael Collins started his education, Lisavaird National School. My teacher there was Jeremiah O'Mahony. I later had the privilege of saying a few words when he was buried, this great man. He instilled patriotism and love of the country in us, and from his schoolboys came most of the company of Volunteers that were first formed there. He was not a soldier, and he hadn't a soldier's outlook, but he had that patriotic outlook of doing good for his country and instilling in the boys something that they hadn't before – that was to improve their homes, improve their surroundings, to love their country, to learn their language, to do everything possible in their lives to help their comrades, and with their fellow pupils to plant an apple tree, to cut the hedges or set the hedges. He had a beautiful garden which at that time was the pride of everybody. I was only four and a half years when I went to school, but you spent your play hours clearing that garden and planting the flowers. People would come along in their sidecars and they stopped outside his school garden to look and to enjoy the splendid blooms and the way he had that garden, the way he had it arranged.

4

It was the certainty of British support which made the strength of Ulster resistance.

Mr Bonar Law to Mr Asquith

When the century turned, Victoria died and Parnell's Irish Parliamentary Party was reorganized by John Redmond. Redmond depended upon three factors to realize his life's dream of Home Rule: a solid bedrock of support in Ireland, a Liberal government in Britain sufficiently in need of Irish parliamentary votes to dedicate itself to his policies, and weak resistance, if not agreement, from Irish Unionists – particularly in Ulster, where they were most densely concentrated. They all seemed to fall neatly into place when a Liberal government was returned with a diminished majority in 1910, leaving Redmond and his party holding the balance of power. At this time Redmond had enormous influence in Ireland. Even the radicals seemed willing to give him a chance and, remarkably, in Ulster there was a parliamentary majority in favour of Home Rule under his leadership. The British people too, in returning a Liberal government committed to Home Rule, had endorsed the principle of self-determination in Ireland. Home Rule at last seemed a practical certainty, as well as a democratic right.

But, however carefully he may have laid his plans, it was to be John Redmond's tragic destiny to be left behind by historical forces which simply outpaced him. Matters first came to a head when the Liberal Prime Minister Asquith presented the Third Home Rule Bill to the House of Commons on 11 April 1912. Though it was an eminently cautious document which fell far short of the Irish demands, it met with instant and outraged resistance from Ulster Unionists, British Tories

18

and the army, who soon found themselves drawn together in a conspiratorial alliance to subvert Home Rule. They saw, or pretended to see, in that mild bill a chain of sinister consequences: the dissolution of the Union; a pernicious example to the further reaches of the Empire, particularly India; the exposure of Britain's western flank; the subverting of the prerogatives of the Crown and Lords; and the undermining of the Protestant hegemony. The forces of history seemed to be swinging away from them: oligarchical rule was being pushed out of the way by the principle of self-determination. The triple alliance of Tories, Ulster Unionists and the army hierarchy dedicated itself to freezing time before this transformation could be completed.* They were to have no qualms about sedition, mutiny or the formation of private armies.

They turned their attentions to Ulster, which they claimed was being 'coerced' into Home Rule. On 29 September 1912, Ulster Unionists under a Dublin-born barrister named Sir Edward Carson came together to sign the Ulster Covenant. This document pledged its signatories to use *any* means at hand to prevent 'the present conspiracy to set up a Home Rule Parliament in Ireland'. Carson signed first with a silver pen, followed by distinguished lords, prelates, MPs and some 450,000 Ulster men and women – some dropping to their knees to sign, others doing so in their own blood. The Tories launched a similar campaign in Britain, which enjoyed phenomenal success, and, in the person of their leader Bonar Law, exhorted the King to sack the Liberal government because of its policy of Home Rule. F. E. Smith (later Lord Birkenhead) announced, 'Should it happen that Ulster is threatened with a violent attempt to incorporate her in an Irish parliament, I say to Sir Edward Carson, "Appeal to the young men of England." ' By January 1913, a long tradition of violent secret societies in Ulster dedicated to the protection of

---

* It is ironic that in the Six Counties today the Unionists there have purloined the slogan of self-determination as a means of retaining their old privileges.

Protestant Unionist dominance culminated in the formation of a highly disciplined militia called the Ulster Volunteers. With its right-wing bias, its secret oaths, its abhorrence of democracy and its almost mystical symbology, it might be called Europe's first modern fascist army. Then, in an infamous incident in March 1914, the army threw in their hat when British officers stationed at the Curragh in Co. Kildare refused to obey government orders to secure arms depots in Ulster against raids by Carson's Volunteers. Vladimir Lenin, profoundly interested, like Marx and Engels before him, in events in Ireland, wrote about the Curragh Mutiny: 'March 21st 1914 will be an epoch-making turning point, the day when the noble landlords in Britain smashed the British Constitution and British law to bits and gave an excellent lesson in class struggle.'

The pressure from these three sources – Tories, Unionists and army – was relentless: it pushed the battle for Home Rule out of John Redmond's domain; it shook the British Constitution as it was struggling to evolve, and it monopolized British policies until the outbreak of the Great War. The government, its capacity to rule being steadily undermined, helplessly offered the partition of Ireland as a makeshift compromise. More importantly, a more violent, lawless strain was becoming the more representative in Irish political affairs.

5

We now have a literary movement, it is not very important; it will be followed by a political movement, that will not be very important; then must come a military movement, that will be important indeed.

Standish O'Grady, father of the Literary Revival, 1899

There is in Ireland the murmur of men marching.

Patrick Pearse in Brooklyn, New York, 1914

Elsewhere in Ireland the mood of militancy spawned in the north-east was taken up with enthusiasm. As the reintroduction of the gun into Irish politics eroded the groundwork of Redmond's grand design for Home Rule, so it also radicalized peaceful nationalists.

One of the most significant events of the period was the revitalization of the Irish Republican Brotherhood. Following the ill-fated rebellion of 1867, the Brotherhood faded out amid sporadic and unpopular violent acts and eventually became a kind of harmless, forgotten club for wistful old men. But extra-parliamentary nationalism again became popular in the first years of the twentieth century and the IRB could not remain stagnant. Three young northerners – Sean MacDermott, Denis McCullough and Bulmer Hobson – joined up and soon began to shake the organization out of its despondent torpor; the old guard were removed, new recruits were both more impatient and more dedicated and the IRB began carefully to extend their influence throughout the existing nationalist organizations. They were joined by one of the most dedicated of the veteran Fenians – a slight, balding, grey man with a walrus moustache who ran a newsagent's and tobacconist's in Parnell Street: Tom Clarke. Clarke had successfully endured some fifteen years of torment in Chatham prison for his part in a Fenian dynamiting campaign in the 1880s and had emerged with, if anything, an even colder sense of purpose.

MARTIN WALTON: When Tom Clarke came out of jail – and strangely it was John Redmond and his influence that got him out – between himself as an elderly man and Sean MacDermott, the younger man, they brought in a new spirit. The older men were content to meet and discuss and try and keep an eye on things and put the odd word in here and there, but they had no intention of creating a rising. It wasn't until Clarke and MacDermott got working hard and brought in men like Pearse and Peadar Kearney, the man who wrote the 'Soldier's Song', that things started to move.

All over Ireland, the action of the Ulster Volunteers was forcing choices and awakening previously dormant souls.

MAIRE COMERFORD: I was about fourteen or fifteen when my father died, and I think I was the first woman in my family who was told she had to work for a living. My mother said that girls got very good employment as secretaries to important people, so she gave me what money she could for a course of training in a secretarial school in London. The head of the school was a lady from County Meath who was an acquaintance of my mother. This was about 1912, and she was a bitter Unionist. The signing of the Ulster Covenant was going on and I was probably the only Catholic in the class. She was teaching us shorthand, and she would dictate to us speeches by Edward Carson and people like that. Then she would turn on me very aggressively and say, 'What have you got to say about that?' I felt entirely set back, but I felt there was something I had to know, so I bought books about Ireland. I had a bicycle, and my only liberty and happiness was on the bike, and after reading the

books I began to look for the homes of the absentee landlords from Ireland who had big houses out of the money
they got from Irish tenants. Places around Hyde Park and
Belgravia. I remember seeking out the houses and just looking at them for a long, long time and thinking about the
people back home who had been rack-rented and whose
poverty had provided these mansions in London. So I decided I would never be a secretary to anyone except in
Ireland.

One by one the old nationalist groups left behind the business of recreating Irish culture and were transformed into
militant organizations poised for war. The Gaelic League and
Gaelic Athletic Association, manoeuvred by the IRB, grew
increasingly political. Even the Gaelic League's temperate,
non-violent president, Douglas Hyde, was moved to presage
the violent upheavals to come in a translation he had made
from an old Irish poem:

> There is a change coming, a big change
> And riches and store will be nothing worth,
> He will rise up that was small-eyed,
> And he that was big will fall down.
>
> The time will come, and it's not far from us,
> When strength won't be on the side of authority or law,
> And the neck will bend that was not bent,
> When that time comes it will come heavily.

Other poets of the Literary Revival went further, writing of
the cleansing effects of blood.

Women too were mobilized, as Maud Gonne's Inghinidhe
na hEireann became the Cumann na mBan, a more military
and purposeful organization. Patrick Pearse, now emerging as
a leader, was moved to comment, 'I would not like to think
of women drilling and marching in the ordinary way, but there
is no reason that they should not learn to shoot.'

BRIGHID LYONS THORNTON: Every Friday evening we went

23

to Cumann na mBan, as it was called. They still call themselves Cumann na mBan. A *cumann* is a gathering or an association, and the Cumann na mBan was the company of Irish women. There were first-aid classes held there and drilling and marching and – what do you call these things with flags? – semaphore, and my aunt, the wife of Joe MacGuinness, was very proficient in it and she was one of the leaders and teachers. Then sometimes over from Parnell Square, number 51 where the Volunteers met, some of the officers came over. It was a big night if Commandant Daly or Commandant O'Sullivan or Commandant Paddy Houlihan came. Paddy would usually line us up and march us up and down doing the quickstep up and down the hall. Then we had Commandant Daly, later executed, a brother of Mrs Tom Clarke. He was very austere, very withdrawn I thought, but a man you would never forget. He would come in and sit around and talk to some people who knew him and with Commandant O'Sullivan, who later married his sister.

The Fianna Eireann, the nationalist boy scout organization and recruiting ground for future activists, had been founded in 1909 by the unlikely duo of an Anglo-Irish lady, Constance, Countess Markievicz, and the IRB man and middle-class Quaker from Ulster, Bulmer Hobson; it too was growing in numbers and vigour.

SEAN HARLING: In 1909 an announcement appeared in the Irish papers that the British Baden Powell, the Boy Scout movement, was about to be formed in Lord Iveagh's grounds here, just across from Harcourt Street. Well the Countess Markievicz was very annoyed with this and she said, 'Why should a British boy scout movement be organized here to recruit Irish boys?' and she formed an organization known as Fianna Eireann, the Irish national boy scout organization, to train them in Morse code and everything else the Baden Powells were doing. It took on very

24

well. There were companies in the north side of the city and in the south side. Sean Heuston was in charge in the north side – he was executed in 1916 – and Con Colbert was in charge of the south side, and he was executed in 1916. It was not until 1913, four years after Madam's boy scout movement had started, that I went to join. I was born in 1902, so that would have left me eleven years of age. I was living in the Phibsborough Road, and I went down to the north side headquarters with a pal of mine named Bobby Tweedale to join and there was this woman sitting on the stage. That was the first time I ever saw the Countess Markievicz. I got very interested. We were buying our own uniforms and getting the green shirts made and attending parades twice a week.

The Irish trade union movement likewise found itself evolving into a militant, nationalist organization. Dublin then was choked with verminous, overspilling tenements, and plagued with corrupt government, vast unemployment and catastrophic rates of infant mortality and tuberculosis. Revulsion at such conditions drove thousands of unskilled workers into the Irish Transport and General Workers' Union. But, as with the Land League of the recent past, the purely economic issue could not be prised loose from the enduring National question. The new trade unionists directed themselves not merely against their employers, but also against the entire British connection with Ireland. They were led by Ireland's first twentieth-century revolutionary – the electric, almost daemonic mob orator Jim Larkin, a nationalist as well as a socialist.

SEAN HARLING: My father was a real Labour man, a real Jim Larkinite, and he was with the Midland Railway. I remember a funny thing, some years later when I was working for Mick Collins I had £3 10s. a week and my father was only on 35s. in the railway. I differed from me father's money nearly more than he was earning himself.

25

I met Jim Larkin once. I was in the house one Friday evening and there was a knock on the door. A tall man came in and he said, 'Can I have a loan of the chair?' So I said, 'Yes, Mr Larkin.' He said, 'How do you know me?' And I said, 'I seen you speaking in O'Connell Street.' So I handed him out the chair. What he wanted was to stand on it and address the railwaymen coming out.

In 1913 Larkin organized a transport strike against William Martin Murphy's Dublin Tramway Company. It was late August and, as it was Horse Show week, Dublin was full of wealthy English visitors and Ireland's own aristocracy. The Dublin Employers' Federation, under Murphy's guidance, responded approximately a week later with a lockout against all employees who would not officially abjure Larkin's union. Over the following months the slums of Dublin were slowly starved and brutalized, with the eager help of police batons, into submission. The strike finally collapsed in February 1914.

But an unforgettable lesson had been learned. On 13 November 1913, Larkin's colleague James Connolly proclaimed to assembled trade unionists, 'Listen to me, I am going to talk sedition. The next time we set out for a route march, I want to be accompanied by four battalions of trained men. I want them to come out with their corporals and their sergeants and people to form fours. Why should we not drill and train in Dublin as they are drilling and training in Ulster?' It was with such bellicose rhetoric that the trade unionists formed their own self-protective militia, the Irish Citizen Army.

The most significant and enduring event in this period of increasing militancy was the formation on 25 November 1913 of the Irish Volunteers, the immediate predecessors of the IRA. This was an initiative primarily of Bulmer Hobson and a radical Gaelic Leaguer called The O'Rahilly. They and others had been somewhat transfixed by the brazen manoeuvres of the Ulster Volunteer Force, and believed that the nationalist movement should have a similar body at its disposal. They approached a moderate nationalist named Eoin MacNeill, Professor of Early and Medieval Irish History at University College, Dublin, to write an article for the Gaelic League journal, *An Chlaidheamh Soluis*. Whether the solicitation specified the subject of volunteering is not certain, but the result was a piece called 'The North Began', which called for the formation of a national volunteer movement and applauded the Ulster Volunteers' independence of mind and defiance of the British Parliament. MacNeill was accordingly invited to preside over the formation of the Irish Volunteers, which he did at an overflowing meeting at the Rotunda in Dublin on 25 November 1913. Three thousand men were enrolled at this opening meeting; within six months the membership figures had jumped to over 100,000.

There was a profound ambivalence at the heart of this new organization. It had been engendered in part by what some of its members took to be the sterling example of militarism implicit in the Ulster Volunteers, and in part as a defence against the usurpation of Home Rule by that very force. It was ostensibly a passive body, yet the provisional committee which ran it was loaded with IRB men who saw it as a tool of revolution. Internal dissensions eventually brought about a rupture which sent a large number of Volunteers into the British army and thence to their deaths in France, and others into open rebellion against the Empire. But for most of their first year, before the Great War forced such choices upon them, they were able to abide together in some amity as a loose confederation of nationalists wary of Britain's commitment to Home Rule.

The extra-parliamentary ante was upped when the dummy wooden rifles used on parades by both Ulster Volunteers and Irish Volunteers were replaced by real ones. Both Unionists and nationalists turned to Germany, with whom Britain was on the edge of war, and accordingly, on 24 April 1914, the Ulster Volunteers successfully landed 10,000 Manlicher rifles, 9100 Mauser rifles and 2 million rounds of ammunition purchased in Hamburg. In London, Eoin MacNeill met with some prestigious Anglo-Irish Protestants, including Sir Roger Casement and Alice Stopford Green (an historian for whom Maire Comerford was soon to start work as a secretary) and, perhaps provoked by the success of the Unionists, they decided to respond in kind. On 26 July, the nationalists ran a far more modest consignment of arms, also purchased in Hamburg, to Howth, just outside Dublin. They were carried in a yacht belonging to Erskine Childers, yet another Anglo-Irishman who had previously served Britain with distinction. Seven or eight hundred Volunteers marched out of Dublin to Howth that morning; with them was a small detachment of the Fianna.

SEAN HARLING: One morning in 1914 we were mobilized, about fifteen of us, and I was called upon to take part in my first action. We had a trek-cart – it's a hand cart with a canvas top and a long centre shaft – and we were to proceed with this to Howth. We didn't even know what was going on, but do you know what it was? It was the gun-running. The *Asgard*, that's Erskine Childers's yacht, it pulled into the harbour with himself and his wife on board and they started to unload the rifles. There was companies of Volunteers there but we filled our trek-cart full of rifles and ammunition and started back for the city. When we got near the end of the Clontarf Road we were told that the Scottish Borderers had taken the bottom of the road. We didn't attempt to go through them or we would have lost the rifles so we went back to the village of Coolock. We found a place there, Redden's fields, and all of us started digging and we buried the cart there with the rifles and ammunition in it. We went back some time later when it was safe and dug it up and brought the rifles into Dublin.

A small, truculent crowd pursued the Scottish Borderers into the centre of Dublin, jeering at them and finally throwing a few stones and bottles at them as they turned into Bachelor's

Walk. This rather listless riot had tragic consequences when the Borderers fired a volley into the crowd.

SEAN HARLING: That same day, maybe because they hadn't stopped the gun-running, the Scottish Borderers opened fire on a crowd and they killed some people down at Bachelor's Walk, along the quays. And not many people know this, but they had to be taken out of this country afterwards and they were sent to France. When they were there the Dublin Fusiliers mowed them down for killing those people in Bachelor's Walk.

Four people were killed and thirty-eight were wounded. The Ulster Volunteers were meanwhile openly parading their own smuggled arms, undisturbed by the government; Irish people were acquiring a sharper sense of government priorities.

6

The United Irishmen repudiated Grattan. The Young Irelanders repudiated O'Connell. The Irish Volunteers have repudiated Redmond.

Patrick Pearse

Things began to fall apart very rapidly for John Redmond. He found himself caught in what was effectively a pincer movement, the constituent elements of which had by now passed from his control: not only was the dark alliance of Tories, Ulster Unionists and the army stealing by extortion the Home Rule he was so certain he had achieved, but a terrified Liberal government, bargaining desperately for the survival not only of themselves but also of the Constitution, was quickly capitulating to all their demands. Perhaps worst of all, his old bedrock of support, the nationalists at home, were passing into the control of those radical separatists, the IRB. The British political process on which he staked his authority was coming undone, through no fault of his own, and the same forces which were bringing him to the edge of his political grave were propelling those of revolution forward.

The first of two disastrous decisions made by Redmond occurred in March 1914, when he agreed with Asquith to the partitioning of Ireland, a matter on which he had previously claimed to be immovable. It was to take the form of an Amending Bill to Home Rule. Initially it excluded six of the nine counties of Ulster for a period of six years; Redmond was then manoeuvred with increased pressure to agree to permanent exclusion. When Britain entered the war in August 1914, he struggled desperately to get Home Rule placed on the statute

30

books and also to recover the lost six counties. His partial success, what might be called the realization of his life's work, had a terrible hollowness to it: the Home Rule Bill was passed but immediately suspended until after the war and with a crippling qualifier that all but guaranteed permanent partition. When the Bill received the royal assent on 18 September, a few MPs, confident that British generosity and good sense had once again prevailed, struck up 'God Save the King'; a Labour member called out 'God Save Ireland!' and Redmond, perhaps with some embarrassment, piped back 'God Save England too!' – words which aptly characterized him in the eyes of many of the new nationalists at home.

The Great War put a sudden end to the drift towards constitutional collapse in Britain by removing the disturbing Irish question from the public mind and House of Commons and replacing it with the patriotic fervour of the war effort. Winston Churchill wrote of the effect of immense relief which this had on the Cabinet:

The Cabinet on Friday afternoon, July 24, sat long revolving the Irish problem. . . . The disagreements and antagonisms seemed as fierce and hopeless as ever, yet the margin in dispute upon which such fateful issues hung was inconceivably petty. The discussion, which turned principally upon the boundaries of Fermanagh and Tyrone,* had reached its inconclusive end, and the Cabinet was about to separate when the quiet grave tones of Sir Edward Grey's voice were heard reading a document which had just been brought to him from the Foreign Office. *It was the Austrian Note to Serbia.* He had been reading or speaking for several minutes before I could disengage my mind from the tedious and bewildering debate which had just closed. . . . The parishes of Fermanagh and Tyrone faded back into the mists and squalls of Ireland, and a strange light began immediately, but by perceptible gradations, to fall and grow upon the map of Europe.

* This dispute, related to the partition scheme which the Liberal government was being forced into, was about which parts of Fermanagh and Tyrone – both of which had Catholic majorities – should be included in 'Northern' Ireland and which in 'Southern' Ireland.

The war was also the occasion of John Redmond's second fatal political decision. With his proprietorial bluster regarding Irish nationalism, he had managed to secure partial (and short-lived) control over the Irish Volunteers. Noting the crisis in Europe and trying to ingratiate himself to a Britain that at this point had still not made Home Rule law, he announced in the Commons on 3 August that he was offering his men as home defenders, with the Ulster Volunteers, of Ireland's shores, thus releasing the British army stationed there for service at the front. This was received initially with some enthusiasm in Ireland, an Ireland that sympathized with poor, small and Catholic Belgium suffering at the hands of the Germans. But Lord Kitchener – one of a long line of Irishmen who fought well for Britain – made it clear that all he wanted from Ireland was recruits and recruits only, that Redmond's notion of an armed home defence force was a preposterous joke, that Irish volunteers would not remain intact as a regiment but would fight where and with whom they were told, and, finally, that there would be few if any commissions for Irishmen (Redmond's brother Willy, who later died in France, was denied one when he joined up). Redmond, with ever less room to manoeuvre, suddenly found himself cast as a recruiting agent for the British army, much to the disgust of many of his former supporters. In a famous speech at Woodenbridge in County Wicklow, Redmond announced, 'Your duty is two-fold. I am glad to see such magnificent material for soldiers around me, and I say to you, "Go on drilling and make yourselves efficient for the work, and then account yourself as men, not only in Ireland itself, but wherever the firing line extends, in defence of right, of freedom, and of religion." ' The other Ireland saw it differently. Sean O'Casey wrote in a satirical ballad:

'Now scholars, hurlers, saints and bards,'
Says the Grand Old Dame Britannia,
'Come along and join the Irish Guards,'
Says the Grand Old Dame Britannia.

> 'Every man who treads on a German's feet,
> He gets a parcel tied up neat,
> A Home Rule badge and a winding sheet,'
> Says the Grand Old Dame Britannia.

The Volunteers could no longer stand the strain and accordingly split in September 1914. It took recruitment to finally radicalize some, but many had previously been disaffected from Redmond and his parliamentarians by the inadequacies of the Home Rule Bill.

JOSEPH SWEENEY: My father was a very keen politician and he followed the progress of the Home Rule Bill in the House of Commons at Westminster. We often had discussions and arguments at home about Home Rule and what it would mean to the country. When Carson started the Ulster Volunteers, the Irish Volunteers were started up here as a sort of counter-blast. My father became one of the principals there.

At that time in west Donegal where I lived there was an organization called the Ancient Order of Hibernians, and my father was the president of the local branch. They were very powerful and while they were to a certain extent political in content they were organized originally as a sectarian fraternal brotherhood because of the difficulties in the north. They had no interest in militancy as such at all. They were just bluffing, getting the Volunteers together and getting token arms from various places, old Italian rifles and one thing and another. They were just trying to bluff the Carsonites. As far as I could see they wanted political power more than anything else. They wanted to come in under the umbrella of the Home Rule Act when it became law and get all the jobs for themselves.

We young people regarded them as being useless. You couldn't argue with them at all. You were only young and they pushed you aside. We got a draft of the Home Rule Bill, which we read with avidity, and saw that it was all restrictions. We had no freedom at all. We had no control of the fiscal side of things, we had no control over our police and of course we had no army. The economy was the one thing that we should have had control of and that was a reserved power to the British government. We came to the conclusion that it was useless. Accordingly when the split came in the Volunteers in Dublin, I took up the side of those who split with Redmond and went on from there to join the Volunteers in the local company out in Rathfarnham.

Redmond's side remained vastly superior numerically to the more radical group nominally under MacNeill, but as the former was simply siphoned off to the trenches in France, the latter grew with that single-minded sense of purpose accorded to revolutionaries. Redmond had gambled everything – he had agreed to the severance of Ireland and had pledged its manhood to the Imperial war effort – in return for a suspended, truncated bill which fewer and fewer people really cared about. Time had passed him by, and though he retained a measure of enthusiastic support for some years to come, his commitment to the British Empire rendered him a spent force.

BRIGHID LYONS THORNTON: We counted a great deal on John Redmond, and John Dillon of course and some others, working out Home Rule for us. They carried the balance of power as far as I remember at that stage. John Redmond said that if they put Ireland on the statute book he'd rally all the Irish boys and people to go out and fight for the British army. Well that killed his standing in the country for most people. But a great many did go, they went and they were buried in the Somme and all the other places. Thousands . . . a tremendous number of our best people were sent to that war.

SEAN KAVANAGH: Up to the beginning of the war, when we started recruiting for the British army, I had been a Home Ruler, like 99 per cent of our people. I didn't think we should be recruiting for the British army, sending our people to a war which didn't concern us, and I began to change my mind. I didn't consider us so much taking action against Britain as action for Ireland, for the liberation of Ireland.

7

The general state of Ireland, apart from recruiting, and apart from the activities of the pro-German Sinn Fein minority, is thoroughly satisfactory. The mass of the people are sound and loyal as regards the war, and the country is in a very prosperous state and very free from ordinary crimes.

Major Ivor Price, Director of Military Intelligence in Ireland, 10 April 1916 – two weeks before the Easter Rising

Ireland did not have to wait so long for new leadership as it had after the fall of Parnell. The times simply threw up a host of eager agitators and the IRB, though intensely, obsessively secretive in their workings, began to shape the ripening nationalism in Ireland into an armed revolutionary force. The future heroes of the Easter Rising – the old Fenian Tom Clarke and younger men like Sean MacDermott, Eamon de Valera and Eamonn Ceannt and the poets Thomas MacDonagh, Joseph Plunkett and Patrick Pearse – began to achieve a certain prominence and under their guidance militaristic manoeuvres such as mock battles became commonplace in the streets of Dublin. James Connolly, a man of tremendous intellectual force and moral commitment, likewise pledged his disgruntled trade unionists to insurrection.

One of the most compelling and extraordinary of the new leaders was Patrick Pearse, a quixotic, mystical figure much taken with the vision of renewal by blood that was spreading with the war throughout Europe. Having forsaken both a career as a barrister and the policy of Home Rule which he had once guardedly endorsed, Pearse used his considerable eloquence as a poet, pamphleteer and orator to promote the cause of a free and Gaelic Ireland. Though he wrote apocalyptically about 'the old heart of the earth [being] warmed with the red wine of the battlefields', he was nevertheless a gentle humanist, and was perhaps happiest when teaching. He was an outstanding educator, having founded two bilingual schools – St Enda's for boys and St Ita's for girls – that in their open, experimental approach were long in advance of their time.

JOSEPH SWEENEY: I had the great advantage as a boy of being sent to Pearse's school, to St Enda's in Rathfarnham. I remember the first time I laid eyes on him when I arrived at St Enda's and he came out on the step to greet me. I thought he was a very young man to be the president of a college, because I had done a year and a half prior to this in Letterkenny where all the teachers were priests, and they were pretty old men. The contrast between the headmaster in Donegal and Pearse shook me forcibly from the beginning. He took me in and he sat me down and we had a long conversation. He sort of assessed what he was going to do with me with regard to education. He was a magnificent teacher, one of the two best teachers which I have met in my lifetime, the other being an old priest in Letterkenny who taught English.

Pearse ran the school on the honour system. If something happened that was out of the way you were supposed to stand up and admit it right then. This worked quite well, though we had an intake of maybe two or three fellows a year from other schools who didn't understand this, and who didn't want to understand this, and then we had to deal with these fellows ourselves. One fellow was very difficult, we could make no headway with him at all, and eventually we seized him, four or five of us bigger fellows, and then went down to Pearse's office. One fellow opened the door and we flung him in there and closed the door behind him and he had to explain himself then to Pearse. That was the system we lived under. If you wanted any privileges of any kind you went to Pearse and asked him in

Irish. You hadn't a hope of getting anywhere if you asked in English.

Every night after tea Pearse came into the study hall. He stood at the middle rostrum there and he took up a particular episode of Irish history and gave us a lecture on it. All in Irish of course. I went through the whole gamut, from preparatory, junior, middle grade, and I passed senior grade in 1915. All that time I came very much under the influence of Pearse, as most of the older boys did, and I acquired a very deep insight into history from him. We were committed completely to the idea of separation, the old Wolfe Tone definition of freedom – to break the connection with England.

Pearse himself described the elements of his imaginative nationalist concoction:

When we were starting St Enda's I told my boys: 'We must recreate and perpetuate in Ireland the knightly tradition of Cuchulainn, "better is short life with honour than long life with dishonour" . . . the noble tradition of the Fianna, "we, the Fianna, never told a lie, falsehood was never on our lips" . . . the Christ-like tradition of Columcille, "if I die it shall be from excess of love I bear the Gael" ' . . . I have seen Irish boys and girls moved inexpressibly by the story of Robert Emmet . . . and I have always felt it legitimate to make use for educational purposes of the exaltation so produced.

As Pearse's status rose with the increasing revolutionary fervour, his school came to resemble a training ground for the coming battle.

JOSEPH SWEENEY: We had a man called Slattery at St Enda's who taught chemistry and mathematics and we helped him in the manufacture of explosives. They were a little more sophisticated than these fertilizer things they've used in the North. I used to be sent downtown to Boileau & Boyd's to get all the right chemicals. We ground them up with pestle and mortar and he mixed them and weighted them and we put them into various types of landmines and canister bombs. I used to test them occasionally on the grounds of the school to see if they were effective and at the subsequent inquiry after the Rising a doctor who lived on the neighbouring estate spoke of the terrible explosions he heard from time to time in St Enda's.

BRIGHID LYONS THORNTON: There was a Sunday outing, an *aeraiocht*, at Pearse's school, St Enda's, and Countess Markievicz was expected. You went over there and you walked round the grounds and you met everybody and you had a wonderful day. That was all. I remember seeing all the boys lined up and they had little green shirts and little caps, and I was waiting to hear and to meet the Countess. The boys were all alerted and all enthusiastic and what I could never forget was the adoration they had for her. I hadn't met any countess in my life and I expected her to come in with a tiara and a few ermine robes. And this withered hag came in, gaunt and ugly and with prominent teeth. That's not unkind, I don't mean to be, but she was sallow, you know, and anything but what my idea of a countess was like. But they rallied round her and the emotion and the enthusiasm for her made a greater impression once I'd got over the first.

Redmond continued to tell the Irish people that his promise of Irish manhood to Britain had in fact been a noble and patriotic act. Those who had gone to France, he said, would return, hardened by war, to join their brothers who had stayed at home and would once again assert the Home Rule principle. The British would be grateful for their service in the war, he assured them, but even if they weren't, they would use their new strength to achieve a free and united Ireland. But it soon became clear that the cream of the Volunteers was being slaughtered on the European front and that the new wartime coalition government was hardly well disposed to the implementation of Home Rule for all of Ireland. Bonar Law and, incredibly, Sir Edward Carson were in the Cabinet and Asquith proposed to appoint J. H. Campbell, a most fanatical Unionist who was reported to have signed the Ulster Covenant in his own blood, to the post of Lord Chancellor of Ireland. A profound sense of betrayal began to work on the Irish consciousness; on 1 August 1915, when tens of thousands of Irish men and women took to the streets to mourn the death of the old Fenian O'Donovan Rossa, Pearse captured this sense in his graveside oration and transformed it into one of exhilaration.

BRIGHID LYONS THORNTON: The first of my big outings was the funeral of O'Donovan Rossa, the great Fenian. He died in America and his remains were brought home. They were all organizing then. Flags were being made, banners were being made – all sorts of activities. On that day – it was a lovely Sunday morning – I sold flags and badges all the way from Gardiner Street to the fountain in James's Street. Then we marched to Glasnevin Cemetery, myself and a lot of my colleagues who were a lot more elderly than I was. I was only a teenager; that's when I could walk, before I lost the use of my feet. And I stood beside the grave and listened to Pearse delivering the oration, the famous speech. Now I was very impressed when I was told it was Pearse. I was standing quite near him. Everybody was impressed and you had the feeling that things were happening around you and going on and that you were part of it. That was a great sensation.

Pearse concluded his oration with the words:

The Defenders of this Realm have worked well in secret and in the open. They think that they have pacified Ireland. They think that they have purchased half of us and intimidated the other half. They think that they have foreseen everything, think that they have provided against everything; but the fools, the fools, the fools – they have left us our Fenian dead, and while Ireland holds these graves, Ireland unfree shall never be at peace.

40

The radicals of the new generation were not of sufficient numbers to be called a truly popular movement, but they now had the confidence of one. No one, not even Connolly or the Supreme Council of the IRB, knew precisely what would happen, but however indomitable the British Empire, they had taken irreversible steps to engage it in battle. The history of Irish resistance was fast approaching its climax.

BRIGHID LYONS THORNTON: They were a lovely, happy people, young and old. I was the youngest of the group, with my uncle Joe MacGuinness, the Conlans, the Lynches, all the various other people. We never seemed to meet anybody who moved in any other circle, who wasn't one cohesive company with the one objective of making the gesture of getting rid of the British. We were all geared up and training and preparing for a rebellion. I didn't know what a rebellion would mean, but it would mean a change. After that we might have our freedom and the world would be a different place. We went out on Sundays on picnics up the mountains and met some of the boys who would be camped there and they'd give us tea in their little tents. There was great joy and unity and fraternity and happiness amongst everybody. Everything revolved around training, organizing, preparing. They bought their own uniforms, they bought their own guns, they bought their own equipment, as many of them as could afford it, and they paid their fees to their various companies. There was rivalry between the companies, as was healthy and good of course. There was nothing mercenary about it. There was nothing vicious or there was nothing personal in it beyond their love of getting their own country into their own hands.

PART TWO

The loud silence

Easter 1916

'And then Saturday morning, louder than all the noise was the silence that descended on the city.'

Brighid Lyons Thornton

1

How deep in Irish hearts lies this passion for insurrection.

Augustine Birrell, Chief Secretary of Ireland, in a letter to
Prime Minister Asquith

Physical force, for better or worse, has been one of the cardinal principles of the struggle for a free Ireland since the forces of the Crown first unsettled the pattern of life there in the twelfth century. It has, however, never been resorted to with ease or indeed, until this century, with success; political activists have careered deliriously from moral persuasion to pacifist resistance to parliamentary pressure in avoidance of it. But it has nevertheless been an implicit assumption of each of these strategies that if they failed, violence would be the only possible recourse. It has hung thickly in the atmosphere around even the most explicit parliamentarians, giving them a much-noted ambivalence. Parnell in his dying days called finally on the old spirit of the Ribbonmen, that violent secret society, and even Redmond spoke of the battle-hardened troops who would return from the trenches of France to secure Home Rule. The English could never be certain when the debate would be removed from the Houses of Parliament to the streets and hillsides of Ireland.

To a dedicated republican, 1916 must have seemed a propitious year for a return to the persuasions of armed insurrection. The forces of history seemed to be moving in this direction. There was a distinct restiveness in the air which was making efficient rule impossible; in recent years there had been violent labour disputes, spates of gun-running and related events such as the slaughter by British troops of unarmed civilians on Bachelor's Walk. Republican and socialist papers

45

were openly advocating revolution. More important still was the tenacity of the war in Europe, with its terrible, insatiable hunger for men.

MAIRE COMERFORD: When the Great War broke out John Redmond made a great act of faith, because Home Rule had been granted to Ireland. He pledged the Irish nation to fight for England in the war. The situation was enhanced by President Wilson's attitude to the war, to the conditions for American involvement. I don't think it's realized now by anyone how tremendously important President Wilson was to the unfree world at the time. I think probably historians and people are ashamed because the poor man collapsed. At that time, in the setting of Home Rule, his principles made a tremendous impact on Ireland because they brought our cause, which had been, as it were, a domestic problem for the British, it made it a duel between Ireland and England – a very unequal one, for more than 700 years at the time. This brought the freedom of Ireland onto the world stage. Everything that Wilson said – government by consent of the governed, war for small nations, open agreements openly arrived at . . . what else? – anyhow, go right down Wilson and it was a litany of things which stirred up the Irish people right through. They were in the middle of the war, and by that time England had receded from the Home Rule Bill and had promised to Northern Unionists that Ireland would be partitioned. . . . Meanwhile, Irish manpower was haemorrhaging into the British army. This group of patriots, very noble men, in Dublin saw that, and saw that nothing they could say or do would save the Irish nation from just bleeding into the British army, unless they did something so drastic that it would halt everything.

Ireland would have to strike before the end of the war, not only to save the lives of Irish recruits, but also because only then would the English garrison be sufficiently diminished to offer the Irish some remote prospect of success. Connolly, among others, argued that only through an insurrection, by Ireland's becoming one of the war's belligerents, could it hope to be represented at the peace conference which would follow the war. There, at last, its representatives would have the chance to argue its case in an international context.

Tom Clarke had long nursed a dream of a rising, and it now seemed an idea that had once again come of age. He could see the growing strength of the Volunteers, their open parades and thousands of new recruits. And the IRB, which Clarke and Sean MacDermott had done so much to revitalize, was present at all levels of the Volunteers, including the head-quarters staff where Pearse, Bulmer Hobson, Eamonn Ceannt and Joseph Plunkett, all IRB members, held key positions. Not since the United Irishmen at the end of the eighteenth century had there been such a well-developed revolutionary organization in Ireland.

But Clarke was neither an orator nor a propagandist. He had only his unflinching resolution, and knew that leadership would have to be found elsewhere. Pearse and Connolly provided the answer. They could hardly have been two less likely comrades-in-arms: Pearse, the mystic nationalist born of the Gaelic League, with his vision of a free, pre-Conquest, almost timeless Ireland; Connolly, the pragmatic progressive born of the labour movement, an internationalist with the idea that a revolution in Ireland would signal the end of European capitalism. But their common ground was their love of Ireland, their profound sympathy for the dispossessed, and above all their uncompromising belief that the rightful owners of Ireland were the people of Ireland. The fusion of their ideas, so apparent in the Proclamation, was perhaps the most remarkable achievement of the time.

2

O Wise Men, riddle me this. What if my dream
Come true? And millions unborn shall dwell
In the house I have shaped in my heart –
The noble house of my thought?

Patrick Pearse, 'The Fool'

Towards the end of 1915, the Military Council of the IRB, a secret grouping within that most secret society, determined that the Rising would take place on Easter Sunday, 1916. It was an auspicious date and the symbols of redemption and resurrection, they felt, would not be lost on the Irish people. They were a tiny minority, really infinitesimal when compared to the number of Irish people still dedicated to the war effort as a means of securing Home Rule, and, militarily at least, they faced insurmountable odds. But it was thought that Pearse's miraculous synthesis – between pagan and Christian, Cuchulainn and Christ, valour and blood sacrifice – would reveal to the Irish people their true destiny as members of a united, sovereign nation, and not simply a province of Britain with devolved powers, which was all Home Rule would bring. The Rising could not fail as a noble example, and even if it was defeated militarily, it would provide the groundwork for a later movement which would triumph. It was an audacious supposition, all the more extraordinary because it proved to be correct.

The intervening months had more than their share of blunders, absurdities, false leads and deceptions. The IRB Military Council had first of all to deceive not only the English – and, indeed, there were no informers – but also their own leadership. Both Eoin MacNeill and Bulmer Hobson believed that an insurrection at that stage, with such insignificant numbers of men and such paltry armaments, was not only imprudent but also immoral. Such action could only be justified, they argued, if the people as a whole called for it or, on the other hand, if conscription were applied to Ireland or the Volunteers disarmed. The country was slowly coming around to their side and they must suspend all action until they held a true majority. Pearse and his colleagues circumvented them by ordering apparently innocent manoeuvres for Easter Sunday and then verbally informing selected Volunteer officers that they were in effect mobilization orders for a Rising. In the meantime, Connolly, who had been endangering the IRB's delicate preparations by loudly and relentlessly calling for revolution, was co-opted onto the Military Council and thereby brought, with his Citizen Army, into the plans for Easter.

Elsewhere, a three-cornered arms conspiracy was evolving in Dublin, New York and Berlin. John Devoy and his Clan na Gael, a highly determined and ferociously nationalistic group of Irish-Americans, provided both funds and a base of communications for Dublin's efforts to secure arms and troops from Germany. In Berlin, Roger Casement and Joseph Plunkett both dealt with the German High Command. They were eager, but hardly professional revolutionaries; both were desperately ill, both poets – Plunkett a romantic adventurer and mystic devotee of St John the Divine, always adorned with an assortment of rings, bracelets and bangles, while Casement was a knighted member of the British Consular Service, deliriously in love with Ireland and vainly striving to preserve a modicum of dignity. They nevertheless managed to negotiate for the shipment of 20,000 rifles, 10 machine guns and 5 million rounds of ammunition. These were to arrive in Tralee Bay just prior to Easter.

On the Tuesday of Holy Week, MacNeill was shown a 'secret Castle document' – doubtless an IRB forgery but probably a reasonably accurate reflection of Castle contingency plans – which detailed instructions for the arrest of Volunteer leaders and the suppression of the entire organization. He reacted, as hoped, by ordering the Volunteers to prepare to defend themselves. On Thursday he learned from Hobson that a Rising for Easter Sunday had been in preparation for some time. Enraged and appalled, he paid a midnight visit to Pearse and told him he would do everything in his power to stop such an initiative. Then on Friday, Sean MacDermott and Thomas MacDonagh informed MacNeill about the imminent arrival of the arms shipment from Germany and, realizing that the great event was now a *fait accompli*, he agreed to go along with them.

However, the delicate fabric of deception now came undone. The German arms ship, disguised as a Norwegian trawler and called the *Aud*, was not met in Kerry as planned, due to some appallingly bungled communications, and was duly captured by a British naval patrol; it sunk itself, along with the badly needed 20,000 rifles, in Queenstown (now Cobh) harbour. Casement, certain that the Rising would be a disaster without sufficient German help, hastened to Ireland either to dissuade the leaders or, if it was too late, to die in battle. He was put ashore at Banna Strand from a submarine and, soaked to the skin, his entire German adventure a disaster, he took refuge in some brambles near an ancient fort and listened blissfully to the Irish skylarks until he was apprehended by a local constable. A German railway ticket was found in his pocket and he was eventually identified as the notorious Sir Roger Casement. When MacNeill then learned on the Saturday that the 'Castle document' was a forgery, that Casement had been captured and that the precious arms were now lying at the bottom of the sea, he instantly sent messengers all around the country with instructions that the Volunteers were not to rise and then had published in the *Sunday Independent* an order explicitly countermanding the instructions for manoeuvres to take place that Sunday. The countryside, starved of the anticipated German arms and reeling under the series of conflicting orders that they could not hope to comprehend, was effectively paralysed and Pearse, Connolly and their colleagues, feverishly debating their prospects in Liberty Hall, decided they had no option but to suspend all activity until the following morning. It was unanimously agreed that they had come too far to turn back at that stage.

3

We are going out to be slaughtered.

James Connolly on the morning of the Rising

As most Dubliners pursued their pleasures in the holiday sunshine of Easter Monday morning, the Volunteers and the Citizen Army assembled at Liberty Hall to await instructions. Some were armed and in uniform; others affected an impromptu military appearance with puttees and riding breeches and carried shotguns or even pickaxes and pikes. They were detailed to their respective stations and then at 12.02 p.m. the main body marched under Pearse, Connolly and Plunkett to O'Connell Street, where they were met by Tom Clarke and Sean MacDermott. When they reached the General Post Office, James Connolly shouted, 'Left turn – the GPO. Charge!' They quickly dispersed a bewildered assortment of stamp buyers and clerks, ran up flags of the Republic on the roof and finally, at 12.45, Commandant-General Pearse stepped under the portico and read to a largely indifferent or jocular crowd that splendid document, the Proclamation.

IRISHMEN AND IRISHWOMEN: In the name of God and of the dead generations from which she receives her old tradition of nationhood, Ireland, through us, summons her children to her flag and strikes for her freedom. . . . We declare the right of the people of Ireland to the ownership of Ireland, and to the unfettered control of Irish destinies, to be sovereign and indefeasible. The long usurpation of that right by a foreign people and government has not extinguished the right, nor can it ever be extinguished except by the destruction of the Irish people. In every generation the Irish people have asserted their right to national freedom and sovereignty; six times during the past three hundred years they have asserted it in arms. Standing on that fundamental right and again asserting it in arms in the face of the world, we hereby proclaim the Irish Republic as a sovereign independent State, and we pledge our lives and the lives of our comrades-in-arms to the cause of its freedom, of its welfare, and of its exaltation among the nations. . . .

In an atmosphere of confusion, with no prospects of victory, but with gusto and a lethal seriousness, the Easter Rising thus began. At that stage the forces of the Irish Republican Army, as the combined forces of the Volunteers and Citizen Army then called themselves, were outnumbered three or four to one; on the following day the odds would go up to twenty to one against.

Of our nine veterans, four took part in the fighting – Joseph Sweeney, Brighid Lyons Thornton, Martin Walton and Sean Harling; one, Maire Comerford, was an inspired eyewitness; four, with some regret, were far away from this newly established front – Sean Kavanagh and John L. O'Sullivan in County Cork, David Neligan in west Limerick, and Tom Barry, as a member of an ill-fated British Expeditionary Force, in far-off Mesopotamia.

JOSEPH SWEENEY: It was quite evident to us that the leaders intended to take action. At the time I was doing a course of study as an engineering student at University College and I lived out at Pearse's school. In 1915, Pearse himself swore me into the IRB, and then in 1916, in the early spring, he told a number of us – there were about eight of us attending university – he told us one night in confidence that the Rising was fixed for Easter Sunday. It was felt that it had to come in our generation or never, that we would never get an organization like it again. Of course none of them had any idea that it would succeed. Pearse often talked about the sacrifice of blood that had to be made in order to awaken the conscience of the Irish people. None of them expected to survive.

We had various activities going on and we were all geared to have them completed by the time Easter came around.

Because of the fact that I had a bicycle I was invariably chosen to act as a runner carrying messages from Pearse to other men who eventually became the leaders in 1916, and I also had to transport munitions like shotgun cartridges and chemicals for the manufacture of explosives. And of course we knew that the Citizen Army was making its own preparations. Desmond Ryan was with us at St Enda's and he kept us in touch with the activities of Connolly and the labour movement. It was very interesting for us to try to liaise with them as best we could. Pearse's idea was that we all belonged to various parts of the same country.

On Easter Sunday morning then I got up early to go to Mass and cycled down to Mount Argus, and on the way back I saw posters everywhere: 'The Volunteer Parade Cancelled by MacNeill'. So I went back to St Enda's and of course there was consternation there. Pearse had gone off a few days before to stay with Sean T. O'Kelly's mother in order to avoid arrest, and Eamonn Bulfin, who was the senior man there, went off into town on a bicycle to contact him. He came back then in the afternoon with the message that the Rising was off for that day but that we were to stand by for further orders. The next morning then we were awakened at seven o'clock and told to mobilize and a few of the lads went out to round up the local company and eventually we assembled at the Yellow House, a pub beside the church in Rathfarnham. A lot of them had gone off to the Fairyhouse races, but still quite a number began to trickle in and as they did Eoin MacNeill and Sean Fitzgibbon arrived on the scene to try to persuade us not to go, that we would all be shot down. Eamonn Bulfin eventually told them to buzz off, that he was taking his men into town.

While waiting there I was told that some of the gear belonging to the company had been left behind at the college, so I got on my bike and cycled back, but when I arrived back at the meeting place they had all gone. They had taken a tram from Rathfarnham and gone to war. So I set out for Liberty Hall and on the way I collected a lot of strays from other units, so that by the time I passed Jacob's I nearly had a whole platoon. We could see that Jacob's was being put into a state of defence by the Volunteers and when we turned into Dame Street we heard the firing at the Castle, which was the attack led by Sean Connolly, who was killed there. I knew then that we were pretty near the appointed time.

When I got to Liberty Hall I found that my company had moved again, this time to the GPO, so I sent a young lad up there with a note to Pearse to the effect that I was there and was awaiting instructions. I was told then to put the place in a state of preparedness, which wasn't easy because by this time Liberty Hall was a mass of people, hangers-on just getting in the way, and I had a terrible time getting them out of it. Then I got further instructions to report to the GPO. So about a dozen of us started off up Abbey Street and when we were about halfway up there was a burst of fire from O'Connell Street. This was the attack from the GPO on the Lancers who were coming down from the top of O'Connell Street. They immediately wheeled around and galloped off, but some were shot and they left a couple of dead horses behind.

Eventually we got into the GPO and began the task there of filling mailbags full of coal, mainly dust from the basement, blocking up the windows and generally getting ready for what was to come.

MAIRE COMERFORD: I went out to lunch on Easter Monday, and this involved going from my cousin's house in Rathgar into Dublin and walking down Grafton Street. I remember stopping there to admire a party of the Citizen Army who were marching up the street and were later to take over the College of Surgeons. So I went out to Blackrock to the luncheon party and when that was over, at about three or four o'clock, I suppose, I came back into town by Balls-bridge, and there were people there in knots discussing things, talking about the Rising in Dublin. A tram man who had been held up said something about 'Streets up to your knees in blood'. So I plodded on into the city, up Grafton Street, where I saw British soldiers peeping around the corner, and into Stephen's Green. Opposite the Russell Hotel at Harcourt Street I met a young volunteer in the Citizen Army who was on sentry duty and he told me that the cause of Ireland was not lost. I had been led to believe that perhaps it was, and that only things like Home Rule could be depended on now, but here were men in insurrection and what was happening connected immediately with what I had read of Irish history. This young man told me that the Countess Markievicz was inside, which I found intensely interesting, and would I like to come in. I said, 'No, I'll come back tomorrow,' because I hadn't the heart to leave my poor old cousin, who was a cripple.

SEAN HARLING: On the Monday I was selling race cards for the Fairyhouse races down here at Broadstone Station, and there were two ticket checkers on the gates who were in the First Battalion of the Volunteers. So this cyclist came up and told them they were to report to North Brunswick Street. They immediately started off, and then myself and some of the other lads – Sean Howard, his brother and Bobby Tweedale – we went with them. We were stationed in the North Dublin Union, and there wasn't much going on there. We just brought capfuls of ammunition up to the snipers on the roof.

SEAN KAVANAGH: In 1916 I was working in Fermoy, County Cork as a young railway clerk, and news of the fighting in Dublin came as a complete surprise to me, to everybody outside of Dublin, and even to the Dublin people themselves. It was so unexpected, especially after the cancellation of the activity of Easter Sunday by Eoin MacNeill. I read that in the Sunday paper, but I wasn't in the Volunteers at the time and it didn't convey much to me. By Tuesday the trains had stopped running and there were no newspapers or news of any kind from Dublin for the first few days. I was very excited, of course, and proud, and felt that this was Irish history repeating itself.

MARTIN WALTON: I joined the Volunteers just three weeks before the Rising. I was only fifteen years of age at the time, though I had grown to six feet and so was taken in as a man. I think I attended two meetings, had instructions on how to handle a rifle, and we had one bit of field drill. I remember Thomas MacDonagh taking our names in case we were shot, so that the relatives would be looked after. We all knew there was something big on for Sunday, though we didn't know what. I found out afterwards that our job was to have been the taking of Ship Street barracks – that's the barracks behind the Castle – but of course owing to historic events known to everybody now it was cancelled. We were then mobilized for the following morning, but I missed that as I was only a latecomer to the Volunteers. I believe that Captain Colbert called to the house that morning with a message that I was to go to such and such a place, but I never got it. I had a desperate toothache that day and I went down Drumcondra Road to get my tooth out, but because it was a bank holiday the dentist wasn't open, and I remember coming back home and my father putting whiskey on it. About four o'clock in the evening then we heard a terrible burst of machine-gun fire and my cousin, an orphan girl who lived with us, she became terribly worried. She was very attached to Tom Cotter, who was one of three sons in that family who were out in the Rising, and he to her, and she said, 'O my God,' she said, 'he's out in that.'

My plan then was to get into town by pretending to go to work on Tuesday, but I found out my parents had taken the valves from my bicycle because they didn't want me to get involved. But I insisted I'd be sacked if I didn't go to work, and I managed then to get into O'Connell Street. I could see looters emptying the shops out, and there were some dead horses that had been shot under the Lancers, who had tried to take the GPO on the Monday. Hamilton Norway had just renovated the GPO from top to bottom and had done a terrific job on it, but all the windows were knocked out and the place was barricaded. There was an upturned tramcar too. A general scene of desolation. So I called in to the GPO and asked where C Company, Second Battalion was, and I saw all the lads in there and all the hustle and bustle, and I was told it was in Jacob's Factory, the biscuit factory in Wexford Street. It's very hard for people today to believe that a man living on the north side of Dublin had hardly ever been across to the south side, but I had no idea where Wexford Street was and so I had to inquire my way across. Trinity College at this time was held by the Officers Training Corps and the GRs.* They had an armband with GR on it in honour of the King, but we used to call them the Gorgeous Wrecks or the God's Rejected. The whole of Dame Street was completely held under fire by them. Now I had no uniform or rifle, no arms of any description, but as bad luck would have it I had a green suit which looked damned like a uniform and I was nearly shot at the Lower Castle Gate.

When I arrived then at Jacob's the place was surrounded by a howling mob roaring at the Volunteers inside, 'Come out to France and fight, you lot of so-and-so slackers.' And then I started shouting up to the balustrade, 'Let me in, let me in.' And then I remember the first blood I ever saw shed. There was a big, very, very big tall woman with something very heavy in her hand and she came across and lifted up her hand to make a bang at me. One of the Volunteers upstairs saw this and fired and I just remember seeing her face and head disappear as she went down like a sack. That was my baptism of fire, and I remember my knees nearly going out from under me. I would have sold

* The GRs were a reserve training force comprised primarily of middle-class, over-age Irishmen.

my mother and father and the Pope just to get out of that bloody place. But you recover after a few minutes.

BRIGHID LYONS THORNTON: Rumours began to go around. There wasn't much in the way of media then. Out in the country where I was people would only get a paper once a week. I came into Longford to my uncle on the Sunday, and the following day some of the staff belonging to him had gone off to Dublin. It was the thing to do to go to Dublin on an Easter Monday excursion. They didn't get back that evening at seven o'clock, the time the train was due, and we were all very concerned. When the train finally did arrive at ten or eleven o'clock they said that Dublin was in flames and there was shooting and they only barely got out with their lives. There were dead horses in the street, they said, so many people had been killed and the British had multiplied their garrisons.

So everybody was up all night standing in the street waiting for rumours and the next day the thing went on. There were no trains or communications then at all with Dublin. So that morning, on the Tuesday, my uncle said to me that he'd like to go to Dublin to see what was happening. Now he was a mature man and I would have expected more sense, but the next thing he said to me was, 'Would you like to come?' Well, I said I'd love it. 'Well then go and ask your aunt,' he said, and I did. She said, 'Surely he's not going,' and I said, 'He is, and I'd love to go with him.' 'Oh no, no, no,' she said, 'it would be too dangerous.' And then she came to me after a while and said, 'Maybe you'd be safer if you were with him.' So I had on a little grey costume and the car came down to pick me up and we set off for Dublin. There was my uncle and myself, a Mr Farrell, whose wife was ill in Dublin, and Tom Bannon, a teacher and a *Gaeilgeoir* – a great, you know, supporter of the movement. It was a lovely day, and the loveliest country-side. Birds singing, trees blossoming, everything glorious and peaceful and happy and there was no sign of trouble or bloodshed or anything. But it was then we came to McKee Barracks – it was Marlborough Barracks then I think but it was renamed later – and we were stopped by a tremendous gathering of troops. They were looking over the wall, over sandbags and barbed wire and rifles and bayonets and all sorts of things. We were told to get out then, and the soldiers started whistling at me. It was rather flattering I suppose. Then my uncle was called forward and he produced his warrant of appointment for them – he was a Peace Commissioner, you see – and he told them that he was wanted at the Castle. It was a lie of course, but then what was a lie here and there to the British. So we were told all right, that we could go ahead, but that we were to leave the car there and walk into Dublin.

So we set off over fields, across through Drumcondra around where the Archbishop lives now and then we finally got into Dorset Street. Well one thing that impressed me very sadly was the number of young people sitting along the footpath just relaxing in the sunshine. No work I presume. And we could hear the guns booming and we could see the smoke, the pall of smoke over the city. So then we walked up to Gardiner Street where my uncle Joe MacGuinness lived, and his wife was there with two or three friends, other members of Cumann na mBan, and they were very frightened and very shattered and they said, 'Oh, it's not going to succeed,' they didn't think it could, and they were sure that all the men would be shot. They had been to the Four Courts where my uncle Joe MacGuinness was, and then towards evening that day a message came out that he wanted me to go down, that my cousin, who had been sent on dispatches, had fallen and cut her hand on a lemonade bottle. So I was only too delighted to go down, and that evening Tom Bannon and myself set out, and we walked down Upper Dorset Street, Bolton Street, North King Street, then down into Church Street, sheltering in doorways every now and then when the bullets were flying. We went through barricades of barrels and dustbins across the road and you had to give the password 'Antonio' to get through. First we went down to O'Connell Street and looked at one of the horses, a dead horse, and we saw the GPO and all the fires. And then we got down into the Father Matthew Hall and I met a lot of other friends there. It was very dark there, they had only candlelight and you couldn't see much, but what I did see then was a pillow stained with blood and I said to myself, This is the rebellion at last.

4

The defensive is the death of every armed rising.

Karl Marx

The war plan, devised by Plunkett and modified by Connolly, was designed less for military victory than for a noble display of valour and endurance. Victory would be measured by how long the insurgents could hold out – six months was thought possible by Clarke, which might take them to the end of the war and thence directly to the conference table – and how vivid a symbol they could create in the process. It was propagandist poetry of the most extravagant order.

Each of the battalions of the Dublin Brigade, along with the Citizen Army, was assigned an outpost in a ring around the city and in rough correspondence to British army barracks. The GPO, headquarters for the Military Command and the Provisional Government – lay at the centre. The obvious lines of reinforcement from England or garrisons and posts in the country into the city were covered, however sparsely, and it was hoped that the rest of the country, operating under previous directives and inspired by the activities in Dublin, would spontaneously rise and, having held the line of the Shannon, march on Dublin. At least with regard to the capital itself, it was as static a plan as could be conceived: there was no provision for rudimentary street fighting or any of the more effective tactics of urban guerrilla warfare, and however strenuously more experienced warriors like Major John MacBride might have advocated taking to the streets, the insurgents remained in their outposts to the end. It was assumed that the British attack would come in the form of bayonet charges.

The leaders were perhaps aware of the emotional appeal of a besieged garrison, the implicit heroism of defence against a much larger, more professional army. Also, Connolly is said to have argued that British officers, as defenders of capitalism, would not use artillery to destroy property. That might have been the case if the city in question were London, but in the event the bayonet charges did not materialize and it was the ruthless use of artillery which broke the rebellion and demolished the centre of Dublin.

Brigadier General Lowe was the principal strategist for the British during the Rising, and though the British army had not fought within a city since Delhi and Lucknow in the 1850s, it was not a terribly difficult matter to break his opposition by driving a line of troops and fire right along its central axis, roughly along the River Liffey, thus isolating Irish outposts on the two sides of the city from one another. Reinforcements were on the way almost instantly from the Curragh and England, and with the help of these and four 18-pound guns brought in from Athlone General Lowe quickly established control of the line from Kingsbridge Station to Trinity College, as well as taking a number of important buildings in the city from which attacks were launched and fire poured into republican outposts. By Wednesday these forces were aided by relentless shelling from the makeshift gunboat *Helga*, which eventually sailed up the Liffey, the better to reduce O'Connell Street to rubble.

Such activities might have been forestalled had the Irish taken advantage of three crucial opportunities which, though they were not aware of it, lay within their grasp: the cutting of the telephone lines, and the taking of the almost completely undefended Beggar's Bush barracks and that most symbolic edifice, Dublin Castle. Had they pressed the attack they made on the latter on the first day they would have captured Under Secretary Sir Matthew Nathan, Major Ivor Price, head of the Special Intelligence Branch at army headquarters, and Hamilton Norway, Secretary of the Post Office, who were at that precise instant drawing up plans for the suppression of the

Volunteers. But however prestigious and strategically beneficial such victories might have been, they could not have reversed the outcome of the battle.

The first republican surrender came on the Wednesday, when the Mendicity Institute under Captain Sean Heuston, having endured two full days of fierce assault, finally gave in after a bomb attack. Later that day the fortunes of the republicans temporarily changed. Two rather bewildered battalions of the Sherwood Foresters had just arrived as reinforcements that morning from England and, as they stood on the quay at Kingstown (now Dun Laoghaire), some of them had thought they were in France. They made their way into the city along Northumberland Road and as they reached Mount Street Bridge fell straight into withering fire from republicans stationed there. Two Volunteers, Lieutenant Michael Malone and Section-Commander James Grace, fought ferociously for nearly five hours in number 25 Northumberland Road and inflicted enormous damage on British troops before they were bombed and the tenacious Malone was killed. Seven Volunteers in Clanwilliam House at the bridge held out for nine hours against 800 British troops. In the end they too were bombed and three Volunteers were killed. British losses in the engagement were four officers killed and fourteen wounded, and 216 killed or wounded from other ranks, by far the largest of any engagement during the week.

Meanwhile, General Lowe's improvised cordon drew tighter.

JOSEPH SWEENEY: On Tuesday morning I was ordered up to the roof, behind a thick balustrade there of granite at the corner of Henry Street and O'Connell Street. We noticed that the British troops were beginning to encircle us and I could see troops moving about freely on the tower of Amiens Street railway station. I reported back to central control below on the ground floor that these people were there and asked would I fire on them. I was told not to because they were the Inniskillings – an Irish regiment – and they might be friendly. Well, a very short time after that they indicated their feelings to me when they opened fire on me with a machine-gun. I got a right belt from a bit of granite on top of my head.

On the Wednesday, I think it was, the British mounted howitzers in the back of the Rotunda Hospital grounds and they began to lob incendiary shells on the GPO. So we dealt with them as best we could with the hoses available. And then the fire became more intense, they began to come oftener and then they shut off the water supply. So we had to retreat from the top of the roof into the lower floor and we barricaded the window overlooking the street. A young lad called Sammy Reilly, who is now a caretaker of Columbia University in New York, and myself were on sniper duty and we stopped a lot of movement at the top of the street, because when they saw the place on fire they thought they could move in. That night they brought an armoured car that they had built in Inchicore railway works around the corner of the then Great Britain Street – it's now Parnell Street – into O'Connell Street and it proceeded to clank on down towards us. So I said to Reilly, 'You take the right aperture and I'll take the left,' and we concentrated fire and stopped it. We must have killed the driver or injured somebody because it stopped there and eventually that night, when all the lights were out, they came along and pulled it back where it had come from.

From that time on the civilians cleared. There was nobody around at all – although I do remember one fellow who emerged from somewhere down towards O'Connell Bridge, dressed up in the usual businessman's style – bowler hat, rolled umbrella, striped suit – and that fellow walked the whole way up from O'Connell Bridge up to Abbey Street corner – and you could see the bullets knocking the dust up around his feet – and climbed over the barricade at North Earl Street and disappeared from sight. That evening, I think, a couple of drunks wandered out and started to abuse us, shouting up at us, and they were shot down from below

65

by British troops. They showed them no mercy at all, although it was us they were abusing. A Red Cross man ran out to attend to these fellows then, and the British began to fire at him, but he managed to get away safely. Then a fellow appeared at the door of Clery's, the big drapery establishment opposite the GPO. It was the headquarters of the Citizen Army and it had their flag, the Plough and the Stars, on top of it. But this fellow came out with a mattress wrapped around him and he ran like blazes. But when he got to the middle of the street he tripped and fell. We all thought he was a goner because the fire was desperate. But he discarded the mattress then and ran like the hammers of hell for the GPO and got in safely. I found out afterwards that it was Gearoid O'Sullivan, who later became Adjutant-General of the Free State army.

MARTIN WALTON: The British began to close in very fast then. There was a cordon around town and you couldn't get past any of the bridges. When I was moving about then I met at the corner of Dorset Street a school pal of mine, Jack Clancy. He was a medical student at that time and had joined up with the Dublin Fusiliers. He was in uniform and he called me across. 'Are you mixed up in this, Martin?' he says. 'Yes I am, Jack,' says I, 'and I'm ashamed to see you in that uniform.' He said, 'For God's sake get word down to the GPO straight away. We have four guns coming up from Athlone and there's reinforcements. Get the word down as quick as you can.' So I remember crawling down under gunfire with this message.

It became very difficult then to get in and out, but having been a kid and explored all the lanes and alleyways I was able to devise a way. Having been stopped at the bridge in Drumcondra, I went back up the North Circular Road and took a turn down a little walk behind Mountjoy Prison. There was a branch of the canal which ran down there to Broadstone Station. I was able to climb off a footbridge and onto a signal post and then down along the line. This gave me clear passage in and out of Dublin and I used this several times during the week running messages.

BRIGHID LYONS THORNTON: Tom Bannon and I went down further and further until we were brought in through a hole in the wall from Church Street into the Four Courts, and I met my uncle Joe MacGuinness there and I was received with great affection and joy. He was in uniform, puttees they wore, and he introduced me to Captain Fahy, who was later the Ceann Comhairle – that's the Speaker of the Dail – and to Peadar Clancy, who was of course butchered a few years later on Bloody Sunday. Ned Daly, the commandant, was there too, of course. So then he said I was to go down to the kitchen where the girls were and I made my way down through sandbags and Volunteers and got into the kitchen, which seemed to be full of food. There was no light, only little candles, but as far as I could make out there was a big range and there were several girls cooking there. So nobody knew me and I just sat down on a box waiting patiently until directed to do something. Captain Fahy came in after a while and he said, 'Is there any tea?' and somebody said they'd make some for him. So then I asked if I could have a cup too and after that a young fellow came in, one of the Fianna – Sean Howard* I think his name was – and they said, 'Would you like a cup, Sean?' 'I certainly would,' he said, 'I'm frozen.' Well he took it and he spat it right out and he said, 'Well you're Cumann na mBan maybe, but it's Cumann na Monsters you are. You want to kill us off, that's terrible tea.' What happened was that they had cooked a meal of turnips during the day in a big iron pot, and they didn't empty out the water. They just put about a pound of tea into the pot and this was the tea they made – turnip tea. And it was, of course, appalling. I'll never forget it.

So then we were told we could go upstairs and lie down

* For Sean Howard's subsequent fate, see Sean Harling's account on page 69.

for a while, and we went up and wrapped ourselves in the ermine and sable robes of the judges and we got some sleep or rest at least. Then in the morning we heard a movement at the door and a figure appeared and somebody said, 'That's Barney Mellows,' that was the brother of Liam Mellows. Well he came in and he said that Peadar Clancy had taken over a post in Church Street, that there was going to be heavy fighting on the quays and that the British were coming in from the Curragh and Dun Laoghaire. He wanted two of the girls to volunteer to go to the house and look after the men there. Well I thought, 'This is what I would love to do now,' but I daren't speak out of turn. Then one of the girls said, 'My brother Mikey is out there, I'll go.' Then nobody else said anything and I was afraid to speak, and finally somebody said, 'Let that fat girl from the country go, she's not tired like the rest of us.' And that's what I was – a big, fat country girl, you know, with a glorious complexion, which was all I had to recommend me, along with the enthusiasm. So of course I was up like a shot and the two of us went out. And we had a very hazardous trip across. It was ankle-deep in glass, you know, because they'd broken all the windows in the Four Courts, and we went along cops and robbers, stopping and going along the side, with the sniping going on around us and the big gun booming out in the bay. Eventually we got out through a hole in the wall into Church Street and finally into this small artisan's dwelling, a nicely kept little house owned by a Mr Lennon at 5 Upper Church Street. He told me that he had sent away his wife and three children and then he said to me, 'Now, there's going to be a lot of heavy fighting here' – and there was, much more than we'd really thought, you know – 'and we have no stretcher,' he said, 'but we'll manage.' So he took a stepladder and broke all the rungs out of it and nailed a hearthrug onto it, and this made a very excellent stretcher. So he said, 'I'll leave this in the corner and if there's anybody wounded you know where it is.' And within an hour wasn't he on it himself. He was the first casualty.

MAIRE COMERFORD: On the Tuesday morning my cousin was very nervous, and she said that I wasn't to go into Dublin. But I said I had to go in to Mass. I was an awful liar. I knew she couldn't say no to that, she was too holy to say no to that. I wanted to get back to Stephen's Green because I was deeply interested in that young Citizen Army man. I was longing to see him again. But instead of him there was an old man there with a rifle and a great moustache and he told me to go away. So I went down into O'Connell Street then and people were very excited, they were running backwards and forwards. There was a crowd there watching and I saw the harp and green flag flying over Liberty Hall. Somebody came out of the GPO to warn them away because they were worried about looters, and then somebody fired a shot. There was a stampede then and I ran away with all the others. I never got back that far again. I used to try to get in to find out what was happening. One morning I got as far as Stephen's Green again and I remember I walked in some blood. It nearly took my shoe off.

SEAN HARLING: Then on the Wednesday, Paddy Houlihan, who was the OC at the North Dublin Union, gave Sean Howard a despatch to bring to Piaras Beaslai, who was a captain in the Father Matthew Hall. So we were travelling across North Brunswick Street and we came to North King Street, and just when we were in the middle of North King Street Sean Howard shouted, 'Oh,' and I grabbed him as he was about to fall. So I dragged him off onto the path and ran down to the Father Matthew Hall for help. Two lads came out with a stretcher then and we brought him back to the Richmond Hospital, which was quite close by. The doctor there said he was dead. Now he was about the same age as meself, fourteen. I felt terrible then, and it was left to me to go back up to Temple Buildings to tell his mother. I felt that very hard really. The next day a priest came up from Church Street Chapel and he kicked up murder with Paddy Houlihan, he said it was a bloody shame to have children like that out and he insisted that Paddy Houlihan pull us home. But we stayed on. We were only there because that's what we wanted to do.

BRIGHID LYONS THORNTON: So things went on, you know, the bombing was fierce and through it we were making tea, tea, tea and sandwiches and the men were coming in and out. Messages were coming in from the outposts and we heard that Cork was up, Limerick was up and they were marching and that the Germans were on the Naas Road. Now at this time I used to empty the teapot into the fender of the little stove; it saved me going out to the little yard at the back. And didn't one of the girls come up and hit me on the arm with a spoon. 'Didn't I tell you not to do that?' she said. And I said, 'What harm will it do?' 'Well,' she said, 'don't you know it will bring crickets?' You know the crickets, they hide in the turf fires and they cheep-cheep, but there's nothing to fear in them. Well I thought with the naval battle going on in the bay, Cork up and the Germans on the Naas Road, it didn't matter about a few crickets.

One evening I watched the Bridewell, the prison, being taken over. It was a barracks then, I think, for the Dublin Metropolitan Police. And the next morning I went back into the Four Courts and I saw this collection of these huge Dublin policemen, wearing these capes and these helmets with chinstraps and spikes on the top. They looked to me like Germans and my first thought was that the Germans had arrived at last. But of course they were just police they had found hiding in the basement of the Bridewell and they didn't know what to do with them. But at the time I didn't know or care. As long as something was happening it was all right.

Having successfully isolated the north side of the city from the south side, General Lowe concentrated a large part of his fire on the General Post Office in an effort to separate it from the Volunteers' Four Courts garrison under Commandant

Daly and eventually bludgeon it into capitulation. Machine-guns and sniping fire, incendiary shells, two 18-pounders and the gunboat *Helga* poured everything they could into the GPO, leaving it, along with most of Lower O'Connell Street and vicinity, in flames. General Lowe was assisted in his task by Lieutenant General Sir John Maxwell, who arrived at 2.00 a.m. Friday morning, fresh from the Gallipoli campaign. He established his thorough control over the civilian authority, manoeuvred some of his troops around to complete the cordon, and otherwise left Lowe to keep pounding away at the GPO.

JOSEPH SWEENEY: Then Thursday night, as far as I remember, we had the big fire. They shelled the whole lower end of the street and there was one particular place, a wholesale chemist, they hit it and the flames from that were terrific, right away up in the air. Clery's on the lower floor and the Imperial Hotel on the top were on fire and gradually that whole end of the street was on fire. The following day, I think, they opened up again and the fire developed so much in the GPO and the adjacent houses that we had to retreat. We made for a lane opposite the side door of the GPO and came under fire from Jervis Street. One fellow actually got the heel shot out of his boot. It upended him. But nobody was hit, strange to say, though the firing was intense. We got into Moore Lane then, which takes a left turn into Moore Street, and going off it as soon as you take the bend was a lane running parallel to it again and facing the Rotunda Hospital. As soon as we began to run across this lane to get into the houses in Moore Street, fire was opened up on us from the Rotunda Hospital itself. They were firing from the windows and firing from the roof, very intensive machine-gun fire. We could see the lumps of brick flying off the houses and they actually tore the whole side off the end wall. But we managed to get an old cab out of a storehouse there and ram it into the entrance to the lane. We packed it with anything we could get our hands on, mainly empty mineral water bottles, and that gave us freedom up

71

and down this lane. So we ended that night with the whole city on fire around us and I lay down behind the barricade there and went off to sleep. When I awoke in the morning I found myself in a loft. I don't know how I got there.

We had to get into the houses in Moore Street then, and a very tragic thing happened here. The door of the house we were trying to get into was locked and we could hear people moving about inside. We asked them to open the door and they wouldn't. Then somebody shouted in to get out of the room and he put a gun up to the door and blew open the lock. When we got in then we found it had killed an old boy inside.

So we then started to burrow through the houses, first on the ground floor, then on the upper floors and then back again, so as not to leave any clear line of fire, and at this point I was called by our medical officer, Jim Ryan, who said, 'I have a job for you.' And the job was to carry one end of James Connolly's stretcher. He had been shot just above the ankle earlier in the week and the wound had become gangrenous. It was creeping up his leg by this time. And of course we had no supplies or dressings or any morphia to ease the pain, and he was in frightful agony. These houses were very small and the stairs were very narrow and sometimes we had to lift the stretcher over the top and Connolly was roaring with the pain. It was pitiful to listen to him. Eventually we got him to a house that they had selected for a headquarters and I then moved further on towards the top of the street. By this time there was very little in the way of command. You simply moved with anybody you knew.

I got very hungry at one stage and I went back to a shop called Norton's – it's still there I think – and the only thing edible I could see was some bottled peaches. But as soon as I reached out my hand to get a bottle the whole window came down on top of me in a burst of fire. They had spotted me from somewhere or other.

I made my way back to the top of the street then and was

told to fall in with about thirty other fellows. I asked one of them what it was all about and he said, 'J. J. Walsh has some kind of a mad idea to rush the barricade at the top of the street and we're to be the cannon fodder.' So we all sat there in silence, but in the meantime somebody had got to headquarters and it came back that the order was countermanded.

5

I said: 'The Commandant of the Irish Republican Army wishes to treat with the Commandant of the British forces in Ireland.'
Officer: 'The Irish Republican Army? The Sinn Feiners you mean.'
I replied: 'The Irish Republican Army they call themselves, and I think that a very good name, too.'

Elizabeth O'Farrell, Cumann na mBan nurse,
in dialogue with British officer on the occasion of the
surrender

On Saturday morning, 29 April, huddled in their Moore Street headquarters, completely surrounded by machine-gun fire and blazing buildings, the leaders discussed a surrender. Towards noon Pearse watched three civilians dash out of a house in Moore Street under a white flag only to get mown down instantly under a burst of machine-gun fire. Their corpses lay in the road. It was around this time that Pearse decided he had had enough. He sent a Cumann na mBan nurse, Elizabeth O'Farrell, to treat with General Lowe, who demanded an unconditional surrender. Finally, at 3.30 p.m., Commandant-General Pearse, in his slouch hat, presented himself to General Lowe and handed over his sword.

BRIGHID LYONS THORNTON: And then Saturday morning, louder than all the noise was the silence that descended on the city. Everything seemed to flatten out and go quiet, and a few people came in and said there was a rumour of a surrender. And some of the Volunteers said, 'Have you a hatchet, have you a hammer? Nobody is going to get my gun, I won't give it up, I'll die,' and so on, and they began

74

to look out the back to see if there was any avenue of escape. And some of them gave me addresses and said, 'When you get out, if we're taken prisoner, will you call to my mother?' I had a whole list of names. And then someone gave me a gun and said, 'Will you keep that for me?' and I said I would. I had a big skirt that somebody had brought me with an enormous pocket on it. It was like one of these aprons that the women in Moore Street used to wear. So I put the gun in the pocket and kept it. They had all bought their own guns, you see, there were no supplies from Libya or Russia or anywhere else, and they'd do anything rather than give them up. So then towards evening we did hear that we had surrendered. It was a terrible, shattering, chaotic moment. They cried and they wept and they protested and they did their best to destroy their guns. I could see them hacking away at them. But there was no escape for them then.

JOSEPH SWEENEY: We noticed a great lull then. There was no sound coming from anywhere. Eventually somebody came to us and told us that Pearse had sent out an envoy to negotiate with the British. Of course arguments arose then. Some people wanted to surrender, others didn't, but word was passed around, 'Orders is orders,' as one of Kipling's men would say, and we were told to march out into Moore Street. We did this by going up to the top house. There's a laneway near it that's now called O'Rahilly Parade, and we got out into this laneway and as we passed out through the backyard of the house, Sean MacDermott, who was one of the leaders, was standing on an eminence there and he addressed us. He told us that this was only the beginning of the fight, and that all the leaders would be executed, he said, 'But it is up to you men to carry it on.'

MARTIN WALTON: On the Sunday then Jack Cotter and myself decided we couldn't get into town at all, so we went out to Ashbourne. It was the only victorious fight in the

Rising. We cycled out there on the Sunday evening, but when we arrived we saw that they'd just surrendered. We saw them being taken off in lorries and thought, 'That settles that.' That was how I escaped internment, though most of the lads my age just got a kick in the arse and were told to go home.

SEAN HARLING: On the Saturday then the word to surrender came through and all the Volunteers were lined up on the road and they had to lay down their arms. The officer who took the surrender seemed to be a very decent sort of fellow. I think he was a captain. I was just standing at the end of the line and he came along and he looks at me, you know, and he gives me a clip on the ear and tells me to get the hell home. I was very annoyed about not being arrested but that's what happened and I just watched the others being taken off as prisoners.

Dr Thornton and General Sweeney were then taken prisoner.

BRIGHID LYONS THORNTON: I didn't know where home was or where I was in the city, and I just sat on for a while. Then some of the poor people from around there came into me and said, 'Have you any food? We haven't had much during the week.' Well we had stacks of bread and butter and ham and I gave lots of it away. Then I decided I had better go as it was getting on towards dusk and I came out and tried to get through the hole in the wall again. Then Peadar Clancy came along. So I sat down with him and gave him tea and sandwiches and asked him what was going to happen and he said, 'We've surrendered,' he said, 'so I suppose we'll be arrested.' Then he took me back into the Four Courts, over the wall again, and there was terrible confusion. British soldiers were there and British officers. Then I met my uncle, Joe MacGuinness, and he said, 'Get home as quickly as you can and tell Katy' – that was my aunt, his wife – 'tell her that I'll be all right and not to worry.' And everything was toing and froing and I said I'd go, but then Ned Daly came in and said, 'Listen, don't go, the city's under martial law.' That was the first time I'd ever actually spoken to him, and it was the last time too because he was later executed. But in any case he said, 'Lieutenant Lindsay here' – that was one of the British officers – 'has given me his word of honour that all you girls will be taken home in the morning.' Lieutenant Lindsay was quite an attractive young man, nicely dressed in uniform, more spectacular than I was really, and I said, 'Whatever you say, Commandant, I'll do.'

After that we were sent upstairs and some of the Church Street priests came in and lambasted us with abuse all night for doing what we did. They disapproved highly of the rebellion, of the damage to the city and the people who were killed and whose homes were burned. We took it all, we didn't say anything. And the next morning then we were all awakened very early and very tired and we were told that we were not going home, that we were being taken instead to Richmond barracks. Well of course that was a bit of a clanger for us, but we went down anyway and we were put in a lorry with straw on the bottom of it and a hooped thing on the back closing us in and we drove through the city. Most of us were women but there were three or four Volunteers, including Dermot O'Hegarty, who later played a very prominent part in the First Dail. So then we got to Richmond barracks and were taken out of the lorry there and lined up. There were crowds and crowds of Volunteers there by this time. Sean MacDermott was there and so was Ned Daly. Then my friend Lieutenant Lindsay came up and I said, 'I thought we were being taken home this morning,' and he said, 'Just keep quiet, keep quiet.' A girl beside me said, 'Don't talk to them at all,' so I didn't.

That evening then we were told we were being brought to Kilmainham Jail, and one of the girls said, 'That's a terrible place.' So we were all lined up in the barracks square, and one of the first in the rank we joined was the Countess Markievicz, in her green turned-up hat and her puttees and her breeches and her tunic. Now we never had the British to protect us before, but luckily this time the soldiers guarded us very heavily because when the gates were opened and we were marched out there were such shrieks of hatred. Never did I see such savage women. A lot of them were getting the separation allowance because their husbands were off fighting in France and they thought their livelihood would be taken away because of what we had done. A lot of it seemed to be directed against the Countess's breeches and puttees.

And then we were marched, it seemed a very long way, down the road and up the hill and round into Kilmainham – which was a dismal, dreary, frightening place to be on a lovely summer evening. We went in and there were officers inside and a terrible man with a lantern, like one of those things you'd see in a farmhouse long ago for going out to milk the cows. And he held it up and they tried to get more details out of us and then somebody said, 'Take them up and throw them into the cells, we can't get anything.' But then this old fellow with the lantern said, 'Bring them down here first.' So he marched us down some corridors and then he held up his lantern and said, 'Read that.' So we read out, *'Sin no more unless a worse thing should come unto thee.'* 'It's into the drop you should be taken,' he said. 'What's that?' I said. 'The scaffold,' he said. So we protested and we said we didn't sin and then we were marched up the stairs and thrown three or four into a cell. We didn't care where we got so long as we got lying down. We were very exhausted and very tired.

JOSEPH SWEENEY: We filed out onto Moore Street and were lined up into fours and were marched up O'Connell Street and formed into two lines on each side of the street. We marched up to the front and left all our arms and ammunition and then went back to our original places. Officers with notebooks then came along and took down our names. A funny incident happened there. One of the officers just looked at one of our fellows and without asking him anything wrote down his name and then walked on. After he had gone a certain distance, somebody asked this fellow, 'Does that officer know you?' 'That's my brother,' he said.

When that formality was over we were marched into a little patch of green in front of the Rotunda Hospital, an oval patch, and we were made to lie down there. Anybody who put his foot out of line got a whack of a rifle butt. We were kept there all night and a British officer amused himself by taking out some of the leaders. He took out poor old Tom Clarke and, with the nurses looking out of the windows of the hospital, he stripped him to the buff and made all sorts of disparaging remarks about him. 'This old bastard has been at it before. He has a shop across the street there. He's an old Fenian,' and so on, and he took several others out too. That officer's name was Lee Wilson, and I remember a few years later I happened to be in the bar of the Wicklow Hotel and Mick Collins in his usual way stomped in and said to me, 'We got the bugger, Joe.' I said, 'What are you talking about?' He said, 'Do you remember that first night outside the Rotunda? Lee Wilson?' 'I do remember,' I said, 'I'll never forget it.' 'Well we got him today in Gorey.'

During the night the garrison from the Four Courts came in and we were put lying on top of one another. I had two fellows lying on top of me. In one way it was desperate and in another way it was great, because it was a very cold night and they kept me warm.

The following morning we were put into formation and marched down O'Connell Street, past the GPO, which still had the tricolour flying from it, and past Clery's, which still had the Plough and the Stars. We got a very hostile reception along the way. At this stage we had very little sympathy in the country as a whole.

We were eventually led out to the Richmond barracks

and put into a big gymnasium there, where all the detectives
of the G Division or political division came in to have a look
at us. They picked out all the leaders and anyone they knew
to have been previously involved in meetings or demonstrations or whatever. They were all courtmartialled and the
leaders, of course, were shot.

They took us all to barrack rooms then and I lay down
on my back on the floor. I was a fairly good sleeper in those
days and I went right off to sleep. I was awakened after a
bit by somebody kicking me on the soles of my feet and I
looked up to find a British staff officer standing over me.
He had a lot of gold on his cap. 'What age are you?' he said.
I said, 'I'm nineteen.' So he passed on and one of the fellows
said, 'You're a bloody fool. If you had said eighteen you
would have been out by now.' But I was unconcerned about
whether I got out or not because I wanted to stay with the
crowd. I was glad about it afterwards too, because I went
through experiences that I'd never have had otherwise. That
evening then we were marched down the quays and put on
board a boat at the North Wall, down into the hold. We all
got lousy as a result of the trip over to Holyhead, but I met
a lot of fine people in Wales where I eventually wound up,
outside Balla, a place called Frongoch Camp.

The abject surrender and smoking ruins of central Dublin
might have been sign enough that the Easter Rising, conceived
in such heroic splendour, was in fact a dismal failure. But the
men were unrepentant and the leaders thoroughly confident
that their actions would be immortalized. And indeed, during
the two or three years which followed 1916, the Rising received
its mandate in retrospect and became enshrined as the great
turning point in Irish history; it is now heresy in the Irish
Republic to criticize in any way the desperate activities of what
was then a tiny and despised minority. In a telling phrase,
Desmond Ryan – one of the participants who survived to write
a number of valuable historical records of the period – called

it 'the triumph of failure'. But that does not mean that the ghosts have at last been put to rest.

The legal and philosophical base of the Easter Rising was contained in that much-revered document, the Proclamation. The Proclamation evokes a vision of an ideal Ireland, one that it implies existed before the terrible catastrophe of illegal English rule. It declares the right of the people of Ireland to the ownership of Ireland, claims that the tradition of Irish nationhood is ancient, and guarantees full religious and civil liberties, including women's suffrage. It is emphatically anti-sectarian, being at pains to point out that the divisions between minority and majority, Unionist and republican, Protestant and Catholic, were carefully fostered by an alien government for its own ends. And it was asserting that these rights and principles should be defended in arms, as so many generations had done in the past.

Part of Ireland got its republic in 1949, but the ideals of the Proclamation have nevertheless yet to be realized. The Proclamation nurtured a mentality – an insatiable idealism and a corresponding discontent with the mundane – that historical reality has been unable to gratify. Whether or not the Easter Rising led, by direct cause and effect, to the Sinn Fein election victory in 1918, the subsequent Anglo-Irish War, the Civil War and the present conflict in the North is open to question; but what is not is that the participants of each of these events have claimed their inspiration to have been the ideals of Easter Week. The simple, potent graffito '1916' on the walls of Belfast today is testimony to its enduring significance.

But the final element of the military plan had yet to be effected when General Sweeney and Dr Thornton were led off to their respective prisons, and it was not until it had been that these historical processes were set into motion.

6

I am going to ensure that there will be no treason whispered for a hundred years.

Sir John Maxwell to Lord Wimborne

> O but we talked at large before
> The sixteen men were shot,
> But who can talk of give and take,
> What should be and what not
> While those dead men are loitering there
> To stir the boiling pot?

W. B. Yeats, 'Sixteen Dead Men'

Pearse had not long to wait for the full realization of his blood sacrifice. Thirteen of his comrades were, like him, tried by court martial, sentenced to death, and shot between 3 May and 12 May. They were Thomas MacDonagh, Tom Clarke, Willie Pearse, Joseph Plunkett, Edward (Ned) Daly, Michael O'Hanrahan, John MacBride, Con Colbert, Eamonn Ceannt, Michael Mallin, Sean Heuston, Sean MacDermott and James Connolly. Thomas Kent was executed in Cork on 9 May and on 3 August Roger Casement was hanged in Pentonville Prison for treason.

To General Maxwell, they were simply traitors, for whom the only suitable punishment was death. But he cannot carry the sole responsibility. The press, the Unionists and many members of the Cabinet were all howling for blood, and Asquith and even Redmond and his deputy John Dillon were in agreement that the leaders must bear the ultimate punishment.

MAIRE COMERFORD: In every chapter of Irish history we

should be accustomed to hearing of ruthless acts, but this was another. Many had gone before. We had mourned the Manchester Martyrs during the Fenian times, we had mourned many other people who had died in jail or suffered long imprisonments and we are mourning them still. But these executions demonstrated to the country the quality of the men.

Most of the historians seem to accept that we reacted to the Rising in the way we did because of the executions. But it wasn't death, it was the call to freedom which captivated us. We could see the flag of the Republic flying over the GPO, we could read the Proclamation and we could see the sacrifice the men were prepared to make – these were the things which counted more than anything – else. People re-alized that the self-respect of our nation depended on some action such as this. Afterwards, there was no longer any such thing as practical politics.

MARTIN WALTON: I first heard of the executions when I was out walking with my father. He wouldn't let me out of his sight after Easter Week. We were walking down Drumcon-dra Road and as we passed over the Tolka Bridge we met the head of St Patrick's Training College, a big stout man, Father O'Flynn. He had a 'stop press' in his hand. 'My God,' he said – he'd stopped us – 'look at that. They're after shooting three of the men.' From then on it just went on day after day.

Of course anybody who had made up their minds to take part in this fight, all they ever expected was jail or hanging. But this was savage. It was even against the British hand-book on how to deal with rebellions. The people generally in the country had been weaned away from using physical force, because physical force had failed in the past, and had been persuaded to see what they could get by constitutional means. But Easter Week and the executions brought them completely back into the physical force field and unified

Ireland. Whatever bitterness was in your heart just swelled up and made you more and more determined to carry on.

BRIGHID LYONS THORNTON: One morning our cell door opened and two women came in, wardresses from Mountjoy prison. They came to see what types of people we were, they'd never seen the likes of us before. Early that morning then I heard a terrible volley of shooting and I asked the one who came into me, a Miss McInnerney, I said, 'What was all the shooting this morning?' And she said, 'They were shooting some of the men.' Now I didn't know who or what and I didn't believe it. Later that day we were let out for about ten minutes' exercise and we met a lot of other girls who had been at other centres during the week and I said to one of them, 'I heard they were shooting the men.' And she said, 'Don't you worry, they're not going to shoot any of the men. They'd be too much afraid of America.' Well the next morning the shooting was on again and again and again, every morning after that at about five o'clock. I could hear the men marching out down by my cell door, a heavy march and then out and then the volleys. And that was very frightening now, but I was consoled by what this girl had told me. Then I asked Miss McInnerney again and she said, 'Yes, there were more shot this morning.' And then on the Sunday we were led down to Mass and put on the balcony. I saw four Volunteers going to Holy Communion and I leaned over the balcony to peep down at them and of course I got a bite with a bayonet. Well they were all executed the following morning, and they were the last, apart from Connolly and MacDermott. Well for months afterwards I always woke at that hour and I've never forgot those volleys, never.

It was calamitous, shattering. Everybody was gone. I had only known Tom Clarke and Ned Daly personally. We used to spend a lot of time down at Tom Clarke's house with his wife and the young children, and many pleasant days and memories we had from that place. I didn't know the others, but it was as if the head of a family, if both your parents were shot and all your family and you were orphaned. There was no head or leadership or anything left. I never felt so desolate in my life as I did after that. And that was the feeling of most people, that everything was gone and lost. But it helped to unite the people too. Their hostility to the executions brought them together again.

JOHN L. O'SULLIVAN: I was very sorry for the people that were killed. They appeared to us to be men of intellect and vision, visionaries more than anything else, and it was very sad to hear of them being executed. We saw then that we had men prepared to sacrifice their young lives for an ideal – men of education, ability and courage that faced their deaths in a noble manner. I was only fifteen at the time, but looking back now I would say that if you hadn't the executions the Rising might have gone off like all the others before it, through the generations, through the centuries. The people mightn't have given their support. At that time the anti-British feeling wasn't so high as it was in later years. Many people had relatives in the civil service and in the armed forces and in all the other paraphernalia that Britain set up in a fairly big way here, and this had a moderating influence. But after the executions the feelings of the Irish people expanded and exploded, if you like, in the years afterwards.

DAVID NELIGAN: The events at Easter were a bad show. I was horrified at the executions. Horrified. Of course from a military point of view the whole thing was a washout, a farce. Pearse was an idealist, he had no bloody business being a warrior at all, poor devil. But I thought what Bernard Shaw thought afterwards. Bernard Shaw understood the Irish people inside out. When the British executed those fellows after 1916 he said, 'Nothing will stop these people being named as martyrs for the Irish people.' Paddy Pearse said the same thing. 'We have failed,' he said, 'but there are people who will come after us who will succeed.' That was a prophetic remark. Perfectly true.

SEAN HARLING: When I heard about the executions I felt terrible sore, I had a feeling of revulsion. But it was also something that seemed natural to me, you know, because we knew they were going to be punished. But there were some people you'd never think they'd execute which they did, like Sean Heuston. He was just an ordinary person, a young lad who was working in Kingsbridge railway station, and he wasn't of any importance, he wasn't like Patrick Pearse. He did command the men in the Mendicity Institute, and it's said he did play certain havoc with the soldiers coming out of the barracks and around the quays, but other than that I wouldn't say he was the sort of person who should have been executed. An ordinary army would never have shot the likes of Sean Heuston.

TOM BARRY: In 1916 I was in the land called Mesopotamia, which is now Iraq as you know, and I was serving there with the British Expeditionary Force. There was, of course, as always a lot of glorious talk about our noble mission and so on, but behind it all there was a very simple economic explanation for what we were doing, which at that period was oil for the British navy. But when we were billeted or encamped there I went out and I saw that outside the orderly room there was a communiqué up, and it told of this Rising in Dublin, and it told of the executions of men I'd never heard of – Pearse and Connolly and the rest of them. News reached us slowly and this was about fourteen weeks after the Rising. Now I felt afterwards, when I found out what happened, that although I could cut their plan of campaign to pieces these men were really the cream of our generation. But at that stage I was only about eighteen and I didn't know what it was about or what was happening. What stopped me first was the long-drawn-out time they took with the executions – one one day, then two more two days after that, and so on – and that put me to thinking. I got indignant then with the idea of Dublin being shelled and I said to myself, 'What the hell am I doing with the British army? It's with the Irish I should be.' From that time on then, although I went on all fronts and wasn't demobbed until January 1919 in Oswestry in Wales, I was never happy until I could get home.

PART THREE

An Irish Plot

May 1916 to 21 January 1919

'The English said [the members of the Dail] were involved in a "German Plot". No English government of that period could believe that anyone in Ireland could go into rebellion for the sake of Ireland. They preferred to believe that somebody abroad was paying us to rebel. That was, I suppose, confirmed by the arms which Casement had negotiated from Germany. Casement had been hanged in August 1916. Now we were in 1919, and there was still a "German plot" and our people were in jail and the German war was over. The Russian Revolution had happened by this time and the English were able to switch with the greatest smoothness into a "Russian plot" and ever since then we've been haunted by "Russian plots". They could never believe that there was an Irish plot to make Ireland free. They don't believe it yet I don't think.'

Maire Comerford

1

A nation in crisis becomes almost like a single mind, or rather like those minds . . . that become channels for parallel streams of thought, each stream taking the colour of the mind it flows through.

W. B. Yeats

Within two and a half years the country had undergone the metamorphosis Pearse had designed in his mind. Slowly at first, and in some disarray – but with growing impatience – Ireland began to embrace and celebrate the men and ideals towards which it had previously been so scornful. This national reawakening had a composite of direct causes. But the important point is that history at this time took on the *appearance*, if not the actuality, of inexorability: the nation, starting with the Easter Rising, appeared to be on the march, with new vigour and unanimity. Britain, in the meantime, could be seen to be taking an altogether different road, one that was leading directly into a head-on collision with Ireland. Quite soon after the Rising, a final severing of the connection with Britain became Ireland's only viable policy.

2

The people as a whole had not changed; but the new spirit was working slowly, half-afraid, yet determined. . . . Without guidance or direction, moving as if to clarify itself . . . the strange rebirth took shape. It was manifest in flags, badges, songs, speech, all seemingly superficial signs. It was as if the inarticulate attempted to express themselves in any way or by any method; later would come organization and cool-headed reason. Now was the lyrical stage, blood sang and pulsed, a strange love was born that for some was never to die till they lay stiff on the hillside or in quicklime near a barrack wall.

Ernie O'Malley on post-Rising Ireland in
On Another Man's Wound

The men who had been marched off to the Dublin quaysides for internment in Britain – to the accompaniment of jeers – could not have known that this transformation was taking place back home. Yet while in prison they behaved not as participants in an embarrassing failure, but rather as men with no other idea than to continue, and finish, the revolution they had started.

Nearly two thousand of them were sent to Britain and seg-regated there into a number of convict prisons throughout the country. Shortly afterwards, those carrying heavy sentences from courts martial were divided between Reading, Dartmoor and Aylesbury prisons (where Countess Markievicz languished alone), while the internees were all gathered together at Fron-goch in north Wales. There the free association that the pris-oners enjoyed gave them the chance to educate themselves collectively in the ways of revolution and debate remedies for the errors of the past. Men from Dublin met men from Tipperary, Cork and Donegal, making contacts which would prove invaluable in the guerrilla war that was to follow. By the time they were released they were a far more committed, disciplined and determined group than they were when they went in.

Joseph Sweeney was one of the internees.

JOSEPH SWEENEY: When we arrived at Holyhead there were two trains on either side of the platform – one to Stafford and the other to Knutsford. I was sent down to Stafford and I remember particularly an incident which occurred as we were taken out of the train there. We were formed up and marched towards the prison and strangely enough our escort was one of the regiments which had been badly cut up in the fighting here in Dublin during Easter Week. They had borne the brunt of officers' stupidity in pushing on when they could have got around. I was towards the rear of the column, and just as we were nearing the prison a couple of English fellows who were just standing around watching darted up the footpath and tried to assault some of our lads. I remember a great big sergeant made a race at them and shouted, 'Get back, you bastards. These men fought for their country, you won't.'

We were lucky to be sent to Stafford, because it was a military detention barracks, not a jail at all, and although we were kept in solitary for the first few weeks we had the life of Riley there. The commandant was a literary man and when he heard that there were literary men amongst our bunch he used to take them into his own quarters to discuss things with them. We used to kick around a football we made up ourselves from paper and old rags, and we'd have concerts and sing-songs as well. Our policy of course was one of non-cooperation, but the control of the place was really very benign.

We had very bad relations with the visiting clergy, how-ever. I remember the first occasion when word came round that anybody who was a Catholic and wanted to go to confession should get ready. So we jumped at this and were marched down to the church. We made our confessions and then we were asked were we sorry for taking up arms against His Majesty the King. We all said no, that that was our affair, and accordingly we were refused absolution. So we said, 'Well, if that's the way you want it, all well and good,' and we refused to have anything to do with them. Up to then everything had been fine. The chaplain was an oldish man who wasn't able for the duties and he got a young fellow to look after us. We thought the clothes he was wearing were an absolute disgrace for a clergyman, so we took up a collection and bought him a new suit and then subscribed to anything he brought up in the way of charities. Then this thing happened. But eventually they surrendered, they said they would make no conditions on political grounds and everything was all right again. Strange to say, that priest's name was Stafford too, and he became so chummy with us that he always came over to Ireland every summer for his holidays to renew his relationship with all the men he had met in the prison.

After about two months there we were shifted over to Frongoch, which was an internment camp in north Wales. It was an old brewery or distillery which they had added on to another camp. It was all newly erected hutments, everything was very primitive, and we had the place pretty much to ourselves. We set up our own university there, both educational and revolutionary, and from that camp came the hard core of the subsequent guerrilla war in Ireland. It was a continuation really of what we had been doing in Stafford, only this time we were all together. We had Irish classes and different higher education classes for those who were studying for scholarships. Each camp elected its own commandant and every day we had our own inspection roll call in the morning and the evening. We never had much in the way of foot drills, except for lining up in parades, which we did in military fashion, but we went in for all kinds of arms training. We smuggled in manuals of one kind or another and fellows were given instruction in leadership and told what to do when they got home. Most of the top men, like Griffith and de Valera, had been taken to Reading Jail, but Collins was there and I got to be very friendly with him and all the Cork fellows he had gathered around him. Collins was using his time there to find out from fellows all over the country about conditions in their areas and particularly about any policemen they might know who would be friendly to the movement. Gearoid O'Sullivan was one of Collins's Cork friends – he was the fellow I mentioned before who ran across O'Connell Street wrapped up in a mattress – and so was Sean Hales. He was a huge big man who went in for putting the shot. All in all it was very easygoing there. To give you an idea, we had one poor fellow we always had to keep an eye on – he was a bit gone in the head – and he just walked calmly out the front gate one day and into the town of Balla. He could have got away to anywhere he wanted to go, but he walked up to a policeman and said, 'What's the name of this town?' And of course the policeman pulled him in straight away.

Back in Ireland, General Maxwell, with 40,000 troops, continued to impose his soldierly discipline on the country. But his rule by martial law was no more effective or popular than the executions carried out at his behest. The demoralization he and his superiors were perhaps anticipating was only temporary, and those who had been active before – along with an increasing number of new recruits – began to reorganize. Sympathy for the prisoners and their dependants provided a most successful focal point. Within days of her husband's execution, Mrs Tom Clarke took the legacy of gold her husband had left for this purpose and organized the Irish National Aid Association and the Irish Volunteers' Dependants' Fund. Anti-recruiting activity was stepped up, and the organizations which had fed the Rising – the Volunteers, Cumann na mBan, the Fianna, the Gaelic League and so on – swelled with new members.

MAIRE COMERFORD: I got a jolt. I was jolted into national politics by the Rising. I was in Dublin with the romantic idea of looking up the *Book of Kells* and landed in the middle of the Rising. The sight of the tricolour on a pole really stirred me. I remember going to the headquarters of the central branch of Cumann na mBan afterwards – it was somewhere in Parnell Square – and I saw Lilly O'Bannon there, who was a sister-in-law of Eamonn Ceannt. She had been out in the Rising, and must have been released from prison after it. I left my name there and after that I was up to my neck in Cumann na mBan.

Those of us who were at home did what we could. We used to write to the prisoners. I wrote to a man named Sean Etchingham. He was a Volunteer and had been out in the Rising in Wexford. I remember when the Volunteers started I collected all the ·22 rifles we had in the house and brought them down to him. I got into terrible trouble then when they were missed. His father had been a stable boy and he got very little schooling, but he taught himself by the light of the lantern in the stables and he became a journalist eventually. He used to write a very funny satirical column called 'Patsy Pat'. Everybody, even my grandmother – and God knows she wasn't a republican or anything like it – they all used to get together and say, 'What has Patsy Pat got to say this weekend?' Anyway, I used to write to him and send him parcels of food.

In Wexford, which was my native place, I helped organize clubs and branches and meetings. We used to have that kind of festive, outdoor meeting where people could go into competition about Irish history and the Irish language. They flocked to this. They used to sing ballads too, which was illegal. One ballad I would love to sing for the people in jail today is 'Felons of Our Land'. Men got six months' imprisonment for singing that.

We began collecting funds immediately after the Rising. Tom Clarke had left a thousand pounds in gold to his wife to look after any emergencies, the dependants and whatever other need there was, and very soon after his execution she had assembled a band of women to collect money. There was a flag which was sold on the street and the inscription on it was of course 'In praise of Easter Week'. Michael Collins became secretary of this fund when he came out of prison, but before that General Maxwell directed the first proclamation of the English in Ireland after the Rising against the widows of the men they had just executed. Fortunately for us some of the names were in Irish and the police couldn't read the names. They went to the Gaelic League to get them translated and of course the Gaelic League had sense and said they didn't know. I'm very proud of the women, as a woman myself, very proud that it was the women that provoked this first proclamation.

SEAN HARLING: At this time the British were recruiting like hell for men to serve in France, you see, and the whole city was billposted with pictures of Kitchener and 'We Want You' and 'Remember Belgium' and all this sort of nonsense. There was one very big canvas streamer tied across the top of the GPO, also with a picture of Kitchener and him pointing his finger at the people – 'We Want You'. So my commandant came to me and said, 'I've been instructed to get you to destroy that poster.' So I went down and I looked and I thought, 'How the hell am I going to destroy that thing?' It was way up near the roof, you see, and I knew if you put ladders up the police would be on top of you before you knew where you were. Then I had this bright idea. We went into a shop and bought a sod of turf and then let the turf steep in a bucket of paraffin oil. We put some wire around the turf then, because if you put twine on it it would just burn along with the turf. Then we tied some twine on to the wire, lit the sod of turf and fired it up across the banner. Within a few minutes the whole thing was blazing, roaring. It was shocking. The fire brigade came along then. Joe Connolly, whose brother Sean was killed in 1916, was one of them. Well they all looked and saw what was burning and turned around and went back.

BRIGHID LYONS THORNTON: I had to go back to Galway after I was released from jail, and nobody would talk to you there. There was a terrible pro-British element in Galway, and if they didn't scorn you they didn't believe you had gone out in the Rising. It wasn't until the *Irish Times* published a list of all those arrested that they believed me at all.

But gradually then people began to wake up again. The war was on and they were still recruiting for the British army. We used to go up to them and interrupt them and shout at them. It was unladylike, I suppose, but of course we didn't care. It was the highlight of my life going around the town tearing down the recruiting posters. We used to go around at night with black shoe polish and a brush and black out the posters with the big picture of Kitchener with all his medals and saying how you could serve your country best and so on by joining the British army. I remember one Saturday night we did them all, the whole town, and the next Sunday morning people going to Mass were terribly mystified by this. Of course we were very proud of our night's work.

MARTIN WALTON: After the Rising we started to reorganize immediately – to look for guns, try and buck up the language, the Gaelic League and any other organization that wasn't banned and that we could get into. It was a terrible time. There were still thousands of Irishmen fighting in France and if you said you had been out in Easter Week one of their family was liable to shoot you.

With the surrender in 1916 and the immediate raids by the military and the round-up, the country was disarmed. Here and there we managed to hold onto a few guns, but very few, so looking for arms was a very high priority. I remember getting the key of an old Sinn Fein hall from an old Fenian, and we started there, about eight, ten or twelve of us, drilling and organizing. I always thought that was the great test of a man – if he was able to keep coming to meetings, without any arms and with nothing happening, just drilling and going through the long haul until he could see combat.

It was in that hall that one of the most famous of the guerrilla fighters, Ernie O'Malley, was brought into the movement. That little hall dissolved then and we took up headquarters in the painters' union – the Tara Hall, Gloucester Street, which is now Sean MacDermott Street. We met and drilled there. We were under cover of the painters' union, you see, so we got away with it. We more or less just kept in touch until the prisoners were released from Frongoch, because they were the ones who would be able to lay the foundations for the fight to come.

Several of those internees were released in August 1916, and there was a general amnesty declared in time to bring the rest of them home for Christmas. Only those carrying sentences remained behind.

Joseph Sweeney was among the early releases.

JOSEPH SWEENEY: At one stage we were brought before the Sankey Commission in London, which had been set up to inquire into the causes of the Rising and our aims and objects and so on. Of course the word went out that we were to tell them nothing, just our name and address.

I was there on two occasions. The first time I was put into Wandsworth Jail and the second into Wormwood Scrubs. We were there a week and we got to know a lot of our fellow prisoners. Down below they kept the conscientious objectors, and while I was there they kicked two of them to death. Another wing was given over to a military detention barracks, and one day we came across a big guardsman and we asked him what he was in for. 'Breaking windows,' he said. 'What the hell did you want to do that for?' we said. 'Well,' he said, 'I ain't going to France. I'm going to keep myself in jail until the war is over.' Well, the contrast between the treatment of the conscientious objectors and this fellow was terrible.

But anyway, in due course I was brought before Sankey and he had a great big book, a kind of ledger, and I could see that he had very little next to my name. So I duly gave him my name and address and went back to Frongoch. That was in July, and to my astonishment I was released about a month later.

Now we had been enjoined upon leaving Frongoch to do everything we could to get the organization going again and to get our hands on as much arms and ammunition as we could get. So naturally enough when I got to Dublin I wanted to get around to find out the state of things and it wasn't long before I met some familiar faces. I remember walking up to the GPO where I saw a big man, about 6 foot 4 inches, with a very brownish face, smoking a pipe and casting his eye about. I went up to him and I said, 'Tom, where the hell did you get to?' 'Well,' he said, 'when we had to get out of the GPO I pushed on down through the escape route, got into a backyard and climbed over a couple of other backyards and got into a house. I put my gun away there and picked up whatever clothes I could, and when things began to get quiet and people were walking about I just came out and mingled with the crowd. And here I am.' This fellow was Tom Byrne, and he'd also fought with Major MacBride against the British in the Boer War.

After a few days in Dublin I went home to Donegal and to my surprise I got a tremendous reception there. The Ancient Order of Hibernians had been very strong in that part of the world and my views weren't well accepted at all prior to 1916. But when I came back they had the bands out and they put me in a side-cart and pulled the horse out and took me up to my home. From then on it was easy enough to get an organization going. I hadn't known it previously at all, but I found out that in the next town of Dungloe there was already a corps of the IRB in existence.

I remember going to one of the lads there and asking him what the prospects were of getting the Volunteers organized again. 'Very good,' he said, 'you have eight here to start with. There are eight of us here in the IRB.' So we had a meeting and as time went on we got in more and more young fellows. We organized a company – we called them companies but in some cases they were no more than a squad. But we had high hopes that we would build up in strength, and we formed a company in every chapel area, where fellows could meet and get into a corner and talk about things. We were getting on quite well, and we then organized the companies into a battalion, and after that two further battalions in Gweedore and Creeslough. We lost a lot of them during the migration periods, and that made it difficult to keep units together. Migration was the only thing in our end of the country. They'd go over to Scotland twice a year, for the setting of the crops and then for the harvest, and quite a few of them also went over to the mines. But the enthusiasts moved from one company to another and we were able to keep things fairly stable.

Michael Collins was among the prisoners released from Frongoch at Christmas. He has since achieved a unique status in Irish history, for he is revered not so much for his vision or his sacrifice or his unrealized promise – the qualities associated with most Irish heroes – but for his awesome effectiveness. He stands directly in the Fenian tradition of uncompromising republicanism, but with a crucial difference: he had no taste for the vainglorious act. Of the Easter Rising he wrote in a letter to a friend:

[The leaders] have died nobly at the hands of the firing squads. So much I grant. But I do not think the Rising week was an appropriate time for the issue of memoranda couched in poetic phrases, nor of actions worked out in similar fashion. Looking at it from the inside (I was in the GPO) it had the air of a Greek tragedy about it, the illusion being more or less completed with the issue of the before-mentioned memoranda. Of Pearse and Connolly I admire the latter

101

the most. Connolly was a realist, Pearse the direct opposite. There was an air of earthy directness about Connolly. It impressed me. I would have followed him through hell had such action been necessary. But I doubt very much if I would have followed Pearse – not without some thought anyway.

Collins was a large and boisterous personality, with a lavish generosity and engaging humour, as well as a ferocious temper. He had the uncanny ability to seem to be on intimate terms with nearly the entire nation, while apparently remaining invisible to the British authorities; he was widely read; and he could be wistfully romantic, particularly about his native Cork. He was also unequivocally ruthless. But above all he never lost his hold on reality. He had a genius, a passion for extreme detail, and it was on this that his effectiveness was based.

The first step in his ascendancy was his appointment to the secretaryship of Mrs Clarke's National Aid Association. It was a position which he exploited to the full. It allowed him to develop his already considerable talents for finance, and brought him into direct contact with extreme poverty – an experience which remained with him for the rest of his life. It also brought him to every corner of the country, allowing him to develop the IRB contacts he had made at Frongoch and providing him with a profound sense of the relative strengths and weaknesses of the whole nation. Under his guidance, the National Aid Association became one of the principal catalysts in the transformation of the country.

BRIGHID LYONS THORNTON: There was a great campaign started to get help for the dependants of the Volunteers who were in jail, and at Christmas this great fellow came home from Frongoch who was going to clear the whole thing up: Michael Collins. He started collecting money all around the country. His name was on everybody's lips, and he was so fascinating and so attractive.

By the spring of 1917 we had formed a branch of Cumann na mBan in Galway and we were drilling and dancing and getting organized again. People were beginning to speak up and come alive. So we decided to have this concert then to raise money for the prisoners' dependants. We had to get the permission of the District Inspector of the RIC to do it, but we did and we raised £50, which was an awful lot of money then. And then I remember I got this magnificently written and very appreciative letter from Collins about it – and that's what breaks my heart, to think of all the letters and notes I had from him that got lost. He used to ask my uncle after that, 'When is she organizing another of those concerts? That was good money.' But that was the way he was, you know, never forgetting anything anybody ever did like that. And he had no secretary or office or tapes to help him remember, he just kept it all in his head or on little notes in the folds of his trousers. He had such terrific spirit, and he made you want to go out and do everything you could, more than you could do really, to help the cause.

3

How can I convey to the reader, who does not know him, any just impression of this extraordinary figure of our time. . . . One catches in his company that flavour of final purposelessness, inner irresponsibility, existence outside and away from our Saxon good and evil, mixed with cunning, remorselessness, love of power, that lend fascination, enthralment and terror to the fair-seeming magicians of North European folklore.

John Maynard Keynes on Lloyd George

If you want to please Henry & me, settle Ireland. Everyone with a sense of humour must enjoy Ireland, trying as the Irish are.

Mrs Asquith to Lloyd George

Meanwhile, a pantomime of increasing irrelevance was being enacted at Westminster. Asquith hastened to Dublin at the tail end of Maxwell's executions to establish his prime ministerial presence there, visiting a number of prisoners from Easter Week and judging them 'very good-looking fellows with such lovely eyes'. He returned to London full of resolve for a 'new initiative on Ireland', and appointed to the task David Lloyd George. Lloyd George's actions in the subsequent period are not important for any chance of success they might have had – for they had none whatsoever – but for their display of the sheer inventive deviousness of his negotiating tactics. Largely for the benefit of American public opinion, he provided the illusion of intense and sincere activity in pursuit of a 'fair settlement', while giving away nothing from the Imperial design; when negotiations broke down, as they inevitably did, he blamed it on the obduracy of the Irish and invariably emerged unscathed, with even greater levels of personal power.

Lloyd George's first step was the obvious one of reviving discussion on the Home Rule Act already on the statute book. But with it came all the acrimony associated with the question of partition: Carson would accept no less than permanent exclusion of six of Ulster's nine counties, while Redmond would only agree to this desperate measure if it was clearly provisional. Lloyd George's remedy was to negotiate separately with these two irreconcilables, and simply promise them each what they wanted. He then prolonged the negotiations as long as was necessary for them to appear to be genuine, keeping Carson and Redmond apart so as not to expose his deception, and then allowed them to collapse of their own accord. He preserved his own blamelessness by driving a wedge between the Ulster Unionists and their counterparts in the south (who did not want partition as it meant their total abandonment to the nationalists), then coupling the Unionists' internal arguments with Redmond's 'intransigence' and declaring that he was helpless before such Irish quarrelsomeness. In doing so he accomplished his only goal, which was to suspend indefinitely the really crucial question of Ulster while appearing to try to solve it. It was a formula which the British government has monotonously resorted to ever since.

American opinion was central to these deliberations. Britain's losses in Europe made it imperative to entice America into the war. But Ireland remained a serious impediment. Irish-America has always had a significant and highly vocal lobby in American politics – and it was particularly vocal in the aftermath of the executions; likewise, when President Wilson declared that 'no nation should seek to extend its polity over any other people, but that every people should be left free to determine its own polity, its own way of development, unhindered, unthreatened, unafraid, the little along with the great and powerful . . .' the parallels with Ireland were obvious. These were the sole principles on which America would enter the war, and British politicians, hungry for American troops and weaponry, could only murmur their pious assent. Evidently, more strenuous efforts would have to be made to solve the Irish problem.

In Ireland, the American principles were seen to be precisely those which had motivated the Rising, and it was genuinely believed that they would be faithfully adhered to at the peace conference after the war, if only Ireland could gain recognition there. This enthusiasm for the ideals of President Wilson, along with a rejection of partition, were the issues which focused the attentions of the amorphous and somewhat discordant group of republicans and malcontent nationalists who had repudiated Redmond's Irish Parliamentary Party and were now taken up with fund-raising and anti-recruiting activities. But there was as yet no political organization to harness their otherwise wayward energy.

The possibility for a beginning, however, presented itself in the form of a by-election in North Roscommon in early February 1917. The Irish Parliamentary Party had not been exposed to a serious electoral challenge in living memory, at least from non-Unionists, and it was decided to give them one in the form of the candidature of Count Plunkett, an ageing Papal count with a patriarchal beard who was the father of Joseph Plunkett, one of the executed leaders of the Rising. Count Plunkett came to be known as the 'Sinn Fein candidate', though Arthur Griffith's moderate party of that name, begun in 1905 on the principles of self-reliance, repeal of the Act of Union and the old Hungarian idea of non-recognition of the Imperial parliament, was now virtually moribund. But, as the saying went, 'It wasn't Sinn Fein made the Rising, but the Rising which made Sinn Fein,' and, inaccurate as it might have been, the name was foisted not only on the participants in the Rising, but on nearly all those slightly to the left of Redmond's party.

The old Count astonished everybody: he polled nearly twice the votes of the Redmondite. And, in one important sense, he justified his labelling as a 'Sinn Feiner', for he adopted Arthur Griffith's old policy of abstentionism from the British Parliament. Griffith had long argued that the Irish should use the British electoral machinery to demonstrate their desire for their own assembly, and Count Plunkett was persuaded to concur – 'It is in Ireland that the battle for Irish liberty is to be fought,' he declared.

Dublin Castle's response was a series of arrests on such charges as flying the tricolour and singing disloyal songs. And, in a remarkable early acknowledgement of the potential seditiousness of the visual medium, they banned a film, 'Ireland a Nation'. . . . *Plus ça change*. . . .

But the national will was hardening and, as it did, the occasions for expressing it simply multiplied. One of these was the first anniversary of the Easter Rising.

MAIRE COMERFORD: The first anniversary of Easter Week was a marvellous occasion. When the women of the Citizen Army were released they came home determined to wipe out the insults they heard while they were in prison. They gathered up the type of the Proclamation and found a friendly printer, an Englishman, and he printed this. They had it then for the first anniversary and they put it up in places that had been defended by the Volunteers. Then a steeplejack climbed the ruins of the GPO and put a flag up. The police couldn't get the flag down and it stayed up there most of the day. It created great excitement in Dublin. I remember reading an account of this in the paper on the Monday. It must have gone like lightning around the country and if the people elsewhere responded as well as we did, and I'm sure they did, it must have been a great inspiration to them.

The next by-election – and therefore the next test of the country's *political* will – was to take place in the South Longford constituency on 9 May 1917.

BRIGHID LYONS THORNTON: There was a vacancy then for an MP in Longford, and Michael Collins and Tom Ashe, they were great pals, they got the bright idea that they'd run a candidate who was in jail. So Collins wrote to my uncle, Joe MacGuinness, who was in Lewes jail at that time, but he turned the idea down. He wasn't that type of man; he was a quiet retiring little gentleman and he wouldn't have that kind of thing. But they prevailed on him anyway and eventually he reluctantly agreed to come in.

So everybody in Ireland that was worth knowing came to Longford to help fight the election. Cars and contributions came in from nowhere. I remember Rory O'Connor, who was executed later during the Civil War, gave me £2. And we put up posters with a picture of my uncle in his prison clothes and the slogan was 'Put him in to get him out'. Dan McCarthy came up then. He was a dynamic electioneering agent, and he and I worked day and night. I was secretary and I made more buckets of paste and I put posters on cars and on anything I could find. Every weekend they came in their hordes and they slept out in the haysheds and they slept in the streets. It was lovely weather and we just put them up wherever we could.

The next thing was I heard that Collins was coming, so I was up in the air. The crowd came in on the train one evening and all came to the election room in the apartment over my uncle's business, and I looked round at them all and I saw this one handsome man and I heard the accent and the chuckle and I saw the twinkle in his eye and I realized that this was Collins. You'd know him the minute he was in a place. So everybody in the town was keeping people, it was like a big congress in the town, and we had nowhere to put him. But we had found this lovely hotel in Granard, which was run by four beautiful sisters and their brother, and we decided to put Michael there. They were very lovely and glamorous and had all the right ideas and had been to St Ita's, Pearse's school for girls. So Michael went over there with some others and he met Helen, the loveliest of the Kiernan girls, and I think he fell in love with her. But she had other views and married someone else, a solicitor I think. I mean Michael wasn't much of a catch, apart from his charm. He hadn't a house or a job or any-thing, and if you were any way down to earth you wouldn't . . . I suppose I would have at that stage, but the Kiernans were very keen business girls and were more mature than I was.

The day of the count came then and we all went down to the courthouse where the count was being made and we stood in the middle of the street. It was a dismal day and we waited there with bated breath. McKenna, I think, was the Irish Party candidate, the Redmondite, and they had great support in that part of the country and we were very worried. Suddenly then my uncle Frank appeared at the window and there was a cheer, a terrific cheer, and the green flags began to come up. I nearly died because the green flags meant the Irish Party. My uncle eventually calmed us down and shut the window again. Then we heard there was a rumour of a recount, that they had found fifty votes pushed aside, and suddenly then came the announce-ment – my uncle had won by thirty-seven votes. There was great jubilation then and bonfires were lit all over the coun-try to celebrate the great victory. Sean Nunan, who was beside me, charged off to the post office and sent a telegram to Lloyd George. I don't remember what it was but we all thought it was very smart. It was a terrific slap in the face to the British, to put a convict, someone they had in their jail, into Parliament, especially with the peace conference coming and all the talk of the fight for small nations. With that and the rest of the prisoners coming out it was really the beginning of our freedom.

The *Manchester Guardian* referred to the election result as 'the equivalent of a serious British defeat in the field'.

1917 proceeded apace for the republicans. In June the re-maining prisoners from the Rising – many of them on penal servitude for life – were released from the convict prisons in Britain and arrived in Dublin to a spectacular welcome. One of those to return was Eamon de Valera, a former mathematics teacher and hero of the Rising who the following month won a landslide victory in a by-election in East Clare on an uncompromisingly republican platform. In August, another of the released prisoners, William Cosgrave, won in Kilkenny by a similar margin, and, with the display of bonfires and near-hysteria which greeted such victories, it became obvious that Sinn Fein, however amorphous, was simply engulfing the country.

Dublin Castle's predictable reflex was the arrest of eighty-four republicans in the month of August alone. Among them was Thomas Ashe, another of the heroes of Easter Week, who instantly began a hunger strike in protest against his criminal status, demanding, perhaps prematurely, to be treated as a prisoner of war (there was no such thing as political status at the time). The prison authorities embarked on a brutal and inept programme of forcible feeding, and Ashe died on 25 September as a result. His funeral, organized by the Wolfe Tone Executive Committee (an IRB cover), was the largest Dublin had seen since Parnell's.

MARTIN WALTON: Thomas Ashe's funeral was one of the biggest funerals ever held in Dublin, if not the biggest. At this time most of the main buildings, certainly the important ones like City Hall, were held by the military for perhaps two or three years after the Rising, so it was a pretty audacious – some would say foolhardy – move to decide to wake Ashe there. We hadn't any guns. But luckily enough for us someone in the administration – it was probably a Catholic assistant under-secretary there called MacMahon – got wind of this and rather than have a confrontation he persuaded the military to evacuate the ground floor of the City Hall. When we got there all the troops with their machine-guns and everything were on the top and in the basement, while the Volunteers and the body of Thomas Ashe were allowed onto the ground floor. We all expected

a slaughter, that we'd be mown down, but they were chiv-
alrous enough not to interfere.

My company, that was C Company, Second Battalion, we
drew up near the top of Parnell Square, nearly opposite to
where our music shop is now in Frederick Street, and I
remember young Sean Lemass being received from the
Fianna into the Volunteers that morning. I remember him
being a lovely-looking young lad. Four of us – that was all
of us who had guns – lined up in front of the company.
Mine was a little ·32, which was half-rusty, and I had four
rounds of ammunition. In the company at that time there
were about thirty men, or boys – you could hardly call me
a man at that time – but wherever they came from I don't
know, because in our company alone we had about 200 on
parade that morning. Lads joined in, became enthusiastic.
It was a tremendous event. I think Ashe's death had a
greater effect on this country than 1916.

Michael Collins delivered the brief oration over his friend's
grave, following the firing of three volleys: 'Nothing additional
remains to be said. That volley which we have just heard is
the only speech which it is proper to make over the grave of
a dead Fenian.'

If gunshots were the replacement for political rhetoric, for
how long could the young men of Ireland be restrained? Sinn
Fein was rapidly acquiring a new, more menacing edge.

4

When Irish questions, or rather the *Irish Question* (for there is
but one), has been forced on our attention, we have felt, like
a dreamer in a nightmare, oppressed by the consciousness that
some great evil was rapidly advancing – that mere exertion on
our part would avert it, but that we had not the power to will
that exertion.

Nassau William Senior, 1843

Lloyd George had finally ascended to the premiership in
December 1916. Within months his government had reached
a familiar impasse on Ireland, for it could not take the necessary steps to solve the problem there without bringing itself
down. Irish and British interests had diverged to the point of
mutual exclusivity: the British government would either have
to accede to the demands of Sinn Fein, which would soon be
in control of Ireland, or apply sufficient coercion to suppress
it. As his Coalition Cabinet was stacked with Unionists who
were foresworn to give no quarter to Irish nationalism, the
former was impossible; the latter was simply distasteful, not
to mention difficult in the face of demands made on British
troops by the war in Europe.

Nevertheless, Lloyd George's career was based largely on
his negotiating skills, and he applied himself once again to this
middle road. The new Cabinet's first initiative was a further
adaptation of the Home Rule Bill, which would partition the
country but at the same time allow for a Council of Ireland
made up of Ulster MPs and an equal number of delegates
from the Home Rule parliament in Dublin. It had little more
than symmetry to recommend it and it was scrapped before it
got off the ground.

The next proposal was more ambitious and costly, but like-wise designed to give only the *appearance* of fair representation. This was an All-Ireland Convention, which began its meetings in Trinity College in Dublin on 25 July 1917. This had scant prospects of reaching a solution; it was merely an occasion for a large number of representatives to come together to present an equally large number of irreconcilable points of view. It was to have 101 members – 'hand-picked' by the government, as the London *Times* remarked, 90 per cent of whom had already consented to partition. Sinn Fein, widely acknowledged in even the hostile British press as the most powerful force in Ireland, and organized labour were to have five seats each, a total of less than 10 per cent between them. Both naturally declined to attend under such circumstances, though Sinn Fein offered to participate if all solutions were open to debate and if the convention delegates were elected by adult suffrage in Ireland. But self-determination was not Lloyd George's goal; he simply wanted to offload his burden and buy himself generous amounts of time – which is what he accomplished, for the convention bickered and agonized its way to April 1918, finally submitting its report shortly after the death of an utterly broken John Redmond.

Meanwhile, the new Sinn Fein finally came around to consolidating its various elements at an Ard Fheis, or convention, on 26 October. The object was to ratify a new constitution more in line with its revitalized membership, and 2000 delegates came together for that purpose. Joseph Sweeney was one of them.

JOSEPH SWEENEY: It was quite apparent that if the fruits of the action taken in 1916 were to be realized there would have to be some kind of political organization brought into being to carry on what those men had started. Sinn Fein had been set up earlier in the century by Arthur Griffith, and it was obvious that a new programme would have to be devised to meet the more advanced ideas of the membership. The IRB of course was committed to the Wolfe Tone prop-

osition of complete separation from England, and they became very active in Sinn Fein and greatly influenced its
policies. Accordingly, in October 1917 the Sinn Fein organization held an Ard Fheis in Dublin, and a motion was
brought forward – as far as I remember it was brought
forward by Cathal Brugha and seconded by Sean Milroy –
and it proposed a new constitution for Sinn Fein on entirely
republican lines. This was speedily adopted unanimously.
There were three nominations for president – de Valera,
Griffith and someone else* I can't remember at the moment
– and in the event Griffith and the other man withdrew and
de Valera was elected unanimously.

This began the movement to get control politically of the
whole country. Sinn Fein prepared itself then to engage in
elections to all public bodies, so as to get rid of the Irish
Parliamentary Party's hold on the country. The Parliamentary Party had backed Lloyd George's convention in Dublin,
which had achieved nothing and could not possibly achieve
anything because Sinn Fein had been building up steadily
since the executions after Easter Week.

The delegates to the Ard Fheis had represented widely
differing viewpoints, and it was a tremendous achievement to
internalize them all within one organization. The new inner
conflict was the moderate/radical one which besets nearly all
political parties – though in such explosive times reasoned
debate could not always be relied upon to solve it and the
differences finally erupted under British pressure into civil war
in 1922. For the time being, however, the anxiety to present
a united front prevented any open rift.

The contentious issue was the open advocacy of an Irish
Republic, seen by some as an intractable and extremist demand which would lead directly into a military conflict with
Britain, and few at the Ard Fheis wanted to be seen to be
calling for violence. But de Valera made an early display of

* Count Plunkett.

114

manoeuvrability, straining even his renowned mathematician's logic for a formula which would be acceptable to radicals and moderates alike. This was: 'Sinn Fein aims at securing the international recognition of Ireland as an independent Irish Republic. Having achieved that status the Irish people may by referendum freely choose their own form of government.' This ambiguous declaration allowed everyone the comfort, however illusory, of their own interpretation, and de Valera and others continued to labour diligently to strike an effective balance within Sinn Fein. Everyone did their best to pull together, and as a further gesture towards unity de Valera was also made President of the Irish Volunteers at their own convention the following day. Thus, within the space of two days, the political movement had consolidated itself, however uneasily, and also acquired a military wing under the same leader.

5

The British Administration could no longer succeed in governing Ireland; it could only prevent her governing herself.

Y. M. Goblet

By 1918, Britain and its allies had suffered appalling losses in
their mismanaged campaigns in the Dardanelles, Jutland and
Mesopotamia. But it was on the Western Front, under Sir
Douglas Haig, that disaster had reached truly cataclysmic proportions. The resulting hunger for troops put tremendous
pressure on Lloyd George to take a step he had long been
dreading: the extension of conscription to Ireland. He knew
its inherent dangers and had been warned by his advisers in
Ireland – from General Sir Brian Mahon, Commander in Chief
there, to Sir Edward Carson – that resistance to it would be
extreme. It would clarify the choices open to Irishmen like no
other event or policy since the executions, something which,
with public opinion in Ireland moving in the direction it was,
Lloyd George desperately wanted to avoid. Yet his generals,
his right wing and the British public, too, would not tolerate
an idle Ireland in the midst of such an exacting war effort.

Lloyd George's dilemma was an old one, and his solution
was typical: he simply tried to make the problem disappear.
He proposed to soften the blow of conscription by enacting a
new Home Rule Bill, and the two Bills were presented side by
side. But, as ever, an agreed Home Rule formula could not be
found, and conscription could not be applied without it. The
only path he found open to him was to prolong the Home
Rule deliberations until they degenerated into impotency, pass
the conscription Bill but suspend the enactment of it indefinitely, and in the meantime apply coercion to Ireland to keep

things from boiling over. He was able to convince his ministers that the establishment of some order was an essential precondition to any implementation of Home Rule or conscription – a point of view they eagerly assented to, for it let everyone off the hook. It was, of course, not a policy, but merely a postponement of the moment of truth.

The passage of the empty conscription Bill – empty because it required an Order of Council to enact it – drove the Irish Parliamentary Party out of Parliament in protest, with John Dillon, who had taken the place of the late John Redmond, at their head. The Ireland they returned to was in a state of uproar. The Catholic bishops had declared their resolute opposition to conscription and approved all forms of resistance to it; Labour called a one-day general strike, and Sinn Fein and the Parliamentary Party stood together on anti-conscription platforms.

MAIRE COMERFORD: Whether he was moved by 1916 or not, every man in Ireland of military age, particularly with the threat of conscription hanging over him, had one choice in front of him: which flag would he fight under? There was no way out of either being conscripted, carried off by force by the English, or joining the Republic and the flag of the Republic. The tricolour was then being put up on chimneys and on trees and on telegraph wires and we were nearing a state of revolution at home. Anyone who had a choice to make – and no man had a choice to stay at peace – the choice before any man was to fight for somebody. The majority of them of course made the choice to fight with their own soil under their feet in the cause proclaimed by Pearse in the Proclamation, which promised rights and liberties for which the Irish nation had long been struggling.

Coercion took the form of the appointment to the lord lieutenancy of Field-Marshal Lord French, a bluff Anglo-Irishman who declared that his policy would be 'to put the fear of God into these playful Sinn Feiners'. He requested for the purpose a number of bombs, machine-guns and aeroplanes. But it was decided that a pretext for the measures he had in mind was needed, and accordingly a 'German plot' was concocted. It was stated that Sinn Fein was in league with Germany and as a preventative measure it was essential to round up all its leaders. The only hard evidence was related to Roger Casement's activities before the Rising and few believed that there was anything to it, but in the event seventy-three Sinn Fein activists were arrested. This clumsy effort had two consequences highly inimical to British interests in Ireland: first, it generated the usual campaign of sympathy for the prisoners, which was particularly successful when they were run as candidates in the general election later that year; second, by removing such personages as Arthur Griffith, de Valera, William Cosgrave and Count Plunkett, who exerted a moderating influence in Sinn Fein, it left the country in the hands of men who were preparing for war – men like Michael Collins, Harry Boland and Cathal Brugha. Collins, already hard at work on his intelligence network, had been forewarned of the arrests by a sympathetic detective in the G Division in Dublin Castle, Joe Kavanagh, and had passed on the information to the leaders; they agreed among themselves that their cause would be better served with them in prison, but Collins typically found no appeal in such symbolic resistance and instead went on the run. Under his hand the Volunteers likewise went underground and the police quickly lost all capability of assessing their strength.

In August it was decided that a general election would take place in December, though it remained an uncertainty until the Armistice was signed in November. Lord French's own war against Ireland, however, remained unaffected: Sinn Fein, the Volunteers and Cumann na mBan were banned; their leadership was in prison; Sinn Fein press and election material was suppressed, its Director of Elections was arrested and meetings were broken up by the police; aeroplanes flew over the country scattering leaflets warning of the consequences of voting Sinn Fein. These were hardly the proper circumstances for a democratic election; Sinn Fein, nevertheless, waged an enthusiastic campaign, their platform being the ideals of the Easter Rising Proclamation, abstention from the British Parliament and the establishment of a native constituent assembly, and representation at the Peace Conference.

MAIRE COMERFORD: In the second-last paragraph of the Proclamation of Easter Week, it said that a Provisional Government was being appointed which would look after the civil and military affairs of the nation until such time as the Irish people, all the Irish people, men and women, could elect a government, a parliament of their own. That was the key thing, because the general election which followed the war was foreseen. At this time England was engaged in a war which was supposed to be for the freedom of small nations – for democracy, for peace, for a world which would never be the same again. It was a thing which seemed to open up a new world, and for a number of years we were engaged in cultural activities, in flying the tricolour flag, in having meetings, in appealing to the people to depend on the outcome of the war. The Armistice duly came and we then had the general election. I was in the polling booth and I was very active. I remember pikemen marching in that election, just as they did in 1798. They made them in forges and put them on long sticks. It's one of those things I cherish, having seen the pikemen marching by moonlight. We had no arms, of course, at that time.

Sean Harling, though only sixteen years old at the time, was an active campaigner.

SEAN HARLING: When we were making the barricade during the Rising at the bottom of Church Street and Brunswick Street, there was an old coach-builder had a place at the corner. We went in there and took out one of the coaches and put heavy barricades at either side of it so that anyone going past it would have to go through the cab. After the

Rising the cab was pushed back into the coach-builder's yard because it was badly damaged. But when the election came up in 1918 I took out the cab and got the loan of a horse and we went all around the area shouting, 'Come and vote in the 1916 cab!' We were campaigning for Michael Staines. He was running against John Dillon Nugent, who was the Redmond man.

John Dillon Nugent lived in the first house at the corner of Rathdown Road and one night we came along with white lead and put a ladder up against his house, a red-bricked house, and rubbed it with paint and wrote 'Vote for Staines' on the wall. He stuck his head out of the window to tell us to get away and Paddy O'Hanrahan, he's dead now, he hit him in the face with the brush. So we got down and he must have had a telephone because as we got near Phibsborough church four policemen were running up from Mountjoy and they tried to grab us. So we let them have it with what was left of the white lead and cleared off down the Phibsborough Road. That was about two o'clock in the morning, and we took a short cut then into what we called the Committee Rooms and we laid down there on some blankets and had our sleep.

JOSEPH SWEENEY: Following a bout of the very bad influenza in 1918, which I contracted in Galway and which prevented my sitting for examinations in the university there that year, I went home to west Donegal. I realized that my return to Galway would probably result in my arrest because a man who afterwards became famous as one of the police murder gangs, Head Constable Igoe, was taking particular notice of my activities in the area, and I was warned by the son of an RIC man to watch what I was doing. So I went home, and after a lot of thought I told my father that I was going to abandon my studies. I took up employment with him then as an office accountant. I joined up with the local *cumann*, and I also attended the *comhairle ceanntair*, or district council, meetings when they were held.

My first impression of the organization was that while it was strong on ideals, it was very short of leadership. I had already found this in the Volunteer organization. Up until the very end in our area that was the position. We just hadn't enough educated young fellows. But we decided to make the best of it.

Eventually, in December 1918, the British government declared a general election, and we called a meeting to select a candidate for West Donegal. Now I was never approached by anyone prior to that meeting, or had any serious talks with anyone about who the candidate should be. In my mind the most influential man in that part of the country was a cousin of mine named John E. Boyle, but to my consternation he said that under no circumstances would he go forward, for personal reasons. The nomination was thrown back on the assembly and one of my senior officers then proposed that I should be the candidate. Before it was seconded I got to my feet and demurred and said that I was not a politician and that I thought they'd be better off to select somebody who would have more of an idea of political matters than I would. But I was voted down anyway and my name was put forward formally and seconded and adopted by the meeting. This threw me into a bit of a quandary because I already had charge of the Volunteers there and my area was extending all the time. I then had to go and take personal charge of all the arrangements for the election. I was successful then in getting some very useful members in different districts of the constituency, and things seemed to be going fairly well.

The major problem we had was with transport, with getting the voters out, because we knew that if we got the young people out we couldn't possibly be beaten. That was the feeling in the country at that time. We got some help anyway, and in the event I was returned by a two-to-one majority.

Sinn Fein really fostered a wonderful spirit of cohesion among its members, and it enlarged on the friendships

121

which were formed in the internment camps and prisons. Our greatest rivals up where I was in the northern part of the country were the Ancient Order of Hibernians. They were a very strongly knit organization, and they were based on purely sectarian lines. Sinn Fein, on the other hand, accepted anybody, no matter what religion they were. As time went on Sinn Fein grew to such an extent that the AOH faded out in that part of the country, except in more sectarian-minded areas of the North where there were always conflicts during the different marching periods they had. But I'm glad to say that as far as my area of the country was concerned that type of thing was discouraged and eventually people of any religion could walk about freely without fear of intimidation or insult. Of course Sinn Fein, with all the momentum of what had happened in 1916, with the executions and other events after that, it just swept the whole country in those elections.

MAIRE COMERFORD: The British of course were prepared for intimidation and corruption and that the votes wouldn't be properly watched and counted. We were given a seal to put on every ballot box and we sealed them up. We were told not to leave them out of sight and to send a guard with them wherever they went. The next day I went by bicycle to where the train was and we sent them off to the counting centre. The republicans sat on one side watching the boxes and the police on the other side and nobody was able to put a finger on them until the count was made.

The result of the election in Ireland was what elections had always been since about 1885 on – it was held by nationalists. But in this case the old-fashioned nationalists had been replaced by republicans in the tradition of Pearse and Connolly. It gave Irish republicans the mandate to confirm the Proclamation of 1916, to declare independence and to set up an independent government.

When the election results were declared on 28 December

1918, it could be seen that the new revolutionary party had been spectacularly vindicated: out of 105 seats in Ireland, seventy-three had gone to Sinn Fein; the Unionists won twenty-six. For the Irish Parliamentary Party, who only managed to secure six seats, perhaps the only blessing was that John Redmond had not lived to see this final and unmistakable consignment to oblivion. In Ulster, the Unionists held a popular majority in only four of that province's nine counties, and even in those the nationalist minority was of great significance, certainly far greater than the Unionist vote in comparison with the rest of Ireland. The message to Britain had been made brilliantly clear: no partition, total self-determination. No British party in the history of parliamentary politics there had ever received such a decisive mandate.

Sinn Fein quickly enacted one of the elements of its platform by convening an assembly, Dail Eireann, at the Mansion House in Dublin on 21 January 1919. All representatives elected in Irish constituencies the previous month were invited to attend but only those from Sinn Fein accepted, and, of those seventy-three, nearly half remained in prison from the 'German plot' arrests. At this meeting, presided over by Cathal Brugha in the absence of de Valera, who was in Lincoln jail, Dail Eireann declared its independence from Britain and also proclaimed itself to be the legislative branch of the only legitimate Irish government. It ratified the establishment of the Irish Republic made in the Proclamation at Easter 1916, reiterated the ideals contained in that document, and made its implied socialism more specific in the 'Democratic Programme of Dail Eireann'.

The Democratic Programme, like the Proclamation, was a visionary document, a thing of the mind. To implement it would require not only the defeat of an empire fresh from a victorious war, but an overcoming of reality itself, for no government has ever achieved the degree of purity it described. Ireland, unarmed and inexperienced in self-government, could of course do neither. But the Democratic Programme was nevertheless an assertion of legitimate rights and aspirations towards which any properly constituted society should be moving, and only something so bold and profoundly different could have uplifted the people for the tremendous struggle ahead of them. If they were being asked to risk everything – and Lord French's military government had clearly indicated the punitive consequences of the fight for self-determination – then it must not be for just a green form of British misrule. Ireland had travelled a tortuous and sometimes bloody path since the death of Parnell in 1891, and with the meeting of Dail Eireann it had taken its most significant leap on the way from moderate nationalism to revolution. History was accelerating; the impossible appeared to be happening – why not Utopia?

MAIRE COMERFORD: The Irish nation at this time was thinking of nothing else except its freedom. We all thought that however many generations had failed and died in the 700 years that went before, that we were the generation that was going to see this out. It seemed that nothing could stop us. We were totally committed to it. The setting up of our government then coincided with the arrival of President Wilson in Versailles. Everyone assumed that something would happen, because of what had been promised during the war.

It was in this atmosphere that the first Dail Eireann met. Only about a third of its members were there because the rest were all in prison. The English said they had been involved in a 'German plot'. No English government of that period could believe that anyone in Ireland could go into rebellion for the sake of Ireland. They preferred to believe that somebody abroad was paying us to rebel. That was, I suppose, confirmed by the arms which Casement had negotiated from Germany. Casement had been hanged in England in August 1916. Now we were in 1919, and there was still a 'German plot' and our people were in jail and the German war was over. The Russian Revolution had happened by this time and the English were able to switch with the greatest smoothness into a 'Russian plot' and ever since then we've been haunted by 'Russian plots'. They never could believe that there was an Irish plot to make Ireland free. They don't believe it yet, I don't think.

The emptiness of the war promises was then revealed when President Wilson said in an interview that the four great nations had agreed among themselves that the consent of all of them was necessary before any small nation could get a hearing. That of course meant that Ireland had no chance. So it was only when everything collapsed and the promises were broken and proved to be worthless that we had to follow our own instincts in the protection of our own people.

TOM BARRY: I didn't get back to Ireland from the war until January 1919, the day after Dail Eireann issued a pronouncement that they were setting up an Irish Republic. I immediately set about learning what had been happening in Ireland for all those years. I read everything I could get my hands on, and naturally enough I got in touch with some of the republicans around west Cork, where I was from. I could see that after the military defeat of 1916 and the handing up of arms they were trying to reorganize. And I also looked around and I could see the British troops and police, and their terrible arrogance, and anyone could see that there was going to be a collision. It was easy enough for me to make my mind up as to what I would do because I had three clear choices: one, I could join the enemy – the enemy I'd just left – and be a traitor; two, sit in a ditch and be a louser, but I wasn't built like that; or three, join my own people and do the right thing. I met Sean Buckley, who at that time was the brigade intelligence officer, though I didn't know it, and I told him that if they were going to start a fight that I'd fight with them.

SEAN KAVANAGH: In the period after the Rising there was a reorganization of the Volunteers as a military body, and

125

there was also a great growth in the political activity of the country. I joined both Sinn Fein and the Volunteers, as well as the Gaelic League, and I started teaching Irish on a purely voluntary basis. I used to spend my holidays in Ring, County Waterford, where all the people spoke Irish. I was active too in Sinn Fein and I remember I represented my Sinn Fein club from south Kilkenny at the Ard Fheis at the Mansion House in Dublin. It was there I met Collins for the first time. As time went on I became more involved, and I learned a lot about the Volunteers from my friend Michael Staines, who was Quartermaster in the Dublin Brigade then. Eventually, by 1919 I was a full-time teacher in Naas, County Kildare, and things were becoming more tense and I felt anxious to help the movement in any way I could.

JOHN L. O'SULLIVAN: The Rising was really over before the ordinary people in the country heard anything about it, and though I didn't join the Volunteers until 1919, when I was eighteen, I remember my mother and father back then being very sceptical about taking on the British Empire. They were very patriotic, as the majority of Irish people were, especially rural populations, and they had the traditions and the songs of the past, but they always, in any discussion they had with us, said, 'In the name of God, are you mad taking on the British Empire?' They thought that it was impossible, that we were foolish to go up against the might of Britain, which ruled so much of the world at the time and had everything at its disposal. When they spoke of Ireland and its freedom they were in deep sympathy with the ideals but they were very dubious about the results. As is well known, right down the centuries there was never a century which passed without some uprising taking place, and everybody knew that it always ended in failure, and in death, and on the end of the hangman's rope or, as happened many times, in banishment to foreign countries. But gradually we got the spirit and we got the men and we got the leadership and we became a formidable organization, strictly disciplined, under strict control. There was no such thing, as easily happens at times like that, of a man getting hold of power and using it in his own interests or against some neighbour who wasn't a friend of his. The whole country came behind us and they were prepared for the sacrifices and they felt they had to make this last fight for freedom.

PART FOUR

Darkened minds and bleak outlooks

21 January 1919 to 11 July 1921

'We were now hard, cold, ruthless, as our enemy had been since hostilities began. The British had been met with their own* weapons. They had gone down into the mire to destroy us and our nation and down after them we had to go to stop them. The step was not an easy one, for one's mind was darkened and one's outlook made bleak by the decisions that had to be taken.'

Tom Barry, *Guerrilla Days in Ireland*

1

If this is the state of affairs, we'll have to kill somebody, and make the bloody enemy organize us.

Sean Treacy, 1918

Nothing is ever done in this world until men are prepared to kill one another if it is not done.

George Bernard Shaw, *Major Barbara*

War at last entered the political void in Ireland in January 1919. Its opening shots are thought to have coincided with the first meeting of the Dail when, on 21 January 1919, at Soloheadbeg in County Tipperary, a party of Volunteers including Dan Breen, Sean Treacy and Seamus Robinson ambushed a Royal Irish Constabulary escort guarding a load of gelignite being transported to a quarry. In the mêlée, the Volunteers seized the gelignite and shot dead two policemen who had raised their carbines to fire.

The incident had a cathartic effect on Ireland, for it seemed to release other Volunteers who had been restraining themselves with difficulty from violence far beyond the point where they believed a political solution was possible. Over subsequent months, in sporadic acts throughout the country, more policemen were shot.

This first stage of the campaign that extended over two and a half years of mounting terror had about it a buoyant, chaotic enthusiasm. It was more a brimming over of the increased militancy in Ireland than part of a national plan – more a parallel activity to the political ferment which brought the

131

Dail into being than a policy legislated by it.* The generation then coming of age had participated in the post-Rising national upsurge. They were as confident – some would say overly so – as their forebears were timid, and they were desperately eager to test their strength. They fired the first shots of the war on their own initiative.

Following Soloheadbeg and throughout 1919, the campaign against the RIC was stepped up: in the Dail de Valera advocated their social ostracization, while in the countryside this often took the ultimate form of armed attacks, usually for badly needed rifles and ammunition. The RIC, it should be remembered, were not ordinary constables. They were a paramilitary force, fully armed and living in barracks, and of a size grossly disproportionate to the needs of a relatively crime-free country. They were also the grassroots of the British intelligence system in Ireland.

MARTIN WALTON: The country was studded at the time with small police barracks every few miles. The constabulary started off as the Irish Constabulary, but for their zeal during the Fenian rising Victoria graciously gave them the term 'Royal'. And they were the eyes and ears. You couldn't travel from Dublin to Swords – that's a distance of about seven miles – without going into three RIC outposts, and everybody passing up and down the road was noted carefully. In fact when Augustine Birrell, who had been the Chief Secretary here during the Rising, when he was questioned about the activity of the revolutionaries, he said that the Royal Irish Constabulary had Ireland under a microscope.

We thought that with our meagre supply of arms and

---

*The Dail did declare at its inception that a state of war existed between Britain and Ireland, though many of its members had ambivalent feelings about what that war should be like. The Dail's dilemma was nevertheless disturbingly plain: its members had been elected to secure an Irish Republic, something which they all knew they could neither wish nor negotiate into being.

ammunition and trained men that the best thing to do was to make life impossible for the smaller police barracks. These were ruthlessly attacked and they were then driven into larger formations. This left about thirty miles of the country free. These were then driven into still larger concentrations. It was a very carefully laid-out plan. I was on some of these attacks myself.

JOSEPH SWEENEY: Things began to get very tight. We knew the British were building up their own intelligence system and you had to watch where you slept and who you spoke to and what you said. We did our best to make life impossible for the police force in our area of the country. We trenched the roads to prevent them from patrolling in their cars, we attacked parties of RIC and burned their barracks. By the end of 1920 we had cleared them out of the whole area of the Rosses and Gweedore.

The Volunteers who effected these operations were by habit a self-regulating body. They had acquired the more official title of the Irish Republican Army and they became tenuously tied to the Dail by oath and through Cathal Brugha's Ministry of Defence; but they had nevertheless evolved in part from the old agrarian secret societies such as the Ribbonmen and retained some of their characteristics. Unlike the Ribbonmen, who simply avenged, in singularly brutal fashion, the misdeeds of landlords, the Volunteers were motivated by a national political ideal, but like the Ribbonmen they were unpaid, ungarrisoned and, for the most part, without uniforms. Their only methods were the only ones at hand, those of stealth and surprise. They lacked a command structure in the conventional sense and, largely because of poor communications, most of the decision-making devolved on to local company leaders.

Their campaign did, however, take on a kind of coherence on a national level, largely due to a design in the mind of Michael Collins. Collins had a rare gift for perceiving the

British system of rule in Ireland in vivid totality, and he systematically set about paralysing it. He secured arms, organized brigades and deployed the most eager of his IRB men around the country to invigorate the more reluctant areas. In Dublin, he formed his private 'Squad' from the hardest men among the Dublin Brigade and put them on full-time duty. As a cover they rented a shop in Middle Abbey Street in central Dublin and posed as builders' merchants; when on missions they carried their guns around under their aprons. Most important, and most lethal, was the intelligence network which evolved under Collins's control. Here his deputies were Liam Tobin, Tom Cullen and Frank Thornton. These worked tirelessly to secure sources of information from all sections of Britain's administration in Ireland, from post office clerks to Castle detectives. Britain had always secured its rule in Ireland with the help of infiltrators and informers, but Collins, with his enormous finesse for conspiracy, achieved a stunning reversal.

David Neligan was at this stage working for the British as a member of the Dublin Metropolitan Police.

DAVID NELIGAN: In 1918 the British had emerged victorious from the most terrible war in all their history. They had tremendous forces here in Ireland and they weren't prepared to give it over to a handful of Sinn Feiners who had no guns, whose armaments were derisory – a ·45 revolver here and there, a few old, broken-down rifles. 'Twasn't worth a farthing. I remember one time later on during the fight, the quartermaster of the Dublin Brigade took up the paper one morning and he saw where some spy or somebody was found riddled with bullets. He was a very serious individual and he said, 'Christ God, have they gone mad? "Riddled with bullets." Wouldn't one bullet have been enough to finish him?' And he didn't mean that as a joke. We wouldn't have lasted five minutes in any kind of open fight with the army the British brought against us. They had fleets of armoured cars, aeroplanes, machine-guns and thousands of conscript troops. They had a tank inside the Castle, a 20-ton tank. I saw the tommies turning it around one day and they knocked down a wall which had been there for hundreds of years. I heard an old Dublin apple-seller saying when she saw it clanking down the street one day, 'Begod! Butt Bridge going for a walk!' We hadn't a chance against them.

But Collins was a genius at the other game, the underground war. Any kind of uprising we'd ever had before was always betrayed by informers and spies. The Castle always had us by the back of the neck. The British have been authorities in espionage since the time of Cecil and Walsingham. Everyone who made a move against them fell foul of spies. Castle informers sunk us every time we opened our beaks. I saw the files myself inside the Castle. They had their eye on every single Irish organization, even the innocent ones.

The people who were most active against the IRA were the G-men, the political detectives. And this is where Collins shone. There were only a few of them who were very active. Hoey was one of them, Smyth another, Barton another. Collins warned all of these men that if they didn't give up their spying activities they would be shot. But they'd all had long service and they thought Collins would be beaten the same as the Fenians had been beaten, the same as everybody else had been beaten. So they kept up their nefarious activities and duly got shot. I was on duty as a uniformed policeman one night in Pearse Street as it is now – Brunswick Street then – and I heard some rattling out in the street. I thought it was someone pulling a stick along the railings, but it was machine-gun fire shooting down Detective Hoey. We found him lying dead in the street.

SEAN KAVANAGH: The real beginning of an effective intelligence service for the Volunteers ironically came from within the ranks of the G Division itself, the political wing of the Dublin police, when two young detectives sympathetic to the militant movement passed on some advance information on raids and arrests. These were Eamon Broy and Joe Kavanagh. Broy worked in the G Division headquarters in Brunswick Street and Kavanagh worked in the Castle. They were later joined by a third detective, James McNamara, who also worked in the Castle, and then by Dave Neligan. They provided the nucleus of a very powerful counter-intelligence system, which Collins kept strictly under his control, even though he wasn't at that time Director of Intelligence. When he was appointed to that post, some time in the summer of 1919, I think, he concentrated a great deal of energy on building up an effective intelligence system because he thought it to be the most important department of the Volunteer organization.

An intelligence network was set up by degrees throughout the country, and Collins kept in close contact with all the brigade intelligence officers. He had a number of men in the Dublin police and the RIC, some of them in key positions, who kept him regularly informed of their activities. He had quite a few men and women in the Post Office too, particularly the Dublin GPO, and they were able to pass on official telegrams sent by the military and police. For some reason they always used telegrams for important communications, rather than the telephone or normal postal system. Collins was able to keep his principal agent in the GPO supplied with the current code keys so that the agent could decipher these messages himself. He did the same with all the brigade intelligence officers. He seemed to have people in all branches of the administration and services here who were able to help. Many of the staff in the prisons, particularly Mountjoy, were sympathetic, and through them he was in constant communication with political prisoners and was able to arrange the sensational jailbreaks of that period. He had several people working on the railways too, and they provided his most reliable means of communication. They carried highly confidential letters, as well as arms and ammunition.

Collins himself was the only man in Ireland who had a complete picture of all these activities. He only let people know what was essential for their own particular work. This was true even of his most intimate staff. He used to say, 'Never let one side of your mind know what the other is doing.'

Both Sean Kavanagh and David Neligan soon found themselves enrolled in Collins's service.

SEAN KAVANAGH: I first became involved with Collins and his intelligence network towards the end of September 1919. I was teaching Irish for the Gaelic League in Naas, and I heard from a couple of the Volunteers there that there was an RIC sergeant in Naas who appeared to be sympathetic. His name was Jerry Maher, and he was the Chief Clerk to the County Inspector. So I mentioned this to my friend Michael Staines, and he passed it on to Collins, because a week later Staines came to me and said, 'Mick Collins wants to meet you.' So I went to Dublin, where I was taken to number 46 Parnell Square, and it was there I met Collins. I told him about Maher, and he said that he could be very useful because the RIC had produced a new code in which they sent their most secret and urgent messages by telegram. Up until then Collins had been able to crack the word code, but he couldn't break this new number code. So I went back and called around to Maher's house that evening. He lived in a quiet part of town. When I told him I'd been asked by Michael Collins to see him he said, 'You're the man I've been waiting for for years.' I told him that the most important thing to do was to get the new code key, and he said that the County Inspector himself decoded all the messages and kept the key in a safe, but that he would do his best.

I called around again a few days later and found that he'd made quite a bit of progress. He found out that the system worked by giving each letter of the alphabet between one and six two-digit numbers, and he had found quite a few of the corresponding numbers for the letters by taking the original telegrams in code and comparing them with some decoded messages which he'd salvaged from the County Inspector's waste-paper basket. That way we were able to build up quite a bit of the new code.

I brought this to Collins and of course he was delighted to have it. But the trouble was that the code was changed every month, so Collins suggested that Jerry Maher make a wax impression of the key to the County Inspector's safe. So this was done, and as a result Collins often had decoded messages re-despatched to the brigade intelligence officers before the County Inspector could do his own decoding. This was also true of the code key itself. I believe that when Terence MacSwiney's office was searched when he was arrested, a copy of a new code key which hadn't even come into use was found on his desk.

Sometimes circulars were sent out to county inspectors and Maher would give me the originals. I would then stay up all night or half the night copying them out so they could be put back in the morning before they were missed. When Collins heard about this he offered to come down and help me with the copying. He would have come down each time and then gone back to Dublin again in the morning, but of course I persuaded him that it wasn't necessary to take such a risk. He would have had to go through barracks full of Black and Tans. I heard later that he'd spent a whole night with Broy in the headquarters of the G Division in Brunswick Street.

DAVID NELIGAN: There were no jobs to be got around the country at all during the First World War, but I used to notice some of the local men from where I came from in west Limerick coming home from their jobs in the Dublin police, the DMP. They used to be home on leave wearing fine suits of clothes and high stiff collars and riding bicycles, and I used to envy them this, you see. I thought they were paid for walking around the town and doing nothing. So I applied for the Dublin police. My father didn't want me to leave the place at all and he burned my papers when they came down from Dublin Castle. The revolution was livening up at the time and he didn't want me to get mixed up with anything like that. He wanted me to stop at home and be a vegetable. But I wanted to shake the dust of the place off my feet, so I gave a neighbour's address and the papers came down and I found myself on the way to Dublin for a medical examination. My father gave in and handed me £5, all the wealth he could spare, and the following day I was sworn into the DMP.

The Commissioner of Police at the time was an ex-British officer, Colonel Edgeworth Johnstone, DSO. Fine old fellow. Swords champion of the British army. He cut a sheep in two at the swipe of a sword. He took his orders from the Kildare Street Club, a landlord and Unionist coterie that ran the country. The Irish people didn't have any power. But I wasn't about to change anything because I knew nothing at all about it. All I wanted was a soft plank to lie on.

So then I was sent out to patrol the town. I soon found out that police weren't paid for walking about and doing nothing else, as I thought when I was an ignorant gobdaw down the country. I had to go on night duty, 10 p.m. to 6 a.m. every night for a solid month. And at three o'clock when I was half dead even the prostitutes had gone home to rest. There was nothing there only a sign swinging in the wind. The British had their post in the Telephone Exchange and the poor British tommies at four o'clock in the morning used to invite me in for a cup of tea. That was the only luxury they had.

Well of course I soon get fed up with the old uniformed job because it was too difficult and I didn't like night duty. And it was a dull, boring performance. So I decided to join the G Division, looking for adventure. 'Twas easy for me to join because they were all getting shot by revolutionaries and they were taking on practically anybody. It didn't mean that I had got credit for my proclivities as a detective.

Things got very hot, and my brother Maurice came up from Kerry to Dublin, to Liberty Hall. He was a labour organizer, and he persuaded me to resign. His argument was that I had no business being there, working for the British government, while there was a revolution going on. He wanted me to clear off out of it. So I decided to resign, but before I did that I met a neighbour of mine named Paddy Sheehan. He was an ex-pupil of my father's, who was a schoolmaster – so was my mother for that matter – but anyway, Sheehan was de Valera's secretary and he was such an extreme Sinn Feiner that he wouldn't speak to me when he met me on the road because I was a Castle hack. But I sought him out and I said to him, 'If I can be of help to the revolution I'll stay on, but otherwise I'll resign.' So Sheehan went away and said, 'I'll make inquiries,' and he came back the next day and told me to resign. What I think happened was that he got in touch with de Valera and de Valera off his own bat without consulting Mick Collins made up his own mind. So I went home, and I was no sooner at home than a man named Tim Kennedy from Tralee down in Kerry sent word by my brother that he wanted to see me. He was an accountant at the county council, a small little man about four feet nothing in height. But he was a Jekyll and Hyde – we were all Jekyll and Hyde characters in those days. He was an accountant by day and a revolutionary by night.

So I wended my way down to Tralee and he told me he had a letter from Michael Collins. He said, 'Collins wants to see you.' 'What does he want me for?' says I. Collins was only a legendary character as far as I was concerned. So he said, 'I think he wants you to go back to the police to work for the IRA.' So I thought that over for some time and I told him that I'd go up to see him anyway. So I said to him, 'You know the British will be wondering why I've come back, if I go back. I think what you should do is send me a couple of threatening letters telling me to clear out of the place.'

So the letters duly arrived, charging me with high crimes and misdemeanours, to get out of Limerick by order of the IRA. So I put those in my pocket and took off for Dublin. I put up in a yoke called the Clarence Hotel, down in the quays. Austin Stack came to see me. He was a Kerryman and he was Minister of Home Affairs in the Dail, a small little fellow with a battered-looking face, like a man who had smallpox. But he was a nice little fellow. He told me he'd get in touch with Collins. So then Joe O'Reilly turned up. He was Collins's aide. He brought me down to an old third-rate pub in Upper Abbey Street, owned by two brothers named Bannon, and we knocked on the private door and one of the brothers brought us upstairs into an old beer room smelling of stale beer, a cobwebby old place, and there was this handsome-looking man sitting there in an old shabby suit and an old dust coat thrown over the back of the chair. This was the famed Michael Collins.

So Collins got up and said, 'I know all about you, Dave, and your brother and yourself are all right.' He meant we were friendly to the revolution. And he said, 'I have something to ask you. I want you to go back, back to the G Division.' I didn't fancy this role of spy at all, so I said to him, 'Mr Collins, I'll do anything rather than go back to that bloody place. I'll do anything, I'll join a flying column.' 'Listen, Dave,' says he, 'we have plenty of men to join flying columns. The British trust you and we trust you. If you want to serve this country and the revolution then go back.' He was a very persuasive kind of man, and a very magnetic character. So against my better judgement, I went back.

So then I wrote to Colonel Johnstone, telling him that I wanted to go back, and he sent for me. 'Neligan,' he says, 'you want to come back.' 'Yes sir,' says I, 'I do.' 'Why is that?' says he. So I said to him, 'These fellows threatened me,' and I produced the threatening letters. He was horrified. So then he asked me what the situation was like in my part of the country, and I said to him, 'The King's writ no longer runs in the south of Ireland.' This was something I'd seen in the *Daily Mail* the day before, with which I fully agreed. 'Too true,' says he. So we had a discussion and he said, 'Neligan, you're a good man. Where do you want to go? I'll give you any division you want, any station you want.' So I told him I wanted to go back to the G Division. 'All right,' he said, and we parted, and to this day I'm ashamed of deceiving the poor old fellow. He met an Irish fellow in Brighton, in England, after he'd retired, and he said to him, 'The one man that disappointed me was that bloody fellow Neligan.' So that's how I started my nefarious career as a double agent.

In the field, the fighting units of the IRA grew in strength, size and striking ability. In west Cork, Tom Barry, then twenty years old, began to improvise the training sessions and form the units which would make him probably the most effective rural guerrilla leader the British faced.

TOM BARRY: Sean Buckley, our IO, knew that I had plenty of war service and experiences on different fronts, and he proposed that I take charge of training. But I refused him because I didn't think I was competent. People were saying that it was an advantage to me to have seen war service, but of course I knew that the worst training in the world for a man who is going to be a guerrilla is to have served in the regular army. The only thing you learn there is firepower and the use of arms. Other than that you were only a cog in the wheel – you went where you were told to go, you advanced when you were ordered and you had no say in it. You had lines of communication, officers did the thinking for you and soldiers were paid. But we were faced with entirely different circumstances, and all that was inhibiting, you had to wipe it right out of your mind. We hadn't telephones, we hadn't transport, and above all we hadn't arms or ammunition, or at least enough to make any impression. Right through to the end our General Headquarters didn't know what a flying column was doing until they read about it in the paper.

But the major difference in circumstances between ourselves and the British was that we were fighting for our freedom. Irish people who had been sent to the front in the British army had been told they were fighting for freedom too, but they weren't. They were fighting a war of bloody economic survival – Germans, French, British and Americans, the whole lot of them were just looking for expansion. But in 1918 the Irish people had voted their own government into existence, and it was up to us in the IRA to protect it and prevent its destruction.

And I would like to make one thing very clear before I go on with this. I am not one to believe that war is a glorious thing. I think it is bestial, and the First World War taught me that. There's nothing romantic about war. The only war that I can justify to myself is a war of liberation. People get the idea that chaps who are at war actually like it. But they don't. They're the very people that don't like it because they know the bestialities of it and they know the hardships and they know the suffering, not alone of the soldiers but of their kith and kin. It often struck my mind when we killed Britishers that there were women and children maybe left without a husband, without a father. I want to make that very, very clear.

Anyway, Buckley and the others wouldn't accept my refusal, and they came after me again. I was in college here in Cork trying to complete a badly needed education, having hopped it at the age of seventeen to join the British army. It didn't last long, however, before I was whipped out of it again and into another war. A man I dearly loved, Charlie Hurley, came to me to try to persuade me to take the job. I wanted the Brigade Officer Commanding to take it, and he wouldn't, and I wanted the Vice OC to take it, and he wouldn't either, so after two days' pressure I gave in and

143

became the brigade training officer. I told them that I knew damn all about it but I'd do my best.

Above all I was struck by the paucity of arms and ammunition, as well as their state of training and discipline. It was shocking. If I had my way there wouldn't have been a shot fired until 1920, until they were properly ready. The few shots that were fired only prepared the British for what was coming. We knew we had to devise a faster and more effective system of training, and around the time we were discussing this the word came down from GHQ in Dublin that we were to form flying columns within the brigades. What we had then was a succession of columns, of which I was the only one that was with them all as commander, and these columns grew out of the training camps we held.

The training camps lasted for a week. They were drilled in security movements and arms training, not moving about in fours and that sort of rubbish, which would have been useless to us. Security was really drummed into them. They were taught to expect an attack at any minute of the day and if they didn't move fast they heard about it. All the officers of a certain area, forty of them say, would be brought together in an isolated area, the first lot sleeping in a barn, the others in empty houses, derelict houses, and we'd work from the first thing in the morning to about ten at night. The last couple of hours would be a lecture by me, which I had to improvise because I had no precedent. There was no precedent for the war we were fighting. They were taught discipline, and they were taught to move quickly and silently. And they had to think for themselves. Each man was given problems to work out as though he was the column commander. At the end of it then they had to go out looking for a fight, and that way they qualified themselves for service in the column.

None of this made me very popular of course, because I demanded strict discipline and strict security. I put it into them until they were more afraid of me than they were of the British, because I'd have shot them as quickly as I'd have looked at them if they were guilty of carelessness or cowardice. I was often told by some of my fellow officers who were junior to me, 'We thought you were the greatest bastard that God ever cursed us with.'

Every man that was allowed onto the column had to be selected, and you had a good calibre there, a fine lot of good, decent Irishmen. They were volunteers in the best sense of the word – small farmers' sons, shopkeepers' sons, who would have been happy in their jobs if it hadn't been for these British terrorists. There were a lot of brave men amongst them. I would say at least nine out of ten of them were prepared to give their lives, even though they might have felt it would end like all our struggles, in disaster. But they were going to make the British pay once it started. I must say that I was very lucky in the quality of the men that came under my command. I made it clear to every one of them that they'd have to live hard, they'd have to sleep where they could find it, in a hay barn or in a field, and above all they'd have to accept the discipline of me as the column commander. The secret of a good column commander, if there is a secret, is in two things: one, that he leads from the front, and two, that he'll live the life of the men. He sleeps when they do, he gets food when they do, and he goes without it when they have to go without it. That is the only recipe if a man wants to be an efficient column commander, because that's the only way to get their respect and their confidence. And while I don't say that we were world masters in military matters, we did finish up an organized and disciplined and self-respecting force of 104 fully armed guerrillas, and with the strength of a hundred guerrillas you can take on anything if you apply it properly. And that didn't mean rushing in and attacking the enemy any time you saw him. The most important thing for a flying column to do is to stay intact, because its very existence moving around the countryside demoralizes the enemy and uplifts the people we were fighting for. We'd only strike when we could be sure we could get more of them than we'd suffer ourselves. Our job was to inflict as much damage as we could upon the enemy, and that included their civil administration, and to protect our own people and government. It wasn't to go around waving flags and dying gloriously. And I'm glad to say that with these men we never had a defeat in the field the many times that we met the British, and I never had the slightest bit of trouble with one of them. They're all dead now nearly, but they were all men that you could be proud of.

1919 drew to a close with the attempted assassination of Lord French at Ashtown on the outskirts of Dublin. He and his guard escaped, but a Volunteer, Martin Savage, was killed. Collins was reportedly furious at this failure, but he and his troops could take some consolation in what was otherwise a good year, for not only had they enjoyed some spectacular successes, but the conflict was finally achieving the clarity of war. Thousands of British soldiers were arriving in Ireland as reinforcements, parading the streets with trench helmets and with bayonets fixed and Cork, Limerick, Roscommon and Tipperary became military areas. The IRA, in the meantime, raided for arms, drove the RIC into larger and fewer concentrations and organized prison breaks. In March an effort to free a particular prisoner named Patrick Fleming from Mountjoy resulted in no less than twenty imprisoned IRA men going over the wall.

In Cork in September the pattern the conflict was to assume in the ensuing years was established. The Cork number two brigade under Liam Lynch ambushed a party of the King's Shropshire Light Infantry who were on their way to church in Fermoy, disarmed them and escaped with thirteen rifles, leaving behind a dead British soldier. The operation showed all the panache and resourcefulness that would characterize the IRA's rural guerrilla campaign under such men as Tom Barry, Ernie O'Malley and Sean MacEoin, and the British, humiliated and bewildered by an enemy which was in all ways indistinguishable from the native populace and which simply seemed to vanish into the countryside, struck back by sacking the town of Fermoy in a fit of impotent rage. The war became one between increasingly undisciplined British troops and the increasingly resistant people of Ireland.

2

The Press Gallery witnessed a solemn act of defiance of the British Empire by a body of young men who have not the slightest notion of that Empire's power and resources. The more quickly Ireland becomes convinced of the folly which elected them, the sooner sanity will return.

> The *Irish Times* commenting on the
> first meeting of the Dail

From its first meetings in January 1919, the Dail did its best to conduct itself like an effective government. A Cabinet was appointed, ministries were created and given offices and policies were formulated. Michael Collins became Minister of Finance and was empowered to raise a national loan of £250,000,* a task to which he applied himself with customary energy and thoroughness. Other governmental activities included the establishment of a consular service, the provision of funds for afforestation, fisheries and for land purchases for dispossessed farmers, and the appointment of a commission of inquiry to look into the industrial resources of the country. Most impressively, perhaps, an entire legal system came into being with a hierarchy of courts from local to supreme level and a special Sinn Fein police department to enforce the legal decisions they dispensed. Their legal base, which evolved from an adaptation of the ancient Celtic Brehon laws to Dail prin-

*The loan was declared illegal by the British Government and strenuous efforts were made to suppress it, but by the time it was closed in July 1920 it was oversubscribed by £129,000; Collins had also taken the precaution of putting in a gold reserve of £25,000 and secreting it in a baby's coffin beneath the floorboards of his friend Batt O'Connor's house.

148

ciples and the existing British system, reflected the idea of the nascent state.

Britain replied first with indifference and then with proscription of these political initiatives. The Dail itself was finally driven underground in September 1919. Sean Harling, then seventeen years old, became one of its civil servants.

SEAN HARLING: When they were having the first meetings of Dail Eireann here in Dublin I was asked to pick out about twenty stewards to go there – there was no pay in it or anything, we were just to go there – and police the place when the Dail was in session. Michael Collins came in and he thought the policing was very good and he asked Dermot O'Hegarty who was responsible for it. So Dermot told him that I was. After that they set up offices for the Department of Home Affairs, the Department of Foreign Affairs, the Department of Local Government and so on. These all had secret offices set up around the city. Then they tried to get the county councils and the urban councils of the country to forgo their allegiance to the British and swear allegiance to Dail Eireann. It was when this was getting under way that I got a message from my OC that Collins wanted to see me in his office at 22 Mary Street. So I went down then and I met Collins. I hadn't even spoken to him up to this, but he asked me would I like to join the staff of the Dail. 'I've been watching your abilities at the Mansion House,' he said. So I said, 'Very well.'

I had to look after the despatches to the various company units of the Volunteers and do the mails and arrange for things like the printing of the headed paper for all the different departments of the Dail. I also had to notify the members when the next session of the Dail would be. These were very few and far between on account of the British being here and they had to be arranged in a private house in Dublin. There was a man in the Dublin Corporation named Alderman Cole and he had a very big house in Mountjoy Square which he willingly gave us the use of to hold sessions of the Dail in. It was very handy because the grass square was just opposite the house and nobody could be there without us seeing them. The system we used then to notify them was that each of the TDs – that was the Teachtaí Dála, or members of the Dail – had a girl assigned to him, and I would write a letter to each of these girls around the country saying that I would meet her in Dublin on such and such a date. I put it in a way like you'd write to a girlfriend. The girls would then pass on these letters to the TDs, who knew then that they had to come up to Dublin on that date and meet me at a house in Parnell Square. It's now the Kevin Barry Memorial Hall, but it was the Foresters' Hall at the time. So when they came I'd tell them that Dail Eireann was assembling at Alderman Cole's in Mountjoy Square the next morning at nine o'clock.

The new Irish politicians continued to look towards America for a political solution, despite President Wilson's disappointing performance at the Versailles Peace Conference. Diplomatic activity there was accordingly stepped up and no less a personage than the new Irish President himself, Eamon de Valera, committed himself to this full time. He had escaped from Lincoln Jail on 3 February 1919 with the help of Michael Collins and Harry Boland and – again with Collins's help – was landed in New York in mid-June. He travelled throughout the United States and generated enormous publicity for the Irish cause, keeping it prominently before the American public for eighteen months until he returned to Ireland at Christmas 1920. He also floated a multi-million dollar external loan.* But Irish-America had its own political system, complete with internal conflicts in which de Valera became unavoidably en-

*One Timothy O'Grady, a streetcar conductor from Caherdaniel in County Kerry who had lived in Chicago since the end of the nineteenth century, contributed to it by purchasing a $25 Republican bond, which remains unredeemed. He had three children, one of whom, Edward, fathered one of the writers of this book.

snared. So encumbered, he never secured recognition for his government.

The revolutionary government continued to hold meetings and improvise policies in the most difficult circumstances. Right up to the truce in 1921, the Dail was able to give coherence and a democratic base to the revolution, though most of its members were either in prison, on the run or, with increasing difficulty, preoccupied with conducting the military campaign. But the initiative in the contest between Britain and Ireland had long since passed from politics and now resided almost exclusively with the fighting men. The Dail, hounded by the British and lacking a permanent edifice in which to conduct its affairs, took on a more abstract than practical significance as time went on and as the momentum of violence superseded almost everything else.

3

There is no such thing as reprisals, but they have done a great deal of good.

Lord Hugh Cecil

In Westminster, British policy on Ireland expressed itself in something called the Better Government for Ireland Bill. This was yet another partition scheme, similar to proposals put forward in 1917 but quickly abandoned. It specified two Home Rule parliaments for Ireland, one for the six north-eastern counties and the other for the rest, with a Council of Ireland containing an equal number of representatives from both parliaments and with powers to merge them into one if the parties so wished it. The minority was thus granted legislative equality with the majority. There was some question about the precise area of Ulster to be excluded from Dublin jurisdiction, but the Ulster Unionist Council – apparently the sole arbitrating authority in the matter – determined on six counties with their existing boundaries as the largest area the Ulster Unionists could comfortably dominate *in perpetuum*. Fermanagh and Tyrone, with narrow nationalist majorities in each, were not consulted. This contrivance was presented to the House of Commons in December 1919 and duly received the royal assent one year later.

Gladstone had said that his mission was to pacify Ireland, but the Better Government for Ireland Bill was intended merely to pacify the new Unionist-dominated Parliament, for the majority of the Irish people clearly wanted no part of it. Their views remained unvoiced at Westminster after the 1918 election because their representatives had convened their own assembly in Dublin. The House of Commons that passed the

Bill was quite overwhelmingly pro-Unionist – a particularly messianic and uncompromising breed of Unionists – and they, not surprisingly, were given everything they asked for. The Ulster Unionists were even given something they did not ask for – their own parliament – but they came to realize that it was their surest guarantee of their own uninterrupted supremacy, for however much the London Parliament might change its views on the unity of Ireland, their own would not. Partition thus finally became a legislated reality, rather than the theoretical bargaining point it had been previously.

The government then applied itself to subduing the rest of Ireland. Sir Hamar Greenwood became Chief Secretary; Major General Sir Nevil Macready, veteran of coal miners' and police strikes, was transferred from the Commissionership of Police in London to the post of Commander in Chief of British forces in Ireland;* Major General H. H. Tudor became head of the RIC. In London, Sir Henry Wilson, in 1914 a Curragh mutineer and now Chief of the Imperial General Staff, endlessly harassed the Government to give these men a free hand. They got precisely that with the Restoration of Order in Ireland Act, which won the royal assent on 9 August 1920 and allowed for internment, trial by court martial, the suppression of coroners' inquests and other immunities from the normal course of law.

The public face of this policy was an effort to make the war appear to be something it was not: a civil disturbance, a matter for the police. The two new forces raised in Britain to preserve this façade were thus amalgamated with the dwindling RIC rather than with the British army. These were the Black and Tans, so named because of their makeshift uniforms, who began to arrive in March and April 1920, and the Auxiliaries, who arrived in September. Both forces were composed chiefly of First World War veterans; they were notoriously undisciplined and brutal, and have become as legendary in Ireland as Cromwell.

*Sir Nevil was the son of the great actor William Macready, a fact particularly painful to one of the authors of this book: KG.

MARTIN WALTON: The Tans and the Auxiliaries were terrible. They put the fear of God into anybody, and of course that was what they were meant for. I don't know if they should get the blame entirely for what they did, because they were well soaked in propaganda. They used to get lectures like, 'Do you remember those wonderful Irishmen you were fighting side by side with out in France? What do you think happened to them when they came home? They found a lot of gunmen in charge of the country. Will you go across and help to free the Irish?'

TOM BARRY: The Black and Tans and the Auxiliaries came from two different strata of life, and the general feeling, even here in Ireland at the time, was that the Black and Tans were the worst. I don't accept that all. The Black and Tans included good and bad, like every armed force you meet, and quite a number of them were rather decent men. One of them was a fellow called William Hill. Well, William Hill and Co. are now the biggest turf accountants in the world, I suppose. At that time he was stationed in Mallow and he was a very good fellow and a very jolly fellow. He'd come in and have his pint and he never insulted anyone or did anything to anyone. He's now a millionaire many times over, of course, but at that time he was there simply because there was no work to be found in Britain. I understand he got on very well with the IRA up in that district. Well you had that type in the Black and Tans, but you also had criminal types who had their sentences reduced on condition that they joined up.

But the Auxiliaries were something else. There was no excuse for them. Every damned one of them had to be a commissioned officer and to have served on one or more fronts. They were far worse than the Black and Tans. They were a more efficient body because they had more experience and they were half mad with bloodlust. I've no doubt that there were a few amongst them that could pass as ordinary decent men, but the vast majority of these were

154

the worst that the British produced at any time. You have the SAS now up in the North, but they're not commissioned officers. Perhaps their experiences in France had driven them half mad. It must be said that the better quality British officer wouldn't join up to go over to Ireland to become a terrorist policeman, which is what they were. They were sent over here to break the people and they were a far more dangerous force than the Black and Tans.

The British campaign, with the help of these new forces, extended itself beyond the IRA and into the economic and political life of the country. The period had seen a burgeoning economic experimentation: cooperative creameries, mills and bacon factories had been established and in some areas militant republicans, prompted by the Dail's Democratic Programme, seized industries and declared soviets. The cooperatives were systematically burned and the soviets quashed, while the ordinary fairs and markets on which the chiefly agricultural economy had traditionally depended were prohibited in martial law districts.

The Dail Loan was also subject to exhaustive attentions from the British. Collins had hidden these assets in a number of bank accounts belonging to republican sympathizers, and Dublin Castle appointed to the task of uncovering them a resident magistrate named Alan Bell, who in his younger days in the RIC had applied his investigative skills to the finances of the Land League and Parnell. Operating under a special dispensation, he carpeted bank managers in the Castle, quizzed them on their depositors and requisitioned all relevant documents.* Troops meanwhile raided Sinn Fein establish-

---

*Bell was shot dead by the IRA in Dublin in March 1920, while in the midst of his investigations. In his book *The Spy in the Castle*, David Neligan wrote, '[Bell] lived beyond the Dalkey tramline and was escorted by RIC men to that tram every morning, and met at the Dublin end by G-men. One of the latter told me who he was and what he was doing. At my meeting with Kennedy in Tralee I told him what I knew about Bell and suggested that he should be investigated. Soon afterwards . . . Bell was shot at Merrion. No

ments in search of the money, but on only one occasion were they successful in confiscating any.

The political persecution was perhaps more obvious than the economic. Local authorities which had sworn allegiance to the Dail were deprived of their funds, and Sinn Fein politicians were jailed, beaten and even assassinated. In March 1920, Thomas MacCurtain, the Sinn Fein Lord Mayor of Cork, was murdered in his home in the middle of the night by policemen in plain clothes and with blackened faces. Lord French announced that the job had been done by MacCurtain's own comrades, but even the hand-picked coroner's jury returned a verdict of wilful murder against French, Lloyd George, Ian MacPherson (the Chief Secretary replaced by Hamar Greenwood), District Inspector Swanzy of the RIC and other members of that force.

Other killings were less selective. Following successful actions by the IRA, whole towns were looted and burned and innocent people were terrorized and often dragged from their homes and shot. This became so much the operating principle of British forces in Ireland, at least in martial law areas, that Churchill, reaching what must have been the nadir of British proposals on Ireland, suggested dignifying it by condoning *authorized* reprisals. This idea eventually won official approval at the beginning of 1921; up until then the government simply did not intervene, either to prevent or to punish obvious offenders of the law.

Maire Comerford, acting at the behest of the Dail, was appointed to investigate some of these incidents.

MAIRE COMERFORD: When the fighting was on I was working for Alice Stopford Green as a secretary in her house on Stephen's Green. She was an old woman writing history,

---

one filled his place. . . . Collins was not the man to allow this war-chest which had been so painfully gathered to be taken from under his nose. Actually what I did say to Kennedy was that it was a hellish mistake to shoot poor devils of police who were at the bottom of the ladder.'

getting up to work in the morning long before I did, and whenever a bomb went off or she heard shooting in the street she'd send me out to see what was happening because she wanted to keep in touch with the history that was being made outside her door. This suited me, of course, because I was also very interested. If Cumann na mBan or anybody ever wanted me for anything she would immediately send me off. I was sent down to Tipperary at one stage to report on some Black and Tan atrocities there, and I remember that when we got to Kingsbridge Station the Black and Tans got all the passengers together and made them all sit in window seats. We were to be their sandbags to stop them being shot. I thought it was a great tribute to the IRA that they were expecting ambushes anywhere.

On this occasion I went to the Upperchurch area and interviewed a family called Gleeson there. They were one of five houses raided on this one particular night. It was a very bad night's work because they killed a number of innocent people. I met the old man there – he was called Black Willie – and I found out that when the Tans came his two boys were out with the flying column. The Tans came into the house and said they were there to shoot somebody, anybody, in the house. When they didn't see any young person they said to the old man, 'All right, we'll shoot you,' and as they were taking him out his wife and daughter put up a fight to keep him there. Then another son appeared. He was sick, he had consumption, and he said, 'Don't shoot my father. If you must shoot someone, shoot me.' There was another fight then, but they took the boy out and shot him dead in the doorway.

A similar delirium took hold in the North, where the meaning of the anticipated Unionist state revealed itself in a series of pogroms against Catholics there. Local government elections in January had left Belfast the only Unionist-run city in Ireland, with twenty-three Ulster towns going to Sinn Fein and nationalists and twenty-two going to Unionists; there was also a nationalist lord mayor in Derry. The Unionist response was to force a Catholic exodus, and on 19 July 1920, without intervention from British troops, armed mobs began a four-day spree through Catholic areas in Derry, firing houses, wrecking shops and leaving fifty wounded and nineteen dead. On 20 July the campaign was extended to the Belfast ship-yards, where Catholic workers were beaten and thrown into the water by a mob which then moved into that city's Catholic areas, leaving, after a five-day riot, seventeen dead and 200 injured.

One of the weaknesses regretted most by the IRA was that they were unable to establish themselves in sufficient strength in the North to counteract these pogroms, though the Belfast Brigade did finally beat off the Orange mobs in that city. But arms were scarce and the very nature of the IRA guerrilla campaign, which relied both on anonymity and local know-ledge, made impossible the deployment of large numbers of troops to unfamiliar regions where their accents would be immediately noticeable.

Elsewhere, however, particularly in the martial law districts, the IRA became systematic in its resistance.* Under the na-

*In that summer of 1920, local people in County Tipperary, clutching at straws, marvelled at what they thought was divine blessing for the IRA's cause. Sean Harling told us the story: 'Did you ever hear the story of the Bleeding Statue? Oh, it was a very funny thing. Many years after it happened I was in Chicago for my youngest daughter's wedding – that would have been 1966 – and there were a couple of policemen sent over in case things might get out of hand, you know. I got talking to an old policeman there. I knew he was Irish by the way he spoke, and I asked him, "How long are you over here?" "Well now," says he, "I'm here since the year of the Bleeding Statue." I couldn't believe he said it, you know, because I must have been the only man in Chicago who would have known what he was talking about. But what it was was that in 1920, in Oola in County Tipperary, there were two young lads in the IRA who got another fellow to make up a statue of Our Lord with the works of an alarm clock inside. And you know the old rubber fillers they used to put inside fountain pens? Well they filled one of these with sheep's blood or something, and they fixed it so that when the clock struck a certain time it would send a spurt of this blood through Our Lord's heart. Then they brought it up to an old woman's house there in Oola, a farmhouse, and they

tional leadership of the Minister of Defence Cathal Brugha, Chief of Staff Richard Mulcahy, and Collins, an 'Offensive Defensive' policy was formulated, which resulted in the establishment of the flying columns, the burning of police barracks and the cutting of lines of communication. On the fourth anniversary of the Easter Rising, in a remarkable display of national synchronization, the IRA burned tax offices all over the country from Belfast to Cork and some three hundred unoccupied police barracks.

The Volunteers were not barracked troops; they had by necessity of circumstance to rely on the good graces of their non-combatant neighbours and fellow countrymen, for after an operation they were either on the run – sleeping out or in friendly houses and getting food where they could – or else they would return directly to their normal pattern of life in shops and in the fields. If British forces had difficulty distinguishing them, their neighbours certainly did not, and they might easily have been given away; despite inducements, however, this rarely happened, and support for the IRA by most people was implicit.

SEAN HARLING: Mick's instructions were that I was never to carry a gun, but this one morning I had a Webley on me and I was coming down Mount Street in a tram and I suddenly seen the road being held up by some soldiers and I looked back and there was another hold-up behind the tram. So I jumped off and went into Hollis Street – that's

---

told her she was to raise the alarm when she saw the statue bleeding. So she did this, and then when all the people came around to have a look these two IRA fellows charged an entrance fee. They were using it to raise money to buy guns for the IRA. It was a terrible thing, you know, and the clergy didn't fall for it at all. In fact they kicked up murder about it. So this one morning I was in the office and Mick says to me he wants me to take the train down to Tipperary and bring this statue back to him. So I did this, and when I got back Mick took hold of the statue and banged it off the side of the desk, and of course out fell the works of the alarm clock. "I knew it," he says. So that was the end of the Bleeding Statue.'

a street off Merrion Square – and there was this girl standing in a door and I walked up to her and I said, 'Good morning.' 'Good morning,' says she. So says I, 'I have a gun and I want it hidden for a while.' So she says, 'Come on upstairs.' It was a tenement house and her mother was sitting by the fire, and she says, 'Mother, this is Jim.' Now she didn't know whether I was a Jim or a John or what I was, because she'd never met me before. So the mother says, 'Hello, Jim,' and the girl took the gun and hid it. I went back the next day and got it from her, and I've never seen the girl since.

BRIGHID LYONS THORNTON: You had to admire all the rank and filers up and down the country – no great names, no great positions, but they worked loyally and fought and gave up everything. There was great unity – all the people in the country, young and old, were involved. It was the people of the country who suffered most. They stood by the men and clothed them and fed them and kept them and took great risks. And they'd hear the roar of the army lorries at night. They didn't know who would be taken away. They were the real heroes of the war.

Conventional military engagements in this war were almost nonexistent, and body counts were relatively meagre. But victory was not to be decided on such a purely physical balance sheet. It was more a question of who could best bear the strain in what was really a war of nerves between Britain and Ireland. Moral pressure was applied relentlessly by Ireland through propaganda about British atrocities and through such means as the hunger strike. In April 1920, sixty republican prisoners in Mountjoy Prison in Dublin went on hunger strike to demand prisoner-of-war status or release. Joseph Sweeney was arrested around this time in Donegal and, with many others, joined the fast in sympathy.

JOSEPH SWEENEY: I was arrested in the early part of 1920,

in March. All during that evening I'd had some kind of premonition of trouble and I'd warned some of the Volunteers not to sleep in their own homes that night. I didn't have the sense to follow my own warning, however, and in the early hours of the morning I was roused by some heavy knocking at the door. I stuck my head out to ask who was there and I heard the constable say, 'That's him.' They hardly gave me time to dress before they took me off to Derry. It was a military party and on the way the soldiers professed to be socialists, so of course I needled them mercilessly for working for a capitalist society.

That same evening they put me on a train for Belfast. I was then put into Crumlin Road Jail there for a couple of days. After that they brought us down by lorry to the docks in Belfast where they deliberately left us standing beside a destroyer for about ten minutes so that the Orangemen there could throw anything they could get their hands on at us – lumps of coal, big rivets, bolts. We were handcuffed in pairs and the fellow I was handcuffed to, I'd never seen him before in my life, he got a whack of something on the top of his head and I had to drag him up the gangway and iron steps myself.

We landed in south Wales and were put on a train to London, where we were taken to Wormwood Scrubs. Now we had started a hunger strike in Belfast in sympathy with the hunger strikers in Dublin, and we continued this inside the prison. A new medical officer, so-called, arrived, and it was quite obvious to me that he wasn't a medical officer at all. So we began to devise ways of frightening this fellow. My idea was to lay down on the stone floor until he was about two doors away from my cell, then hop into bed. By this time my pulse had slowed down to nothing, you see, so when he came in he felt my pulse and went away without saying anything, having conferred with a medical orderly he had with him. So that evening I was taken away to Marylebone Infirmary.

The hunger strikers' victory was almost absurdly easy. Sweeney and his colleagues were allowed to walk out of the Marylebone Infirmary in London, while in Dublin the Mountjoy prisoners, with the assistance of a general strike called by the Irish Labour Party and Trades Union Congress, were unconditionally released only ten days after starting their fast. The bonfires and rejoicing crowds which followed were most of all celebrating this new vulnerability of the British to moral pressure.

But this particular capitulation proved to be the exception and when later that year the British were faced with similarly delicate decisions, they invariably chose the harshest option, regardless of the consequences.

The most celebrated hunger strike in Irish history was that of Terence MacSwiney, who had become Lord Mayor of Cork upon the death of Thomas MacCurtain. Following his arrest on 13 August 1920, MacSwiney started his fast in protest against British harassment of elected public representatives. The British transferred him to Brixton Prison in London and announced their intention to let him starve rather than submit again to what they referred to as moral blackmail. They could not have foreseen, in those early days of hunger strikes, that his fast would stretch to seventy-three days, and that as he lay dying in his cell the whole Irish nation would agonize day by day with him while the world watched with appalled fascination. The British stood by their word and MacSwiney finally died on 25 October. His funeral procession moved solemnly and triumphantly through London, the route lined by large crowds of respectful Londoners; his coffin was then put on board a train for shipment to Dublin, but was diverted directly to Cork through the intervention of Sir Henry Wilson. But avoiding the capital did not prevent MacSwiney's death from becoming an occasion of national mourning in Ireland.

Two other notable cases in the autumn of 1920 involved the town of Balbriggan and a Volunteer named Kevin Barry. In the former case, Black and Tans avenged the death of one of their comrades by storming the small town of Balbriggan, burning twenty-five houses and a small hosiery factory, throwing grenades indiscriminately and bayonetting to death two of the town's residents. Elsewhere in Ireland, the killing of a member of British forces in a town would cause an exodus of its people to spend the night in fields and in barns, so great was the fear of reprisals on the Balbriggan model. In the latter case, Kevin Barry, a popular eighteen-year-old medical student, was caught with a revolver after an ambush of British troops in Dublin and was tortured while in prison. Collins typically strained all his resources to rescue him, but the presence of crowds outside the prison praying for Barry thwarted Collins's plan to blow open the prison wall and Kevin Barry was hanged on 1 November. It was the first political hanging in Ireland since Robert Emmet's in 1803; all of Ireland was yet again moved and outraged, and the net effect for Britain was increased enrolment in the IRA.

Collins, of course, knew very well that sentiment and outrage would not bring the Republic into being, and he worked tirelessly to strengthen the IRA's campaign. In Dublin the war had settled down to a contest between rival intelligence agencies, and here Collins, with ruthlessness, selectivity and vibrant confidence, consistently held the advantage.

DAVID NELIGAN: The most dangerous man the British sent over here was an Irishman named Byrne. Over here he used to use the name Jameson, after a well-known brand of Irish whiskey. He appeared on the scene twice. The first time was in the summer of 1918, when the London police went on strike for higher pay. At the same time there was a union formed for police and prison officers, and in Ireland this union was on the verge of a strike too. Mick Collins had this idea that he could smash up the RIC and the Dublin police as well through union agitation, and he had this madman from Kerry named McElligott, an ex-RIC man who was being financed by Collins to organize the union and break up the force. So Collins sent McElligott over to London to liaise with the strike committee of the London

163

police, and when he was there this suave Englishman turned up, a beautifully dressed man, very polite, and he said he was a delegate from the Soldiers', Sailors' and Airmen's Union, and he was there to say that the armed forces wouldn't lift a finger against the London police in their strike action. So they all thanked him for this expression of fraternal solidarity. Then he turned to McElligott and he said, 'How are things in your country?' Well McElligott was about to make one of his usual hell-for-leather speeches, and just as he was drawing breath he saw over the other fellow's shoulder that Jack Hayes – they called him the 'policeman's MP' – was making mad signs at him to shut up. So McElligott just said, 'Oh, all right,' or something, and afterwards he found out from Hayes that this fellow was not a union delegate at all, but a spy. Hayes had been tipped off by somebody in MI5 that he was there spying on labour for the British secret service. Well the Englishman was in reality the Irishman Byrne.

The next time he was heard of was when the British brought down a detective inspector from Belfast named Redmond to smash up Collins's activities. They weren't satisfied with the progress being made by the G Division. So we were all paraded over to the G Division HQ to be addressed by the new Assistant Commissioner, as Redmond had become. He was a fine-looking man, wearing a bowler hat, more like a stockbroker than a poor devil of a police-man. He brought his own squad of detectives with him from Belfast, and they didn't even show up at the G Division. They just lived around the city as civilians. So anyway Redmond says to us that it was extraordinary that we G-men couldn't catch Michael Collins when a man who had only been over from England for a few days had already met him. I didn't know it then, but this was your man from the Soldiers', Sailors' and Airmen's Union – Byrne. Appar-ently he had come equipped with a letter from a Sinn Feiner in London named O'Brien saying he was all right, and he had in fact met Collins and some other prominent people on several occasions.

But Redmond made one fatal blunder, and that was to appoint as his secretary Jimmy McNamara, a G-man who of course was working for Collins. The upshot was that not long afterwards Redmond was shot dead on his way to his hotel in Harcourt Street. His squad from Belfast got out of town in a hurry. But strangely enough, Byrne stayed on, and for some time Collins seemed reluctant to shoot him. He dodged away from him several times and warned his staff to have nothing to do with him. But Joe O'Reilly ran into him one day in O'Connell Street and Byrne told him that he wanted to see the Big Fellow. So O'Reilly knew he'd get a telling off for this, for talking to the bastard at all, but he told Collins anyway, and Collins said, 'By Christ, I'll fix him.' He fixed up an appointment and told Liam Tobin to meet him. Byrne was never heard of again. They shot him up in Glasnevin. But he was the most dangerous adversary that was ever turned loose on Collins. It turned out he was from the same part of the world as myself, from Limerick. His father was a district inspector in the RIC in the next parish to me at home. Pretty strange thing. I knew lads who went to school with him as a young fellow, but he disappeared off the face of the map and became a star operator for MI5.

Because communications between GHQ in Dublin and the brigades and columns in the field remained so impaired throughout this period, Collins thought it important to bring men to Dublin for conferences whenever possible. Joseph Sweeney and Tom Barry both visited Dublin in the latter stages of the struggle.

JOSEPH SWEENEY: I didn't know where to go when I arrived in Dublin. I went up to a hotel in Eccles Street, Whelan's Hotel. Leo Whelan was a noted artist in his day. I wanted to contact Collins or some of the other Volunteers in Dublin, but everyone I asked refused to admit he knew anything. I was in a terrible state there for three or four days, and I was just making up my mind to go back to Donegal when I met Gearoid O'Sullivan and Liam Tobin. So I was delighted. They asked me where I was staying and I told them Whelan's. 'Well, you'll have to get out of there,' they said, 'because that place is going to be raided tonight.'

So they put me into Barry's Hotel, and the next day I was brought out to Batt O'Connor's in Donnybrook and I finally met Collins there. He had acquired a heavier moustache, but he was still the same man I knew, always ready with a quip. He questioned me about the state of things in the North, and when I told him how short we were he said, 'Why the hell don't you get into the barracks up there and arm yourselves?' So I said that that was easier said than done. We not only had the British to fight, but also the Unionists in east Donegal and the Ancient Order of Hibernians in west Donegal, and 'What's more,' I said, 'I had a hell of a time getting up here.' So he kind of cooled down after that. 'I was wondering what you were up to,' he says.

The following morning he came into Barry's and said, 'Stand on the door there while a couple of fellows come to see me.' So I wasn't there very long before this RIC man with a big moustache and a furtive look under his cap came in. 'I want to see himself,' he said. I pretended to make no sense of this. 'I don't know to whom you're referring,' I said. 'I'll get the porter.' The porter was an old German fellow and I told him that this man was looking for somebody. So the old German ambled off and Collins came out and took this fellow in.

Just after he had gone then another fellow came in. The greatest ruffian you ever saw. He was fit for anything, just to look at him. So we went through the same performance again and after he had gone, Collins came out. I said that I knew the first fellow was RIC, but who was the other one? He told me that the first fellow was from Thurles, County Tipperary, 'a very valuable man', and the second was an

Auxiliary out of Beggar's Bush Barracks. 'Now are you coming?' he says. 'Where are you going?' I says. 'I'm going down to meet another RIC man,' he says, 'he's bringing the police codes down from Belfast.'

So I walked along with him, he was wheeling his bicycle, and near O'Connell Bridge we met this great big hulk of a man. 'This is Matt McCarthy,' says Collins, and then he says, 'We're going down to the Scotch House, will you join us?' So I said that I wouldn't because I'd promised to meet Eoin O'Duffy. 'All right,' he said, and they went off.

The next day I saw him again and he said, 'Just as well you didn't come yesterday.' 'Why?' says I. 'We were just in the little snug,' he says, 'and Matt had just handed the codes over to me when the door was kicked open and an Auxiliary with two guns, one in each hand, came in and said, "Put them up." So McCarthy piped up and said, "I'm an RIC man, my card is here in my pocket." So he handed it over and the Auxiliary looked at it and he said, "OK boys, what are you going to have?" ' He stood the two of them a drink.

TOM BARRY: In May 1921, that would be a couple of months before the truce, I was called up to Dublin, to GHQ, by President de Valera. They wanted me up before that, but I was too busy and I didn't want to chance the journey. They wanted to meet me because I suppose anybody would admit that we were the most successful by far in bringing the war to a different degree of aggression you might say.

The day I took off I was landed down at the railway station by a circuitous route. My pockets were full of medical notes because I was supposed to be a medical student suffering from TB who was going to Dublin for treatment. I had two very hostile papers, British papers, very anti-IRA, the *Daily Mail* and the *Morning Post*, and I was given a first-class ticket. I got spruced up as well as I could. I had a haircut the night before, with a horse shears.

So I got into a first-class carriage and there was another

chap there and he started talking to me. He was a very nice fellow and he said, 'Are you going to Dublin?' 'I am,' I said. 'I'm a TB case and I'm going up to see a specialist.' 'Jolly hard luck,' he said. 'I'm Captain Willis, I'm in the army. I'm going home to England for a spot of leave and I can tell you I'm not sorry to get out of this damned country.' So I agreed with him of course that the country was in a terrible state.

At Mallow then there was a search. Soldiers came on board along with police and this fellow produced his pass and then he pointed to me and said, 'He's all right, he's with me.' This happened twice more on the way up to Dublin. When we got to Kingsbridge Station we parted amicably and shook hands and he said, 'Will you have a drink?' 'No,' I said, 'I'm not allowed to drink.' 'Perhaps we'll meet again,' he said, 'but I hope it won't be in Ireland.'

So I went off to Parnell Place and called into Kirwan's pub, where I was supposed to ask for someone called George. This turned out to be Gearoid O'Sullivan, the adjutant-general. He then took me to a place called Devlin's. Devlin's son was later the Irish ambassador to Rome. He was a poet. Anyway, upstairs in the sitting-room I met Collins. The first thing he said to me was, 'You're the most respectable guerrilla leader I've ever seen. You even look respectable.'

I spent six nights in Dublin, staying with Collins and some others out at O'Sullivan's aunt's place in the suburbs. I visited a number of the Dail departments which they had set up in offices around the city, and met people like Brugha, Mulcahy and of course de Valera himself. We talked about the war, how it was going, and I told them we needed more arms. They were very interested in the different engagements we'd had in Cork because up to then all they'd had was press reports. I saw all these people and it was very interesting. But I also saw a worse thing, and that was the beginning of political cliques in Dublin. It didn't break out until after the Treaty, but you could see it developing before that.

They had an altogether different way of doing things in Dublin from what we were used to in the country. They had their offices and they used to go around like business-men, carrying briefcases. They even got paid, which' of course was a luxury we didn't have down in the country. They didn't take the same sort of precautions we did either, and that used to annoy me. One night Collins, O'Sullivan, Sean O Muirthille and myself were going back to the house we were staying in when we ran into a party of about fifty Auxiliaries. I didn't know what the hell was going to hap-pen, I thought we were all for it, and Collins just leaned over before we got out of the car and said, 'Act drunk.' He put on this extraordinary performance then, joking with them and falling about the place, and in no time they were in very good humour with us. When we got back I gave out to him, I told him the least he could do was put up some kind of advance guard for himself and us. So he just laughed and said I was a 'windy west Cork beggar'. I wasn't feeling in such good humour about it and I persisted, but he ex-plained to me then that that was the only way they could survive in the city. He was right, of course. He was never caught once through the whole war.

Collins of course was the spearhead of the fight. He was a most tireless man. I remember one of the days that I was there he went out early in the morning to see some intelli-gence officers, and before evening he'd attended a Cabinet meeting, met more of the intelligence staff, seen some sailors who were smuggling arms for him, met some of the propa-ganda people and did some work on the Dail Loan. That evening he was in Vaughan's Hotel having conferences with brigade officers from all around the country, and at the end of it he was as fresh as he was when he went out that morning. I'd always heard that whenever anybody wanted anything done they were told to 'see Mick'.

He was very good-hearted and generous, but he was also

a man who could easily be disliked. He was very domineering. He used to organize wrestling to keep himself fit, to test himself out, and I remember one of the nights I was in Dublin he came over to me and he said, 'Get up now and I'll wrestle you, you west Cork so and so.' Well, I was only about 11 stone then and he must have been at least 15 stone, so I said to him, 'Go and wrestle your own bloody weight.' So he said, 'Get up. Are you yellow?' So I got up and we went around the room, but he couldn't put me down and eventually the two of us fell together. The next thing was he caught me by the hair. He had to be top man, you know, but he picked the wrong fellow to be top man with. I caught him by the hair and the next thing was he tried to hit me, so I hauled off, and then we were fighting in earnest on the bloody floor. Somebody separated us, and we were going to keep it up, but within a couple of minutes he was his laughing and affable self again.

He had all the time in the world for anyone who'd put up a good fight, but he couldn't tolerate any kind of laziness. A couple of nights before I went back to Cork we were in Vaughan's Hotel. He was to meet some fellows from the midlands and so I said I'd go out, but he said, 'No, stay where you are.' So these fellows came in and said hello. And he said, 'What do you want?' just like that. 'We're looking for arms,' they said. So he looked at them and says he, 'Ye're looking for arms. What do you want arms for? Four months ago I sent word down that so-and-so who murdered prisoners was transferred into your area and he's walking around the town from pub to pub and not a shot was fired at him. Get out of my bloody sight, you bloody lot of lousers.' After they'd gone he looks over to me and says, 'The bastards,' says he, 'they're useless.'

4

England could always reinforce her army. She could replace every soldier that she lost. But there were others indispensable for her purposes which were not so easily replaced. To paralyse the British machine it was necessary to strike at individuals. Without her spies England was helpless. . . . Spies are not so ready to step into the shoes of their departed confederates as are soldiers to fill up the front line in honourable battle. And, even when the new spy stepped into the shoes of the old one, he did not step into the old man's knowledge. We struck at individuals, and by so doing we cut their lines of communication, and we shook their morale. And we conducted the conflict, difficult as it was, with the unequal terms imposed by the enemy, as far as possible according to the rules of war.

Michael Collins

You that Mitchel's prayer have heard,
'Send war in our time, O Lord!'
Know that when all words are said
And a man is fighting mad,
Something drops from eyes long blind . . .

W. B. Yeats, 'Under Ben Bulben'

The war reached its climax in late November and early December 1920, when its principal characteristics – intricate conspiracy in Dublin, bravado ambushes in the country and insensate reprisals – reached a terrible intensity. Afterwards, military constraints tended to be removed and neither British politicians nor Irish moderates could pretend any longer that what was happening in Ireland was just a skirmish that would soon collapse from exhaustion.

This period began on 21 November – since known as Bloody

Sunday. Collins had been aware for some time that a select group of British intelligence officers had been brought to Dublin and placed in private residences around the city to demolish his network. They had had some successes that autumn and Collins knew that he would have to move fast; 21 November was the day that he appointed for their simultaneous execution.

DAVID NELIGAN: The more of the G-men that Collins managed to bump off, the more the others became demoralized. Some of them resigned and got out of the country, some of them stayed in the Castle or out of harm's way, and as a force the G Division was pretty much decimated. So the British flooded the place with secret service agents. Collins put everybody onto the job of finding out who these people were. McNamara and myself found out whatever we could, the fellows he had working in the Dublin Police made notes of anyone they found with a curfew pass.* Waiters and maids and hotel porters were told to watch out for any suspicious characters. The mails were seized too for any clues. Collins was determined to wipe these fellows out.

He was particularly interested in the identity of anyone carrying out vicious killings. One of these happened when a poor fellow named Lynch – a farmer from east Limerick – came up with £5000 to give to Collins for the National Loan. He was staying in a place called the Exchange Hotel, within a stone's throw of the Castle. Lynch was a civilian, an old man of about sixty years of age, but there was another man named Lynch, Liam Lynch, a general in the IRA who was a thorn in the side of the British down in Cork, and didn't the British get the idea that the man in the Exchange Hotel was your man from Cork, and they went in and shot the poor bastard dead. I got a note from Collins the next

---

*Dublin at that time was under curfew after 10 p.m. Anyone with a 'curfew pass' would have been connected with the British forces.

day: 'Dear Dave, find out what happened in the Exchange Hotel.'

Now when I was a uniformed policeman I was stationed in the local bailiwick in College Street Station, and I knew everything that went on there would be noted down in the Occurrence Book, including the state of the weather. So I wended my way down to this station house, where the sergeant was a friend of mine, and when he saw me he said, 'Just the bloody man I want, Dave. Stay here in the office for a minute, I'm just going for a quick drink.' He was going for a pint in the canteen. So I looked into the Occurrence Book and saw the name of the man who conducted the raid. There was some other rubbish about how Lynch had opened fire on them and they had to kill him, which was of course a blatant lie. Lynch was just a harmless old man. So I passed this information on to Collins. That officer was to pay his debt on Bloody Sunday.

Plans for the operation were finalized the previous night. David Neligan met with Tom Cullen and Liam Tobin in the Gaiety Theatre and Collins as usual held a conference in Vaughan's Hotel in Parnell Square, where he was very nearly arrested.

SEAN KAVANAGH: I used to have an arrangement with Mick to meet him on Saturday nights at Vaughan's Hotel in Parnell Square. This was practically every Saturday night through that period. Men would come in from all over the country and Mick would sit at a big table and call each one of them in turn.

I was in Vaughan's the night before Bloody Sunday. I hadn't any business with Mick that night and didn't actually intend to go there, but I'd come back from visiting some friends in Clontarf after curfew and was locked out of the hotel I'd arranged to stay in. I went along to Vaughan's because I knew that Christy Harte, the 'boots' and general factotum there, would let me in. When I got there Christy said, 'Come in, come in. Mr C is upstairs in the smoke room, and Mr Beaslai, Mr O'Connell and another gentleman are in the pantry under the stairs.' Mick was always called the Big Fellow, but Christy could never bring himself to call Mick a 'fellow' so he always called him Mr C or the Big Man. So I said, 'I have no business with Mr C tonight so I'll join the others.' I sat down for a chat then. The two fellows Christy referred to by name were Piaras Beaslai and Sean O'Connell, both prominent IRA men. The other 'gentleman' was talking to Piaras Beaslai in Irish and I was told by Sean O'Connell that he was from Clare and that his name was Conor Clune.

About half an hour later Dick McKee came down to collect his bicycle and as he was pushing it towards the front door he shouted, 'Goodnight lads!' That was the last time we saw him alive. Shortly after that Mick came quickly down the stairs with Rory O'Connor, Gearoid O'Sullivan, Peadar Clancy and some others. I found out later that Christy had got suspicious and tipped them off that he thought there was going to be a raid. He'd noticed that one of the guests in the hotel, somebody who called himself Edwards, had made some phone calls that night and had left the hotel briefly after curfew. Christy went up and said, 'I think, sirs, ye ought to be going.' Mick never questioned any of Christy's hunches, so he just said, 'Come on boys, quick,' and off they went. Well he was right because a couple of minutes later we heard a commotion in the front hall and Sean O'Connell looked out and said, 'Christ, lads, it's the Auxiliaries!' He and Beaslai went out the back door and over the garden wall and the raiding party of Auxiliaries and soldiers dashed straight up the stairs to the room Collins had just left, pushed in the door and shouted 'Hands up!' to an empty room.

Poor Clune in the meantime was getting very nervous and agitated. He said, 'Sure I can die for Ireland as well as anybody else,' or some rubbish like that. He was absolutely innocent, of course. He'd only come along to talk to Piaras

Beaslai in Irish. He and I just stayed in the little pantry and when the raiding party came back they took us out and lined everybody up. The man in charge there was the infamous Captain Hardy, who was the intelligence officer for the F Company of the Auxiliaries in the Castle. I didn't know him then but he interrogated me again a couple of months later and I was glad then that he'd forgotten he'd met me before in Vaughan's.

I hadn't anything incriminating on me and I wasn't known to the police, so I wasn't really worried. Each of us was searched and questioned in detail. I thought it was safest to tell them the truth, so when Hardy asked me I gave him my correct name and address and said I was in Dublin to see some friends in Clontarf, which was true. Then Hardy said, 'Why isn't your name in the visitors' book here?' But Christy came to my rescue and said, 'That's my fault, sir, he's in number 21. I was too busy to put his name in.' Then they found a toothbrush and a clean collar in my pocket, so they dismissed me as harmless. Poor Clune wasn't so lucky. His name wasn't in the register either, and as Christy didn't know him he didn't want to say anything, so he was arrested, he was taken away. I think he was a bit dazed by it all. They arrested two other men that night. One was the OC of the Sligo Brigade, a man named Pilkington. He's a priest in England now. He was lucky enough to be taken to Arbour Hill barracks, and he escaped from there ten days later. The third was Edwards, the man the Auxiliaries planted there. They made a great performance of that. They took out a photograph and compared it with him, and they began to nod knowingly, saying, 'Oh, that's him,' and they took him away with the others. I saw him in Auxiliary uniform in the Castle later when I was arrested.

Dick McKee, Commandant of the Dublin Brigade, and his Vice-Commandant Peadar Clancy were two of the prime movers of Collins's plan to eliminate the British intelligence officers, but they never saw it implemented as they were arrested that Saturday night following a tip-off and taken to Dublin Castle, as was the unfortunate Conor Clune.

At nine o'clock on Sunday morning eight groups of men from the IRA called at addresses where the British intelligence officers were known to be staying and executed fourteen of them.

DAVID NELIGAN: I remember that day I went over to see how old Tommy O'Shaughnessy was doing – he was the old judge I'd been assigned to guard in my role as G-man – and I saw two Red Cross ambulances outside 28 Upper Pembroke Street. There were five shot in that house, I think. British soldiers were bringing out dead bodies covered with sheets.

I had very little involvement in that episode, though I did meet one of the men who was shot a couple of days before that in the Castle, and I found out where he was staying. He had only one arm. He told me he was in the Auxiliaries and that he was on the run from Sinn Fein down in Clare. I asked him if he was staying in the Castle and he said, 'No, I'm staying in 28 Upper Pembroke Street.' That was the unluckiest day of his life, because when I met Cullen and Tobin in the Gaiety Theatre I told them about him. They found out from the housekeeper there that the one-armed man was staying there and they went in and shot the poor bugger. I was heartily sorry afterwards. I was the cause of his death.

It was a terrible day, shocking. That morning at breakfast Bruton, the chief inspector, came in. His face was as white as a sheet. He said, 'There's been terrible work in Dublin. All the British officers have been mown down.' There was panic that day in the Castle. One of the secret service men who survived shot himself in the Castle that day. For the next week the gates to the Castle were jammed with incoming traffic, with all the military trying to get in for protection. The whole spy network was paralysed, and I don't think they ever fully recovered from this blow. It was a most unexpected stroke. Of course it was a bloody diabolical thing to do, but we were fighting for our lives at the time.

The Black and Tans responded with their most hysterical reprisal to date. That afternoon at Croke Park, where a Gaelic football match was taking place, a party of Black and Tans surrounded and entered the football grounds, set up a machine-gun on a railway bridge overlooking one end of the pitch and fired indiscriminately into the crowd. Twelve people were killed and seventy wounded.

SEAN KAVANAGH: I was still in Dublin on the Sunday, and that afternoon I was going down O'Connell Street – I was going to a concert at about three o'clock – and I saw a line of Crossley tenders going up O'Connell Street, travelling very fast, all full of Black and Tans. They were on their way to Croke Park where there was a Gaelic football match in progress. They were ostensibly looking for IRA men, men who would have been involved in the shooting that morning. But they didn't arrest anybody. They just shot up the place as a reprisal. They went on the pitch and they fired on the teams and they fired indiscriminately on the crowd. They killed . . . I don't know how many they killed, but I know one man named Hogan on the Tipperary team was killed and one of the principal stands in Croke Park is now called the Hogan Stand.

That night the final events of a gruesome day were enacted when members of the Auxiliaries stationed at Dublin Castle tortured and then bayonetted to death Clancy, McKee and Clune. A Castle spokesman fashioned an extraordinary tale about how they had been killed while trying to escape and even piously circulated some contrived photographs to the press, but these convinced no one in Ireland.

SEAN KAVANAGH: On the Wednesday afternoon after Bloody Sunday, I was in Dublin again. The funeral of the men our fellows had shot on the morning of Bloody Sunday was taking place. They were being taken to the North Wall where they were put on board ship and taken back to England where they had come from. I saw this procession of coffins on gun carriages draped with Union Jacks being brought along the quays and across to the North Wall, and while I was there Gearoid O'Sullivan and Frank Thornton, one of Mick's staff, came over and asked me if I could go over to King George V Hospital and claim the remains of McKee and Clancy. So I called a couple of young lads I knew and we went up by tram, up the North Circular Road to the hospital, and I saw their bodies in the coffins. There were marks on their faces, bruises and some cuts which looked like they were made with bayonets or some pointed weapon, but the blood was washed off and of course they were fully clothed so I couldn't see any more.

Their bodies were laid out in the Pro-Cathedral and the night before their funeral Collins and some Volunteers walked through a party of soldiers to dress Clancy and McKee in their uniforms. The next day, with all of Dublin looking on – including police, soldiers and a number of touts – Collins helped carry one of the coffins. On each of them he had pinned a note: 'In memory of two good friends – Dick and Peadar – and two of Ireland's best soldiers.' Within a fortnight the informer who had given them away was traced and shot.

In the immediate aftermath of Bloody Sunday there was a massive intensification of the British war effort: hotels, restaurants and private houses were raided, there were endless hold-ups and searches in the streets, internment camps were established at the Curragh and at Ballykinlar in County Down, and cordons were regularly thrown around selected areas of Dublin while soldiers, Black and Tans and Auxiliaries made minute searches. They wanted above all things the capture of Michael Collins, their *bête noire*, who now had a price of £10,000 on his head. Collins nevertheless continued to move openly about central Dublin, undisguised and unarmed, and if anything appeared to take even greater risks; it was a kind of brinkmanship that some – particularly after the dreadful carnage of Bloody Sunday – saw as a death wish. He himself said simply, 'I do not allow myself to feel that I am on the run.' This apparent invulnerability lent him a kind of super-human aura, so that he was seen throughout Ireland as some latterday Cuchulainn, curiously blessed and fearless. The myth had little to do with the enormous personality – boisterous and businesslike by turns – whose freedom to walk the streets was above all the result of his acute sensitivity to danger, his labyrinth of informers and the ordinariness of his appearance; it was nevertheless an inspiration to the people.

DAVID NELIGAN: There was one situation the night after Bloody Sunday which was really terrifying. The place was crawling with Tans and Auxiliaries and British officers, and I had an appointment with Liam Tobin below, outside Jervis Street Hospital. We were having to meet outside at the time because we'd been turned out of our usual meeting place, Bannon's pub, by the two old brothers who ran it. They were terrified of being caught, and you couldn't blame them. Anyway, it was a dark night, and I heard these steps coming through the darkness. It was Mick Collins. 'Jesus,' says I, 'what brought you here? Are you mad? It's terribly dangerous to be out.' So he told me he couldn't find anybody else to meet me that night and he came himself. He didn't want me to be waiting there, and then be disappointed if nobody showed up. 'For Christ's sake,' says I, 'go away. What I have to say is of no importance.' I thought we were done for. So he disappeared back into the night.

SEAN HARLING: There was one night I heard Mick say to these two IRA officers, 'We'll go up to Vaughan's Hotel.' I was on my way to an office in North Great George's Street, and later on when I was there a lad came in and told me the whole area around Parnell Square was surrounded by British troops, and he told me they were making a house-to-house search in Parnell Square, which is where Vaughan's was. So I immediately got onto me bike and went over to have a look and I could see they had it all closed off. A fly couldn't get in. So I went back to Henry Street, cycled over to Capel Street, came up Capel Street and went into a laneway at the back of Williams and Woods, the confectioners, through there and over to Dominic Street chapel. At the back was a railing gate, where the laneway was that Matt Talbot died in. So I knocked at the vestry and told the priest that it was very urgent to have the gate opened, because I could get into the back gate of Vaughan's from there. So he said, 'There's the keys hanging there. Put them back when you're finished with them.' So I got into Vaughan's then, and sent a message up to Mick. He came down and I told him I'd found a way out. 'Where?' says he. 'It's impossible.' So I brought them across to the chapel yard, locked the gate and hung up the keys. Then Mick said, 'We'd better not all go out at once,' and then he says to me, 'I'll be down at such and such a pub on Bachelor's Walk. Bring the others down there when it's safe for them to come out.' So I did that and when I got there he says to me, 'Sean, if you took a pint, you deserve one for that.'

DAVID NELIGAN: Collins had an old bicycle and the chain was faulty on it; it used to rattle against the frame. And one night a bloody awful fog came down. It was like a London peasouper, you couldn't see a shagging thing. So I was walking along Nassau Street minding my own business, you see, and I heard a rattle, this old banshee wail from the chain. 'Christ,' I said, 'that's Mick's old bicycle,' and I stood in the middle of the tramline. So along comes Collins from Grafton Street corner with his dust coat flying, and when he sees me he says, 'Jesus, where did you come out of?' 'I heard the old bicycle,' says I. 'By Christ, that'll get you shot yet.' So he roared laughing. 'Where are you going for?' says I. 'I'm going over to Batt O'Connor's to sleep,' he says. 'There's about a thousand Tans and British tommies around Parnell Square with rolls of barbed wire colonnading off the whole bloody place.' They were closing in on him and he'd walked right through the middle of them.

Collins had been shaken by the loss of Clancy and McKee, but was heartened a week after Bloody Sunday by news from his native west Cork of the first open engagement with the Auxiliaries – a battle of shocking ferocity that unsettled British forces in the country as much as the Bloody Sunday executions had terrified Dublin Castle. It took place at Kilmichael, near Macroom, and its strategist and leader was Tom Barry.

TOM BARRY: The Auxiliaries first arrived in Cork late in the summer of 1920 and from that day on they spent their time driving into villages and terrorizing everybody. They'd beat people and strip them and shoot the place up, and then go back to their barracks drunk on stuff they'd looted. We knew we had to stop them, and that was what the fight at Kilmichael was all about.

We nearly had to call it off before it happened. I'd selected a spot near Macroom – the only spot we were sure they'd pass – and we had a long march there all night through the rain. We didn't know when they'd come, and we had to wait lying low in the ditches all day without food. By four o'clock – it was the 28th of November – it was getting dark, and I nearly called it off then. But then we heard two lorries of them coming.

There was a bend in the road there, and we had to make sure they'd slow up. So I had an IRA officer's tunic, and the idea was that when they came along the road they'd see an officer standing in the ditch facing them, they'd see this man in a trench coat and leggings, and they'd slow down to see who it was. They might even think it was one of themselves. They were going around in all sorts of dress at that time. And that's what they did, they slowed down about fifty yards away and kept coming, very slow, until they got to about twenty yards away and a Mills bomb was thrown

181

from our side. It landed right in the driver's seat and killed him. Fire was opened up then and it became a hand-to-hand fight. It was so close that one of our fellows caught a spurt of blood full in the mouth from a severed artery of one of the Auxies. We had the better of them there because they were screaming and yelling and our fellows just kept quiet and wiped them all out. There were nine of them dead on the road and all of our men were still alive.

In the meantime the second lorry had come along, and another section of our men was up the road giving battle to them. So I went along the side of the road with some of the men from the command post and as we got up behind them – they didn't see us – they threw away their rifles and we heard them shouting, 'We surrender! We surrender!' Three of our men stood up then from their positions to take the surrender, but the minute they did the others opened fire on them and killed two of them. So we continued up behind them and I gave the order to keep firing until I said to stop, and then after we killed a couple more of them and they saw they were sandwiched in between two lines of fire they started shouting 'We surrender!' again. But having seen the false surrender I told the men to keep firing and we did until the last of them was dead. I blame myself of course for our own losses, because I should have seen through the false surrender trick.

Afterwards some of our men were shaken by the whole thing and I had to drill them in the road, march them up and down, to preserve discipline. I've written all about this and I don't want to go into all the details, but it was a strange sight, with the lorries burning in the night and these men marching along, back and forth between the blood and the corpses. They'd just gone through a terrifying experience and proved themselves to be the better men in close combat. Their clothes were soaking and by the time they marched off they'd gone thirty-six hours without food. But if they didn't keep their discipline we might lose everything. Discipline was all we had.

On 10 December Cork became a martial law area and the following day, after another attack on the Auxiliaries, a combined party of Auxiliaries and Black and Tans entered Cork city at around 9 p.m., forced its inhabitants home at gunpoint and, in a fit of elation, set fire to the centre of the city. Members of the fire brigade were turned away and some were actually fired at. The fire raisers accomplished their task: the centre of the city was left a smouldering wreck and damage was estimated at around £3 million. A court of inquiry was set up by Major-General Strickland, who was in command of the area, but its report was so damning that a ministerial conference in London determined that 'to publish it while Parliament was sitting would be disastrous to the Government's whole policy on Ireland'. Meanwhile, Auxiliaries in Dublin stuck pins through burnt corks and wore them in their Glengarry caps.

5

Historians are apt to reduce to terms of cause and consequence matters about which contemporaries felt in terms of challenging, uplifting, desolating or terrifying personal experience. Destruction, violence, fear, intimidation . . . are apt to figure in sophisticated historical works in the context of general analysis little calculated to pierce the consciousness of their readers. To the generation which experiences it, the effects of force upon their lives are real and tangible and the consequences of its use usually unpredictable; to succeeding generations the reverse obtains, the effect upon their lives becoming unreal . . . with the result that succeeding generations are disposed to exaggerate the consequences and to discount the price. . . .

Nicholas Mansergh, *The Irish Question 1840–1921*

The many dark events of this period exacted a hidden price: a wounding of the mind by the terrible proximity to violence. Fighting in Ireland was at close range; there was none of the neutralizing effect of bombs dropped from aeroplanes or of long-distance artillery. More often than not, lives were taken by point-blank revolver shots. British propaganda described those who pulled the triggers as 'murder gangs', while the Irish preferred to think of them as Spartans; it was not convenient for anyone, least of all themselves, to dwell on their ordinary human susceptibilities. Motivated entirely by ideals, the Volunteers tended on the contrary to be the more sensitive members of the community from which they were otherwise indistinguishable – a community, it must be remembered, with deeply held religious beliefs about the taking of human life. If they emerged from the conflict physically intact, they would nevertheless remain haunted all their lives by the blood and expressions of fear and agony on their victims' faces.

This is an element largely omitted from conventional histories, which, with their detached style of reportage and analysis, cannot admit such immediacy. Historians and even memoirists tend to assemble their material into a grand schema, in which events only acquire importance in so far as they bring about other events, thus acquiring a logic which excludes a given period's less assimilable aspects. The inner wounds of the men who fight the wars have thus become the almost exclusive domain of poets and novelists.

This history, too, in the interest of fashioning a journey from the lives of nine people in a particular period of time, has imposed its own storytellers' selectivity on events, but the terrible price of violence was so movingly and repeatedly apparent in the course of our interviews that it simply forces its way into the narrative. However justified they may have felt about their actions, an unease has remained with them throughout their lives, as the following three stories may help to demonstrate.

DAVID NELIGAN: There were some terrible things that happened in those days, shocking. One night I was just sitting in the mess room minding my own business, reading a book, and Bruton, the chief inspector, sent for me. If you were just hanging around you were in danger of being press-ganged into doing something. So he says to me, 'Neligan, there's a sergeant and a constable of the RIC up here, and they don't know the city at all. They've come up to identify a dead man at the Mater Hospital. It's thought he's Dan Breen.* I want you to meet them and bring them to the Mater.' So I met them and the sergeant was a huge big fat man who I'll call Comerford – that wasn't his name, but his daughter asked me not to divulge his real name, so I won't – and the constable's name was Fitzmaurice. So we went

*Dan Breen was a particularly active IRA man who, among other operations, participated in the Soloheadbeg ambush which precipitated the Anglo-Irish War.

185

along to the hospital and there was a dead man lying there in the morgue and Comerford took one look at him and said, 'That's not Dan Breen. I'd know Dan Breen's ugly old mug anywhere.' Dan wasn't a very beautiful-looking character. But this poor dead man was called Mattie Furlong, since lost to history. He'd been experimenting with a home-made piece of artillery and it blew up and killed him. So we all went off and in my innocence I made an appointment with the two of them for 3 p.m. the next day to show them the city.

As bad luck would have it I had a meeting with Liam Tobin that night in one of his joints and I was indiscreet enough to mention these two RIC men and my appointment with them for the next day. So didn't four members of the Squad show up the next day to say they had orders from Mick Collins to mow down the sergeant. I nearly died. I said, 'For Christ's sake, what has he done?' 'I don't know what he's done,' one of them said, 'but I've orders to shoot him and that's what I'm going to do.'

I begged him not to do it, and I could already see Comerford and Fitzmaurice coming along the quays, and the next thing was of course there was a murderous flare-up and the poor sergeant crumpled up and fell down dead in the bloody road. It was the most terrible episode of my life.

So I went back to the Castle feeling very much the worse for wear, and I was only about five minutes in there when a phone message came in saying that the Inspector-General of the RIC wanted to see me. So I went over across the yard, and all the big brass were there, and the Inspector-General says to me, 'This man Fitzmaurice says he saw you talking to the fellows who shot Sergeant Comerford.' But I got out of it by saying to Fitzmaurice, 'Didn't you tell me that some woman in a bookstall at Limerick Junction station asked you where you were going?' So he said that was right, and I read in the *Independent* a few days later that the poor woman was carted off to jail. The strange thing was that she really was an intelligence officer for the IRA, and I only discovered that years afterwards.

I never found out what poor Comerford had done to deserve his fate, but it was the one day I regretted the role I was playing. There were too many killed. I often wonder if the whole bloody thing was worth it at all. That's the God's truth, and I often ask God to forgive me for having anything to do with it.

MARTIN WALTON: I had been out sick, nearly dying with the flu in 1919, during the spring, and this evening the doctor told me that I could go out for the odd walk, but to take things very quiet. Well on Drumcondra Road I met four lads, two of whom I knew and two I didn't know. They were in the Volunteers. They were not in my company but I knew their faces from battalion meetings and they knew me. So this fellow Liam said to me, 'We're on a job, will you come with us?' 'Ah, I'm not well, I'm not able.' 'Ah, come on,' he said, 'you've experience of these things and you'd be a big help.' 'Well, I've no damned gun.' 'Ach, we've a spare gun.' 'All right, all right, I'll go.'

So we arrived at this place, and it was to be a raid for arms. Now raids at that time were more or less forbidden officially by our headquarters staff. If you got away with it you got a pat on the back, and if you didn't get away with it you were disowned. Anyway, the story was that this particular man, Pearson I think his name was, he had deserted his wife and his sister-in-law had given a tip-off that there were guns in the house. He was ex-British army. We arrived at the house anyway – it was on Richmond Road in Drumcondra – and we surveyed the house and knocked at the door. There was nobody in, but the tip-off was that he was due about 5.00 or 5.30. But he didn't turn up and we were about to give up when this enormous man arrived at the house in the company of two prostitutes. He opened the door and went in with the women.

Now we always wanted to appear as good-mannered,

well-behaved people, with honour and politeness, and we didn't like to make a fuss with the women there so I suggested we go around the back. We posted one man to the left-hand side of the garden and one to the right. Any sign of military or police, one whistle from one side, two from the other. There was another man at the corner in the back. Liam and I went to the door and knocked and out came this enormous man. 'What the bloody hell do you want?' So I said that we were from the Republican Army, and that we had been ordered to go into the house, and that we'd give him a receipt for the guns but that we'd have to take them. He would be paid for them and everything would be in order. So he said, 'There are no fucking guns in this house and get to hell out of this' or what he wouldn't do. Now I was rather particular about language then – I'm not so much now, but I was then – and I was taken aback, but I said, 'I'm sorry, we mean business,' and I pushed my ·45 very close to him. 'All right, all right, come in.'

The first thing I saw inside was a service rifle on a rack. I said, 'I thought you said you had no guns,' and picked it off the rack. 'Oh, that only belongs to so and so, my friend out in the war.' So I told him we'd have to take it and I passed it to Liam who passed it out to the man on the corner outside.

As Liam was coming back this man pounced on him, caught him up in his arms and swung him. I couldn't do anything and there he was, 'Shoot now, shoot now,' he was saying. I couldn't shoot because I'd shoot Liam. So his two hands were engaged, and I had the heavy Webley, and I crashed it down on his head. He collapsed back and we threw him on a bed. I went back into the room and pulled out a drawer and said, 'Any more guns?' He didn't even reply but I went on opening drawers and pulled out a German Luger and brought it out, and just went off my guard for a second and he was off the bed and he had me. I could feel this enormous man, he was about 6 foot 3 or 4, built in proportion, a real titan, a military man and well trained. I could feel my eyes being squeezed out of their sockets, I couldn't get my breath. The only thought that came into my mind was that I remembered a step coming into the room and I managed to get over towards the step and he tripped over it as I hoped he would, and he fell on the floor. But he fell on top of me and I couldn't get my hand on my gun or anything else. Then Liam came back and shouted to the other lads and two of them came in, and whatever happened I got my hand free and on the gun and three of us fired together. He stood up, drew himself up to his full height and said, 'You and your fucking guns,' and just dropped dead.

JOHN L. O'SULLIVAN: This is something that I haven't spoken about much. A war in any shape or form, it grows on you. When you are involved in active operations, it means you have to be disciplined and you have to face every circumstance as it comes. The decisions aren't always your own. This occasion I'm telling you about, I have never given it for publication to anybody, but I suppose our years are getting few and, as you say, it will give people an idea of the kinds of things we had to face and what we had to do about them.

During the height of the war, two members of the Essex Regiment were seen wandering around Bandon. At that time every stranger was under observation and people reported them to our command and they were captured. They claimed to be deserters, and while they said they were prepared to join our column and fight with us, they said they'd rather be sent back to England. Now we couldn't be sure what they were and they were taken to column headquarters to be interrogated. During the interrogation one of them said to the column commander – that was Tom Barry – he said he had a brother in the barracks in Bandon and that this brother wanted to get out too. This fellow thought the brother would be willing to work with us, and the idea of getting arms from Bandon barracks was discussed. So arrangements were made and it was fixed up that members of the column would meet the brother at a particular place outside Bandon. Tom Barry was one of the men who was to go that night, but he was taken suddenly ill – he had a heart attack – and Captain John Galvin, Jim O'Donoghue, who was brigade assistant adjutant, and Joe Begley were appointed to meet this fellow – I think he was a sergeant in the Essex Regiment. Well they went to the rendezvous and they were immediately pounced on by a section of the Essex Regiment. And they were given a terrible time, every bone in their body was broken before they were shot through the head. Somehow or other they were set up.

Now all during this time, the two others, the fellows who said they were deserters, were being held here in this house, my house here. They stayed here during the day and we had to shift them to another place at night. One of them was only nineteen or twenty and the other was older, maybe thirty or forty. My mother, God be good to her, she was a very motherly kind of person, and to her they were just people who were away from home, and she did her best for them. They had the same treatment, the same food as ourselves, maybe better. And we got on well with them too. We used to play cards with them at night.

Then after this murder of our people the order came through that the two prisoners were to be executed. They knew too much, they had talked with Barry and other people at our headquarters, and it was thought they might be intelligence officers, as often happens in war when deserters go over to the enemy. We couldn't hold them as prisoners because that would be too dangerous, and the whole thing was looked at from every angle and it was decided to execute them. I wasn't there for this decision myself, but I can see now, looking back, that it was the only decision that could be made.

So anyway, we were told we were to dig a grave in a particular place. My brother came back home here for a pick and shovel and whatever was necessary. My mother was waiting – as she did whenever we were out, as all mothers do in troublesome times, when things were happening, when people who went out at nightfall never came back again, either killed in an ambush or taken prisoner or something – and she saw the pick and shovel going out and she probably sized up the situation and she said to my brother, 'Listen, Pat, don't ever do anything you'll be sorry for.' Well at that age – at any age – your mother is very important to you, and I can remember the weight of this thing on our minds as we were walking down the road with these two prisoners. We told them we were sending them off by boat and all the time we were wondering what would we do about it. Finally I said to my brother, 'We'll have to get it postponed.'

So we took them up to the spot where the execution was supposed to be, and Moss Twomey was there – he was one of the officers in charge and he was a great friend of mine – and I said, 'They can't be shot tonight.' He said, 'It's very tough, but we have our orders and it must be done.' 'Well,' says I, 'it can't be done, for I'm bringing these fellows home or I'll be dead myself. I'll shoot the man who tries to stop us.' And I'd have done it too. But Twomey marched us up to the grave and just as we got there he said, 'About turn, quick march, take them back home. You'll get instructions where to take them tomorrow.'

So we brought them back home again, and the next night we were ordered to bring them out again. We were told then that they had to be shot, and the punishment we got for disobeying orders the previous night was that my brother and myself were appointed to the firing squad. My brother argued with them and said only one of us would do it, and it was settled that it would be him, because he was older. I think that a man that is in a firing squad should be a veteran who's had some experience of war. The revulsion of taking a human life goes very deep in a person, if he's been reared in a family. So anyway, the commanding officer – he was a different man from the night before – he said to the two prisoners, 'Now men,' he said, 'unfortunately we have to execute you. It won't be possible under the circumstances to get you a minister of religion, but we'll give you time to say your prayers and make your peace with God.' One of them said, 'We have no prayers to say.' 'Haven't you a soul?' said the commanding officer. 'I have,' he said, and he lifted up his boot and he tapped at the bottom of it like that. 'That's all the sole I have,' he said. I'll never forget the blooming thing in my life. He faced it without a whimper. A man that could say that, you know now, before his death, and facing the bullet, he must be a tough man. He was no ordinary soldier. Now the likes of us, fighting for our country, we might face something like that. But an ordinary rank-and-file soldier in the British army hadn't that kind of commitment. They were shot there anyway, the two of them together, and buried on the spot.*

---

*This episode was later transformed by Frank O'Connor into a short story which, following an account of the execution, concludes: 'I stood at the door, watching the stars and listening to the shrieking of the birds dying out over the bogs. It is so strange what you feel at times like that that you can't describe it. Noble says he saw everything ten times the size, as though there were nothing in the whole world but that little patch of bog with the two Englishmen stiffening into it, but with me it was as if the patch of bog where the Englishmen were was a million miles away, and even Noble and the old woman, mumbling behind me, and the birds and the bloody stars were all far away, and I was somehow very small and very lost and lonely like a child astray in the snow. And everything that happened to me afterwards, I never felt the same about again.' Tom Barry, who wrote briefly about the incident in his book *Guerrilla Days in Ireland*, betrayed no sentiments whatsoever about it: 'One of the oldest ruses in war is to send spies, posing as deserters, into enemy lines. The classic example is, I think, the American Civil War, when hundreds of these pseudo-deserters were discovered as spies by both armies and dealt with as such. . . . The two British spies [from the Essex Regiment] were brought to Kilbree, Clonakilty, and there they were executed.'

6

So long as Sinn Fein demands a Republic, the present evils must go on. So long as the leaders of Sinn Fein stand in this position, and *receive the support of their countrymen*, settlement is in my judgement impossible.

Lloyd George, 19 April 1921

Sweep up all motors, bicycles and horses, and make the rebels immobile. Then close the Post Office and banks. And then *drive*.

Sir Henry Wilson

They treat the martial law areas as a special game preserve for their amusement.

Sir Nevil Macready, writing about the Black and Tans and Auxiliaries to Sir John Anderson in February 1921

At Christmas 1920, President de Valera returned home from America. Upon his arrival he looked around him and, though he had received regular reports from his ministers on all military and political activity in the country while away, he was genuinely appalled by the severe bleakness into which the conflict had evolved. It was a truly gothic scene: all across the landscape were the charred remains of farmhouses, shops and police barracks; people were spending their nights in hayricks and henhouses in fear of visits from the Black and Tans; arrested Volunteers were later found shot through the head or bayonetted to death – or, as happened at Kerry Pike near Cork, with their tongues and hearts cut out – while along the roadside were distributed corpses of spies executed by the IRA. Meanwhile, the IRB, with its clandestine world of oaths and intense loyalties, left behind a trail of meticulously executed killings. The people, de Valera began to think, were carrying too great a burden. He suggested an 'easing off' of the war effort. But de Valera, who for eighteen months had been living in a world of speech-making, civic receptions and press conferences, missed the point: the Irish were engaged not in a protest, or in yet another fatalistic gesture at rebellion, but in a final push, an all-out war in which the participants actually believed in their prospects of success. The war depended on the momentum it could generate, and could not be moderated. The lethal finality of the conflict was in itself exhilarating, and no one better embodied that exhilaration that Christmas than Collins, as he raced about Dublin dispensing presents to the innumerable landladies, spies, post office clerks and brigade officers who had served and protected him. David Neligan was given a silver cigarette case in appreciation of his delicate work. Few of the Volunteers or the people they were fighting for wanted an 'easing off', and the war, if anything, grew more intense.

President de Valera did, however, assume great importance as a focus for both political and diplomatic activity. He was a republican who also enjoyed the support of moderates; he had the pedigree of being the senior surviving commander of Easter Week and the last leader to surrender, but he was nevertheless unscarred by the brutalities of the guerrilla war. The British had a cautious respect for him and, sensing an avenue of negotiation, directed that he should not be arrested. Also, his passion for the *form* of political and diplomatic transactions lent a stability to the often makeshift machinery of the Dail. Collins, who had been Acting President following the arrest of Griffith in late November 1920, was being hounded like an escaped convict; but de Valera, having been fêted everywhere in America and now immune to arrest in Ireland, was in a position to invest his office with suitable dignity while conducting its business.

Sean Harling was appointed to assist him.

SEAN HARLING: Towards the end of December 1920, Mick sent for me one morning to go to his office in Mary Street, and he says to me, 'Sean, the Chief' – that was Dev – 'the Chief is back from the States, and I want you to keep him in contact with his ministers and carry any messages for him. It won't be much, about two visits a day will do, and I've arranged for him to see you tomorrow at three o'clock at Dr Farnan's house in Merrion Square.' So I went along there the next day and I met Dev. Kathleen O'Connell was there too, that was his secretary. From that day to the end of the truce I was working with Dev.

He didn't stay long at Dr Farnan's, and then he moved over to a house Mick got for him, a place called Lochnavale on Sandymount Strand, just on the outskirts of the city. So I went there daily and attended to him there for about two months and then Mick bought another house in Blackrock, Glenvar was the name of it, and it was a big house with orchards and greenhouses and conservatories in it. I went to live there permanently then, with Dev, Kathleen O'Connell and Maeve McGarry as the housekeeper.

So I used to go around to all the ministers' offices every day and bring any messages back and forth, and I also used to arrange any of the press interviews for him. These were very important, because I met the Hearst press of America, the French papers, *Echo de Paris*, and all these who were seeking interviews with Dev. Mick would tell me where these fellows were staying – it might be the Gresham or the Shelbourne or the Exchange Hotel – and I'd go there to get their questions. There was always one stock question: 'Would Ireland accept anything but an Irish Republic?' I would be able to answer that one myself – 'No.'

Then if Dev agreed to see these people I had to arrange for a safe house. Once I got them there, I'd just introduce the President to them and leave them talking, and when it was over I'd take the newspaperman back to his hotel. That was how the interviews worked.

Whenever I was travelling with any of the ministerial

documents on me I'd always take the front seat at the top of the tram. There used to be an indicator box there for where the tram was going to and the little trap door for it was always open. So I had a good view of the street from there and the minute a lorry would pull up and the soldiers came onto the tram I'd take me stuff and put it in this little box. I was never caught with anything in all that time.

De Valera introduced an invaluable straightness into diplomacy by declaring that he would consider any reasonable British offer made to him publicly, but would not commit himself to any clandestine deals. This was essential because of the deviousness on the part of Lloyd George which had clouded the earlier negotiations.

The most notable in a series of negotiators was Archbishop Clune of Perth, Australia, an uncle of Conor Clune, who had been murdered with Clancy and McKee on Bloody Sunday. Throughout December 1920, Dr Clune sailed back and forth between Ireland and Britain representing one side to the other. The Irish were constant in their agreeability to a truce which did not involve either a surrender of arms or any hindrance of Dail meetings. Lloyd George, on the other hand, continually shifted his ground: there need be no surrender of arms; peaceful political activity could continue, but certain notorious gunmen must not be seen at Dail meetings; surrender would have to be unconditional; he must deal directly with Michael Collins; Collins would have to be brought to justice as a precondition for peace negotiations, etc. At one point he even declared that a truce could not include 'the perpetrators of the Macroom ambush', referring to Tom Barry's activities at Kilmichael.

Throughout this stage of the negotiations Lloyd George tried to make it appear that he was bringing Dr Clune and, indirectly, the republican government into his confidence by implying that his confusing hardline rhetoric was only a ruse to appease the Unionists and militarists who surrounded him and that he really had the best interests of Ireland at heart.

But the bewildered Dr Clune could not pry any coherent offer from him and he eventually returned to Australia.

Any hope for a reasonable settlement had really ended early in Dr Clune's negotiations when three independent peace initiatives from Ireland reached Lloyd George. These came from: Father O'Flanagan, a Sinn Fein priest who wired Lloyd George to indicate Ireland's eagerness for peace; from the Galway County Council – or rather six particularly squeamish members out of a total of thirty-two, the rest of them being in prison or on the run – which passed a resolution deploring the activities of the Volunteers and seeking peace; and from a moderate TD named Roger Sweetman who wrote a letter to the press echoing this sentiment. Collins repudiated these unrepresentative moves, declaring that only the Dail was competent to negotiate on behalf of Ireland, but Lloyd George instantly leapt at his chance, declaring that the 'terrorists' were 'breaking down' and that all that was needed was a final turning of the screw: martial law would be extended, the death penalty would be employed on a massive scale and there would be no let-up in the escalation of pressure until the IRA laid down its arms.

The level of repression increased again at the beginning of 1921. In January the practice of 'official' reprisals (Churchill's old suggestion) was inaugurated; this meant that houses in the immediate area of ambushes were burned by government order if information on the attackers was not forthcoming.* The 'official' reprisals, of course, did not mean that the 'unofficial' reprisals stopped. Meanwhile, raids, also steadily increasing, were given a new twist when hostages began to be carried about in the open lorries.

All of this took its toll on the hard-pressed IRA. The numerous arrests depleted its ranks and supplies of arms, which had always been inadequate, grew more scarce.

---

*This was a policy which the British had already refined in South Africa when they had failed to defeat the Boers by more conventional warfare from 1900 to 1902.

BRIGHID LYONS THORNTON: I was home in Longford for the Christmas of 1920, and at that time, well at any time, arms were in very, very short supply. The Longford Brigade and Sean MacEoin were very active with their ambushes and everything and they were always in need of more guns. We had no supplies from anywhere, except what we made in backyards or got from a soldier when we took him in and got him drunk or could buy from him. So anyway then, it must have been around the 18th or 20th of December, some of them in the Longford Brigade came to me and asked me would I go to Dublin and get some 'material' – material being I didn't know what, but it would be something they required. So I was given a great big floppy leather case and £50 and I was to go to Dublin and get whatever I could. I was to contact the Quartermaster-General, Sean MacMahon. So I got to Dublin and went to the shop in Pearse Street and he said, 'I'm afraid we're very, very short, there's nothing we can give you now. But if you wait a couple of days we'll do what we can.'

After about four days I got a message to be at Broadstone Station for the twelve o'clock or one o'clock train, I can't remember, to Longford. So I went to the station at the appointed hour and I met Sean MacMahon's brother-in-law, Theo Fitzgerald, and he told me to look out for a small little fellow with a hunchback, that he would have the stuff. 'We've very little,' he said, 'but we've given you all we can.' So I watched out for him and eventually he came in with my big leather suitcase up on his back and he put me into a third-class carriage with a nice wooden seat in it and a place underneath for your luggage. He was about to put the case up on top but I told him to put it underneath because it looked very heavy and I didn't want to have to pull it down. So he went away and the next thing I heard was the whistle of the Auxies. They always came in with whistles.

Theo Fitzgerald came up to me then and said, 'My God, you're caught.' So I told him to get away because whatever would happen to me wouldn't be half as bad as what would happen to him. This was the height of the fighting and if they caught a man they might just shoot him there and then. So he went off.

Then I could see a nice British officer walking up and down and I called him over and I said, 'What's happening?' 'Oh don't you worry,' he said, 'they're just searching the train.' 'What for?' I said. 'To see if anyone might be carrying guns or anything.' So I said to him, 'Haven't you settled all that yet? There's nobody carrying any guns now.' 'Oh,' he said, 'you couldn't trust those Sinn Feiners any day.'

In the meantime four or five country boys got on the train. It was coming up to Christmas and they were probably going home. Well the soldiers picked them up and brought them into the waiting room to search them and of course I was very worried. But they came back after about ten minutes and I was greatly relieved and I thought, Well, we're going at last. But didn't the soldiers come back a few minutes later and take them again. So I was getting weaker and weaker and more pathetic-looking, I suppose, and I said to myself, Now, if I own up to this I'm for it, whatever it is, but it won't be as bad as it will be for them. I thought they would shoot all of them because they were on the train with my leather bag. So I talked to my officer friend again and I said, 'What's the delay now? I'll never get home for Christmas.' I must say he was very gracious and he said, 'Don't be frightened, you'll be going soon.'

The next thing was the country boys came back and the soldiers started taking out the luggage. They were dragging it out and looking at it and shaking it, and I thought, This is it, I've had it. I didn't know what was in the bag, but whatever it was must have been bad. I found out later it was fifty hand-grenades. So they were coming along to my carriage and I prayed and I prayed as I never have prayed before or since, and they opened the door and put their hands in to take out my case and just then my officer said, 'Don't worry,' he said, 'that's the little lady's luggage.'

Well, the little lady just sank back and thanked God for her innocent-looking face.

So the train pulled out safely, but when I got to Mullingar I found I was in the wrong part of the train. I was in the part that went on to Galway. So I had to get off and get over to another platform and to do this I had to go along an underground passageway. Now the case was very heavy and the handle was broken, so I had to take it up in my arms and carry it myself. I hadn't any money to give to a porter and anyway I couldn't trust it to anyone else. But I got on the right train again. I was to get out at Edgeworthstown, which is the stop before Longford, because there were always searches at Longford. But I wasn't met at Edgeworthstown. Apparently the telegram wasn't sent, or if it was it was somehow misinterpreted. Then there'd been a rumour of a raid at Broadstone and I heard later there was great consternation in Longford because they thought I'd been caught.

I finally got to Longford and the little old workman we had came to the station and put the bag up on his back and carried it away. To this day I don't know why he wasn't searched there because he nearly always was. The RIC were very hostile. They knew us and used to take jibes at us, which wasn't very gracious. But this time they didn't stop him and the bag was taken down to my uncle's house. Everyone gathered around then and there was great activity and within an hour the hand-grenades were sent out to MacEoin and his column, wherever they were.

Three of our veterans – Martin Walton, Sean Kavanagh and John L. O'Sullivan – were arrested in the raids which followed the events at the end of 1920. Martin Walton was arrested at this time in the middle of the night and only narrowly avoided being hanged. The two prostitutes who had witnessed the killing of the ex-British officer during the arms raid pretended not to recognize him when they saw him on an identification parade.* Sean Kavanagh and John L. O'Sullivan were beaten following their arrest and they and Mr Walton spent the remainder of the war in prison.

SEAN KAVANAGH: I had an appointment to meet Collins as usual at Vaughan's Hotel on Saturday the 8th of January 1921, but for the first time ever he failed to turn up. So as I was on the train the following Saturday, Jimmy Lennon, who was the ticket collector at Sallins Station in Kildare and one of our chief lines of communication, he handed me three letters that he had received from Dublin. I couldn't read the letters then, I couldn't open them, because the carriage was so crowded, so I just put them in my pocket. I got off the train at Kingsbridge Station, took a tram down to Capel Street Bridge and then went over to the Royal Exchange Hotel in Parliament Street for some lunch. It was a bit late for lunch, but the waitress told me they had some steak-and-kidney pie left, so as I was waiting for that I opened my letters. Two of them were about Volunteer military matters and weren't meant for me. The third was a note from Collins. It was dated at the top and it said, 'Dear Sean.' It ran something like this, 'I am sorry I wasn't able to turn up last Saturday night. Would you meet me at the same time next Saturday?' It was signed 'M'. Now just as I had finished reading this I heard a voice saying, 'Put your hands up,' and I looked around and saw two gentlemen in Auxiliary uniforms. Behind them was a third man, I could just see his face, and I recognized him immediately as a man named Brown whose father was an RIC sergeant who had been stationed at Sallins. This fellow had been absent from the area for some time and it was said he had joined the Black and Tans. Obviously what had happened was that

---

*The Dublin prostitutes were apparently very patriotic at this time. According to Mr Walton, 'Some of Collins's key men – men with big rewards on their heads – used to meet in a pub in the brothel area, and though these poor girls were selling their bodies for tuppence, they never betrayed one of them.'

he had spotted me get off the train at Kingsbridge and followed me to the Exchange Hotel and then went around the corner to the Castle to get the others. He knew that I was on the run, as I had been for a couple of months. I had evaded arrest previously because Jerry Maher had tipped me off when they were going to raid the place where I was living.

The man in charge of the group was the famous Major King, who was OC of the F Company of the Auxiliaries in the Castle. Brown just melted away and I was marched up to the Castle, where I was interrogated by King, Hardy, the man I had met previously in Vaughan's the night before Bloody Sunday, and another fellow called Tiny. He was about 6 feet 6 inches, and he was rather notorious. I think he was in on the killing of Clancy and McKee with the others. So they looked at the letters I had and they immediately guessed correctly that one of them was from Collins. I said that I didn't know anybody named Collins and I told them that I'd just come up from Newbridge and that I intended to return there by train and that the note was from a man I was to meet there. But they didn't believe me. By this time they were beating me up. They didn't mark my face, they just pulled my hair and hit me around the body. This went on for a couple of hours, and then Hardy suddenly got a brainwave that the meeting place must be the Exchange Hotel, where I'd been arrested. Of course I was very relieved that he didn't guess it was Vaughan's, or remember that he had interviewed me himself there some time previously, but I continued to insist I didn't know Collins. They were convinced by now, however, that it was the Exchange.

So at about a quarter to eight I was brought down to the Exchange and put standing on a little porch outside the door. They had about thirty or forty Auxiliaries up and down the street, standing in doorways, and King, Hardy and some others went inside. They put a man on the telephone to make sure nobody would use it, and nobody was

allowed out of the hotel. I was told that when this man 'M'
came along that I was to shake hands with him. I said, 'All
right,' because I knew Mick wasn't coming there. I heard
later that he was getting impatient with me up at Vaughan's.
I waited on the porch there for about two hours, and then
just before curfew a Dublin man I had known in Naas,
who'd shared lodgings with me there, he passed by with a
girl and saluted me. I pretended not to know him, and he
must have thought something was wrong because he came
back and put out his hand. I put my hand in my pocket
and told him to get off quickly, but they immediately surrounded us and we were taken off to the Castle. He was
lucky, however, because a policeman who was standing at
the entrance to the Castle recognized him and vouched for
him, so he was let go. They beat me up again a bit and
berated me for wasting their time, and then put me into the
Exchange Court guardroom, where Clancy and McKee had
been killed.

On the Monday I was transferred to Kilmainham Jail. I
met several Volunteers there, one of whom was Peter Ennis.
He had been arrested with some others when a meeting of
the Dublin Brigade intelligence officers was raided. When
he heard where I'd been he said, 'How did you get on in
the Castle?' and before I could answer he put his hand in
his pocket and pulled out six teeth and said, 'That's how I
got on.' Christy Carberry had been arrested in the same raid
and he still had the remains of black eyes a month after he'd
been arrested.

I was in Kilmainham for about ten days and then one
morning around ten o'clock I was told to pack up. I was
put into an armoured car, up in the turret, and brought
back to the Castle. There I was brought to a very senior
officer, not in uniform, and he questioned me very politely
and quietly for about half an hour. He had a picture of
Collins, not a very good likeness of him, and he went on
about what a wonderful man he must be and how interesting
it must be to know him. I agreed and regretted I hadn't that

privilege. We parted then and I was put into an old prison cell in the Castle, a large cell with three other men in it I hadn't met before. One was an oldish man named Green who was supposed to have been implicated in the Bloody Sunday shootings, another was a young Dublin man named John Noud, and the third was called Vincent Fouvargue. Fouvargue was very talkative and he seemed to think I knew all the big fellows. He mentioned Cathal Brugha, Mulcahy and Collins, and he said he'd been arrested in the raid with Ennis and Carberry. Then we were all brought to Kilmainham again, and one morning I was called to the governor's office. I was questioned again by the same officer who had questioned me at the Castle. Later on that day Fouvargue came up to me and asked me if I'd been to the governor's office and I said that I was. 'So was I,' he said, 'but I don't know why.'

The next thing we heard was that Fouvargue had been taken out as a hostage as they went on their patrol. They often used to do this, take a prisoner and put him up in their Crossley tenders so they wouldn't be shot at. Well, the story was that Fouvargue had escaped during an ambush. But it was only a story because Fouvargue was a plant. Other prisoners at Arbour Hill had found him out and sent word to Collins. What the British did was take him to Dun Laoghaire and put him on the mail boat. When he got to London he contacted some of the Irish there, but they'd received word about him and one Saturday morning his body was found on a golf links outside London. He'd been executed as a spy.

I was court-martialled in the North Dublin Union, out by the Richmond Hospital, and was given twelve months. I think it was for membership of an illegal organization. The prosecution witness was to have been Major King, the man who had arrested me, but he wasn't present because he was himself in custody, awaiting trial on a murder charge. But of course he was acquitted. Shortly after that Ted Herlihy, a guard in the prison who was working for Collins, came into my cell one morning and said, 'I have a letter for you.' It was from Mick, one of his semi-jocose notes. 'Dear Sean,' it read. 'I want to congratulate you on your very light sentence, but of course you know you'll be interned for another few years at the end of it.' He believed the thing was going to go on forever.

JOHN L. O'SULLIVAN: The night before I was arrested I was going off to join Tom Barry and the column at Burgatia here in west Cork. Myself and Con O'Leary, the captain of the company, marched through the night to Sam's Cross, but when we arrived there, at about four o'clock in the morning, we were told it was too late to join the column. They were afraid dogs might hear us or something. So we were to go back home and report back at nine o'clock in the morning. So we came back and dumped our rifles in a hayrick and Con O'Leary said, 'I'll go home and get a change of clothes for I suppose it'll be a long time before we see home again.'

So I went home to bed and later that morning I got up and my people, they were farmers, they were out milking the cows, and I came down the stairs and there was a cycle patrol of military after coming into the house. Now I wasn't on the run at all. They'd arrested my brother a month before but I didn't think they suspected me. But this officer says to me, 'Where were you last night?' So I made up some excuse, I said I'd been in bed for a few days, that I'd had the flu. 'Well,' he said, 'we'll give you plenty of time to cure that now. You're coming with us. There's a bicycle out in the shed there,' he said, 'you get on top of that. And don't chance any tricks for we won't go running after you at all,' he said, 'we'll just pick you off nicely.'

So I was taken to the barracks in Clonakilty then, where the hospital is now, and that afternoon I noticed the military were going out. I heard them moving out in lorries. I found out then they'd been tipped off that the column was in Burgatia House. The postman had gone there that morning and although Barry had held him up and made him swear he wouldn't give them away, he went right back and notified the police. So they started closing in on them, and it looked very bad for them, but they shot it out with the soldiers and managed to escape.

So when they came back to Clonakilty that night, the military, they were under the influence and they were very wild and rough, and some time during the night I was taken out and put up against a wall. There was a British officer there, Captain Cowley, and God, he was 6 feet 4 inches, a terrible big man, and he stood one side of me. He had some other officers to the other side of me and a soldier in the front with a bayonet right up to my chest. So he put his back to the wall like me and he hit me with his elbow in the face and he nearly put my head through the wall. He broke open my mouth and nose. I couldn't stir with the bayonet there and he was going to keep it up, but just then the chaplain of the hospital was passing through, he was on sick call, and he called over this officer. Whatever passed between them I don't know, but I was taken away and put into a cell. The chaplain often told me afterwards that I was a lucky man that he was there that night.

So I was put back in the guardroom then. The soldiers used to give a pick in through the peephole now and again with their bayonets to make sure nobody was looking on. After that I was taken to Cork barracks, to Victoria Barracks as it was called at the time, and I was taken around the city at night as a hostage, inside the lorry. I was put into the guardroom there too with several other prisoners. We were all strangers there and nobody spoke to each other, but once during the daytime a man was put in among us, and he was no sooner there than he started going around from one to the other. 'You know lads,' he said, 'next time the door opens follow me and we'll get out.' But nobody answered him or spoke to him and he was taken out some time afterwards. But some of the lads had an eye on the keyhole and they saw him dressed in a British military uniform. He went out with a raiding party and some time that night he was shot in the city of Cork. I forget his name now but, you see, they'd sometimes put in people to get information from us or to involve us in something that might get us killed.

I was eventually sent out to the prison on Spike Island. It was an old fortress, and when I went there first I was put into one of the cells of the men that were transported to Tasmania back in the last century, the old Fenians. They had their names carved in the limestone in the cell.

Later on, meeting some of the people that were in there with me, what struck me was that here was a group of men you could trust. Some of them were battered before they came in, with black eyes and bruises, etc., but everybody was prepared to take what was dished out. One thing I'll say is that the spirit of the movement at that time could never be approached again – the spirit of self-sacrifice and the courage of these men, a lot of them ordinary working men, many of them professional people, but with the same spirit imbued in them all, prepared to take whatever was handed out without divulging under any circumstances any information that would be of value to the enemy. Some of these people were executed. I remember hearing the volleys in the detention barracks, which was only a short distance away from the guardroom. I also remember when I was in Cork jail the boy in the next cell to me being informed that his two brothers had been killed the night before. They were shot in their beds by a raiding party of soldiers. He just died himself last year, but I remember they brought me out of my cell to be with him, and the grief of that boy was terrible.

Those who managed to avoid arrest were reduced to living perpetually on the run – a life of narrow escapes, overbearing strain and curtailed effectiveness.

DAVID NELIGAN: Dick Mulcahy was Chief of Staff of the

IRA – a small withdrawn little man, very quiet, a silent Irishman, which was a strange anomaly. He was staying with Mick Hayes, who was a scholarly Dublin man, and it was a very dangerous place for Mulcahy to be because Hayes was a fabulous Sinn Feiner. But he had nowhere else to go.

Mulcahy, like Collins, also had a bad old bicycle, and he was belting along a tramline one night and the bicycle gave way, the fork broke, and Mulcahy went flying out on his nose onto the tramline. Some passers-by picked him up and one of them said to him, 'Your dentures are further down the road, sir.' His false teeth had fallen out. So he gathered himself and went back home to Hayes's, and left the old bicycle out in the front of the yard.

He had maps in Hayes's house of the Liverpool dockyard, which was to be blown up, and the Birmingham gasworks and so on, and he always took the precaution of leaving the skylight open in case he heard a rat-tat-tat on the door. So at 3 a.m. he heard the rat-tat-tat at the door and he knew damned well it couldn't be anybody inquiring after his health, so he made a dive for the skylight and he ran across the roofs. He saw a skylight open at the end house and he jumped down through and there was a Jew and his wife in bed. They nearly passed out with the fright. They thought their throats would be cut there and then, and they begged him to go away. So Mulcahy told them what happened and that the tommies were after him, and then it was all right. The Jew even loaned him a suit of clothes because Mulcahy had escaped in his pyjamas, and he got away then. In the meantime the raiding party found all these documents back at Hayes's, and the officer in charge told the sergeant major to go off to Portobello Barracks for reinforcements. So the sergeant major went out and saw the old bicycle in the yard, and he got up onto it and he'd only gone about a hundred yards when it gave way and his head was clapped against the tramline. He was knocked unconscious and the reinforcements never arrived.

In addition to the military pressure on the IRA, the war on the Irish economy was having the most dire consequences for civilians.

MAIRE COMERFORD: Some time after the general election in 1918 they had the local government elections, and the Irish people voted to take over local government themselves. That was a matter involving enormous expenditure. It was the difference between declaring a republic – opening offices and holding courts, things like that which were not very expensive – it was the difference between that and running and subsidizing the hospitals and doing all the things that local government does. Coinciding with this was a depression, and there was enormous unemployment. There were 110,000 unemployed, and that didn't include agricultural labourers. By Easter 1921, hunger was spreading through the country and Dail Eireann founded the Irish White Cross to meet the distress. Now the English should be ashamed of this, because all the social services were normally financed by the taxes of the previous year applied to the services of the present year. Now the taxes which were raised in Ireland were withheld by England, and they weren't available to the local government bodies. The result was that the people who had to take the brunt of the struggle were people like the sick and the old-age pensioners and people like that. That was something which turned our victory and triumph in many areas where we were winning into great sorrow and terrible problems. This made the question of peace more urgent.

7

Despite the military pressure and the driving underground of the Dail's political activity, the republicans remarkably managed to sustain an effective campaign in 1921. In May, 120 Volunteers, the largest on any single operation since Easter Week, 1916, burned the Custom House in Dublin. Through the fluke intervention of a lorry full of Auxiliaries they suffered heavy casualties and the crippling loss of seventy of the best men in Dublin through arrests, but the fire, which smouldered for weeks, was a gesture of defiance on a massive scale and also succeeded in destroying most of the documents and records of Britain's civil administration in Ireland, including the Inland Revenue and Customs, the Local Government Board and Company Registration. Coordinated attacks on both the military and administrative fronts had resulted in the virtual elimination of British rule in some of the more active districts. In May it was reported with horror in Whitehall that the Dungloe district in Donegal, one of General Sweeney's areas of jurisdiction, had become a 'miniature republic'.

Prison escapes likewise continued to counteract the demoralizing effects of the massive arrests.

SEAN KAVANAGH: I was in Kilmainham the night Ernie O'Malley, Frank Teeling and Simon Donnelly escaped. The principal thing was to prevent Teeling's execution. He was due to be brought to Mountjoy in a very short time to be hanged for his part in the Bloody Sunday executions. There was an attempted escape the night before but that failed. Paddy Moran had taken part in that, but he decided not to go the next night because he thought he had very good witnesses for his trial and that he'd be acquitted. He was a bit superstitious as well, and I think he thought that the failure of the previous night was a bad omen.

I wasn't in on the escape plans at all, but that night Paddy Moran came to my cell and he said, 'Some of the boys are thinking of making a dash for it tonight. Do you think you could get rid of the guard for about a half hour or so?' The guard was a Welshman, one of the Welsh Regiment that was on duty that night. So I said I thought I could. I noticed that when he had come on duty he'd already had a few drinks taken. He was a very friendly sort of fellow, and he came over to my cell and told me that his birthday had been the day before, but it was a Sunday and he couldn't properly celebrate. I could see that he was in good form, so I asked him if he'd post a few letters for me. 'Certainly,' he said. I had some loose change on me, which I shouldn't have had, and I gave him a few bob and said, 'Have a drink on me for your birthday.' So he went off, but before he left he said, 'Don't let anybody escape while I'm away!' Well of course by the time he got back the three of them had got away. They'd managed to cut the padlock in the door with some bolt cutters.

When he came back he rounded us all up to put us in our cells and he called out all our names. Somebody answered for Teeling to give them whatever extra time they could to escape, but after a while he came to me and said, 'I can't find Teeling anywhere.' He sobered up very quickly then, but he was later court-martialled and sentenced to eight years, along with another soldier who should have also been on guard duty that night. He was a very nice fellow and I felt bad about getting him into such trouble, but Teeling's life, and probably O'Malley's too, had been saved.*

*By the time the Welsh prison guard was released the British had departed from most of Ireland and Sean Kavanagh had become Governor of Mountjoy Prison. The Welshman wrote to him to ask if there might be a post for him in the Irish army as he could find no work in Wales. This was not possible as only Irish nationals were eligible for military service, but the Irish government sent him some cash to help him.

In March, Collins became obsessed with effecting the escape
of Sean MacEoin, a blacksmith from Ballinalee, County Longford, who had won fame for his romantic exploits as a guerrilla
leader. On 9 January 1921, MacEoin had fought his way out
of an ambush laid by District Inspector McGrath and a party
of Black and Tans, drawing fire away from a cottage containing
women and children and fatally wounding McGrath. A month
later, at Clonfin, he and his column attacked a motor patrol
of twenty Auxiliaries; following an intense battle which ended
in the Auxiliaries' surrender, MacEoin freed the survivors and
arranged for medical attention for the wounded. MacEoin was
then captured in early March at Mullingar; he again tried to
blast his way out and nearly succeeded, but was severely
wounded and taken to King George V Hospital in Dublin. He
was later sentenced to death at a court-martial hearing, though
several Auxiliaries testified as to his compassion and the relatives of District Inspector McGrath made a plea for leniency.
Collins, who had deep admiration for MacEoin, immediately
began to consider escape plans, and Brighid Lyons Thornton
was drawn into them.

BRIGHID LYONS THORNTON: I'd gone one evening to my
aunt's place here in Dublin for tea and when I was there
this man came in. A friend of mine was with him and he
said to me, 'You know this man.' But I didn't, and it was
only halfway through the tea that I realized that it was Sean
MacEoin. He was the most oustanding figure, with piercing
brown eyes that would focus on you and you were mesmer-
ized. Collins wrote about those eyes somewhere afterwards.
He stayed for a while and then when he was leaving he said
to me, 'If I'm arrested tomorrow will you come and see
me?' And then he gave me the names of two or three people
I was to contact and what to tell them and so on. So I said,
'You won't be arrested,' and then another girl came in and
we spent a pleasant hour or two just chatting and then he
went off. Well the next afternoon my uncle came in in a
panic, looking like death. He said, 'MacEoin was arrested

212

and shot in Mullingar.' Now that was a terrible, terrible tragedy for us all, because you'd never know what they might do to a man once they'd captured him.

After a couple of days I got the idea that he must be in King George V Hospital, which is now St Briccin's, so I made my way up there. I met the officers in charge there and I told them that I wanted to see General MacEoin. There were a few little titters then and they said to each other, 'She wants to see "General" MacEoin.' I told them that I wanted to write to his mother to tell her how he was, so they had a little pow-wow and they said it would be all right to send a note up to him and they'd bring back an answer. So the note from MacEoin came back and he said he was all right, but would I send in some sugar because he was afraid of getting sour in there – some little joke like that. I still have that note. I went a couple of times after that and then someone whispered to me that he had been taken to Mountjoy.

At some stage then I got a message from Collins. Joe O'Reilly came in and left a note which said, 'Mick wants to see you tomorrow at 51 Parnell Square at eleven o'clock.' Well that was the day I took to the air. I never was so thrilled or so excited in my whole life. I had a lecture that morning and I remember I just stood there in a daze thinking that if anybody knew where I was going at eleven o'clock wouldn't that be news for them.

I left the lecture room naturally and raced over to Parnell Square and after a while he charged in in his usual way and he said, 'I believe you've tried to see MacEoin.' 'I have,' I said. 'Well try harder,' he said. 'Go to the Castle, get your permit, go in and report to me where you see him, when you see him, who is present. I want all the details you can give me. I'm going to get MacEoin out of there.' That was it. It was a three-minute interview.

So I went over to the Castle and I begged and I pleaded and they would come out on the landing after me sometimes and say, 'Why do you want to see MacEoin?' And I came up against this notorious RIC fellow Igoe, and I thought he was suspicious of me. So I told him that the man was ill, he'd been wounded in the lung, and that I was a medical student and I wanted to see him. I was very simple and innocent and people believed me and they gave me the permits. You could bluff them if you had any little bit of wit to go on.

So then I went along to see MacEoin at Mountjoy. You went through the outer gates and you were in a little court-yard, and then that gate was locked behind you and you were searched by the warders. Then you were passed through another gate and there were cobblestones and you went into the main building and down a long corridor. The deputy governor's office was the second door on the left. MacEoin was brought in there after he had been sentenced to death up at the Castle. He was in the hospital part of the prison, and I used to go in and see him there. I'd go in and put my arms around his neck very affectionately and then I'd slip a note under his collar or under the pillow. Well, it was pathetic to see him in bed in the little whitewashed ward. He looked so virile and he had these amazing deep brown eyes with a lot of fire in them, as Michael said, but to see him so helpless there was terrible. I brought a lot of messages in and out and occasionally a warder, a friendly warder, would also give me a message to bring out. MacEoin sent me out a photograph of himself and a man who was later executed. It was taken by an Auxiliary and written on the back of it was, 'This is for you from Sean, Michael Collins.' I met Collins a few times during that period and he always said, 'Tell me more and get every detail because I must get him out.'

Sean Kavanagh, then a prisoner, like MacEoin, in Mo-untjoy, was also given a part to play in one of the many contingency plans.

SEAN KAVANAGH: I was moved over to Mountjoy along with

twenty-three others at midnight on the 16th of February 1921, two days after the escape of O'Malley, Teeling and Donnelly. About a month later – I think it was the 14th of March – six of those who were transferred were executed, hanged. One of them was Paddy Moran. I'll never forget looking through the spyhole of my cell and seeing six empty coffins being brought up from the carpenters' workshop in the basement.

There were at least three men on the staff of Mountjoy whom Mick had working for him, bringing letters in and out to Sean MacEoin to arrange for his escape, and whatever else they could do. One of them was named Ted Herlihy. He came into my cell one day and said, 'I have something for you. Mr Staines asked me to bring it round to you and asked you to keep it.' Staines was around in the next wing, along with Arthur Griffith, Eoin MacNeill, I think, and Eamonn Duggan. So I brought Herlihy into my cell and he handed me a ·38 Webley revolver, loaded, and he said, 'This was brought around for Sean MacEoin.' I was to keep it until it was needed.

Well it's not easy to hide things in a bare cell. They had an old-fashioned heating system, with hot-water pipes running through all the cells, and you could tap out messages on these things. You could talk to the fellow next door in Morse code. They had a box around the pipe in each corner of the cell. They were about the size of small butter boxes and they were filled with sand, just to try and prevent them from being used to conduct sound. So I just took the top off one of these and buried the gun in the sand. Some weeks later there was an execution to take place in our wing. We used to call it the Hang House. So they transferred us over to Arbour Hill for a few days while the execution took place. I had to leave the gun behind in the cell because I knew we'd be searched going out. Luckily enough it was still in the box when I got back. Some time after that Herlihy came round again and said that Staines had asked him to collect the gun, that the plan had been changed. The idea was that

when MacEoin was being tried in the City Hall he would
smuggle the gun out and shoot his way out of the courtroom.
It was crazy. It was then they got the idea of the armoured
car business.

The attempted breakout was finally made at the beginning
of May.

BRIGHID LYONS THORNTON: There were all sorts of desperate plans made for MacEoin's escape. At one stage a gun
was smuggled in to him and he wanted to shoot his way out,
but then they got this idea of capturing an armoured car.
They found out that the British always sent lorries up to
the abattoir on the North Circular Road every day to get
meat for the various barracks around the city, and they
always sent an armoured car along for protection. So Collins
had somebody take over a house nearby where they could
watch unobserved, and every day they studied their movements – how many soldiers there were, what they did, who
got out, how long they stayed out, how long it took them
to collect the meat, how they lit their cigarette, everything,
every detail. Finally this one morning they captured the
armoured car and a few of them – Emmet Dalton, Pat
McCrea, Joe Leonard and some others, I can't remember
them all – they were all wearing British uniforms and they
drove down to Mountjoy.

The plan specified that the armoured car would present at
the main gate some forged papers ordering the transfer of
MacEoin to Dublin Castle, move into the yard and then swing
around in such a way as to jam open the two inner gates.
Dalton and Leonard were then to enter the prison with their
papers. Everything worked fine up to that point.
    MacEoin in the meantime was to have invented some pretext
for being in the governor's office that morning; he had managed this on the two previous mornings, but that day an
identification parade prevented him. Dalton and Leonard

216

arrived in the governor's office and, finding no MacEoin, passed the time pleasantly with the governor and his staff until he said he would have to ring Dublin Castle for confirmation of the transfer. Leonard then smashed down the phone and he and Dalton tied up the governor and his staff.

Just then they heard an exchange of fire in the yard. A Miss Aine Malone had been delegated to keep the main gate open at all costs by chatting to the guard while handing in a parcel. The guard, however, was uninterested in exchanging pleasantries and a back-up party of Volunteers held him up. A sentry spotted the drawn guns and fired, and Tom Keogh shot the sentry dead. Dalton and Leonard rushed out from the main building and the entire party escaped without casualties, though also without MacEoin.

It was an audacious, ingenious stunt, however, and the effect on the public was almost as if it were a success.

Another coup, perhaps more important as a morale-booster than for its military consequences – was the acceptance of David Neligan into the British secret service.

DAVID NELIGAN: As time went on, Broy was in jail, McNamara was sacked on suspicion that he'd given away documents, Kavanagh was dead, and I was the sole survivor working for Collins in the Castle. And the G Division was finished because the British secret service had taken over the whole works.

So I said to Collins one day, 'Michael, I might as well be in the tramway office for all the good I'm doing in the Castle.' 'By Christ, that's true, Dave,' he said. 'What are you going to do?' 'Well,' says I, 'there's an old saying: if you can't fight them, join them. I'm going to join His Majesty's Secret Service.' 'You must be mad,' he said. 'You'd never be able to get in.' 'My dear man,' I said, 'there are ways and means.'

So the assistant commissioner in the Castle was a very nice fellow named Dennis Barratt, who was very fond of money. So I went along to him and told him I wanted to join the secret service. 'You must be out of your mind,' he said. 'What would you want to do that for?' 'More money,' says I, which I knew was always the guiding force in his case. 'If that's the case,' he said, 'I'm your man.' Two days later I had an appointment to see Mr Cope, who was Under Secretary for Ireland. I also persuaded another fellow to go along with me because I thought it would look better that way.

Cope was a very suave fellow, and his office had very plush carpeting, which I wasn't used to. So I persuaded him that the reason I joined up was that I hated the IRA, and after the two of us got his approval we were sent over to an old red-faced, tough-looking major. He made us swear an oath which said that if I betrayed them they'd follow me to the end of the earth. I'm glad to say they haven't caught up with me yet.

So the old major told me my post would be out at Dun Laoghaire – Kingstown as it was called then – and then he offered me a fabulous sum, £10,000, if I could catch Michael Collins. I met Collins about an hour later and I hadn't even two bob to rub together in those days. Both Collins and the British assigned me couriers. The Collins man was Dan McDonnell and the other one was a little British fellow called Ashe. One day they both arrived at my digs at the same time and we all went off and had tea together, McDonnell posing as my insurance agent.

I asked Ashe one time what brought him over. 'Ah,' he said, 'I had no job.' He used to dress up in a hat and a worsted suit, and I told him that with that rig-out and his accent he could be spotted a mile away. He was a decent skin and I didn't want to see him finished off.

One of the reasons for Collins's success was that he kept all his people in separate compartments so they wouldn't know each other. That way they wouldn't give the game away under torture. But I managed to suggest to the British that they should get all the secret service fellows together so we could compare notes. And they did. They brought us all up to the North Dublin Union. If the major in charge had known anything about military intelligence he wouldn't have done that. All I wanted to do was see who they all were. But I'm glad to say that in the six months I was in the secret service there wasn't one of them shot as a result of me. I said to Collins, 'These people have done nothing here. They're only drawing their pay, trying to make a few quid because they couldn't get any work back in England. They're sick of the whole job and they want nothing to do with it except to be left alone. It would be a mistake to shoot them, a waste of a bullet.' There wasn't a single one of them shot, and that's something for which I'm eternally grateful.

In March, Tom Barry engineered another remarkable victory at Crossbarry, some 12 miles south-west of Cork city. A massive encircling operation involving over 1000 troops and 120 Auxiliaries was mounted to finish off once and for all his troublesome column, which at that time was operating at the fully extended strength of 104 men with only forty rounds of ammunition each. With troops closing in from all directions, Barry took the calculated risk of a stand-up fight and deployed his men into strategic ambush positions at Crossbarry. From the morning of 19 March, with a bagpiper blaring out marching tunes from the opening shots, they met successive British attacks and drove them off, leaving the road strewn with corpses and the surrounding countryside crossed by straggling lines of retreating troops. At the end of the fight there were thirty-nine British soldiers dead and forty-seven wounded, as against three IRA men dead and just a couple wounded.

Throughout the first half of 1921, Tom Barry was steadily increasing the pressure of the conflict in west Cork.

TOM BARRY: The biggest enemy we had out there was Major Percival. He was a sadistic scut, a ruthless killer of unarmed men. In Bandon at the moment you'll find on the side of the road several crosses of men who were brought out of

the barracks there late at night under Percival's direction
and murdered. These were men who were captured unarmed and on the way to the barracks he decided to kill
them. He was a very bad type of man. He had a pincers,
and he'd tear the hair off fellows' testicles and pull their
nails out. One of them he drove mad and another fellow,
Tom Hales, they pulled his nails out. Pat Harte was the
fellow they put into the asylum. He went in there and never
spoke to anyone again.

We tried to kill Percival a few times but we never got
him. Charlie Hurley and I tried. He used to come down
from the barracks because he was going with the bank
manager's daughter, and Hurley and I were great friends
and I said to him, 'You go below now.' He complained that
I'd have the first shot but I just said, 'I might miss and then
you could get him.' But this night that we were laying for
him we found out he was out with a raiding party looking
for us. We'd have done a great service to the British Empire
if we'd succeeded because he disgraced the whole army
when he surrendered at Singapore years later to the Japanese. I heard afterwards that Churchill wanted him shot.
I remember listening myself to 'Germany Calling', that fellow Lord Haw-Haw describing the surrender and saying he
was hoping I was listening because Percival had failed in
west Cork but had made an even bigger failure in Singapore.

Up to the end of 1920 we never attacked any unarmed or
off-duty soldiers and we never touched any Loyalist property, but they were murdering unarmed men and terrorizing
the people and we had to do something. We had very good
relations with some of the regiments, particularly the King's
Liverpool. Colonel Hudson, who had charge of them in
Skibbereen, was a very decent man and a professional, you
know, and he saw that we had a right to fight for our
freedom. He despised the Black and Tans and saved a lot
of our men's lives from their atrocities. He fought us hard,
but he was a fair man and whenever he wanted to go fishing
he got a permit from us. He was mad on fishing. He became

a brigadier afterwards and I had several letters from him
from India. He used to address them 'General Tom Barry,
Cork,' because he didn't know where I was. Actually I was
in prison at the time.

But Percival was something different, and he was informed by me in a letter that from February any member
of his Essex Regiment, because of the murder of unarmed
prisoners, would be shot on sight, armed or unarmed. They
used to go out on their raids, burning up houses or shooting
up the place as the case may be, and then after their rest
they'd go back into the town unarmed, looking for girls and
that kind of thing. But we changed their tune, and we were
pretty successful because a lot of the murders stopped after
that.

I saw something in the paper here not so long ago that I
had started the 'war on property' here. That was the burning
campaign we had here. I never started a war on property,
but what I did do was stop the destruction of our property
by the British. It was Percival started it; they started burning up houses in the martial law area, small farmers' houses,
labourers' cottages. Well the only way you can fight terror
is with terror, that's the only thing that an imperialist nation
will understand. We sent a message to them that for every
house of ours they burned we'd burn two of the big houses,
the Loyalist mansions. That wasn't a policy laid down from
Dublin. If you had a GHQ at the time of seven Napoleons
it wouldn't have done any good because of the lack of
communications. But the British went on with their burning
campaign and they found we meant what we said because
we kept raising the ante. I don't know if you ever played
poker, but I played poker then. When they burned four we
burned eight. And we didn't let them just sell up their lands
and run back to England. We put a ban on all sales of this
property because we weren't going to have them leave Ireland with money in their pockets from land they'd stolen
from the people. You should have heard them screaming
about it in the House of Lords. Appeals were coming in

from everywhere for the burning campaign to stop. All these people had stood by while our own people's homes were burned up and they had to sleep in henhouses or stables, but as soon as the boot was on the other foot they put a bloody quick stop to it. We hadn't a house burned in the last two months of the campaign.

The last places I burned were the workhouse and the Earl of Bandon's castle. They went on the same night. They were taking over the workhouse for extra troops, and they were putting all the inmates out. The 'twin evils of the Conquest' someone called them: one was for the lords of the Conquest and the other was the house of the dispossessed.

Then, on 21 June 1921, three local magistrates and the Earl of Bandon himself were kidnapped and held as hostages to prevent the continued execution of Volunteers in British custody.

TOM BARRY: We took the Earl of Bandon prisoner and held him for six weeks, right up to the truce. And we let the British know that if there was one execution of one of our men held prisoner that Bandon would swing from the nearest telegraph pole. We wrote to General Strickland and the British Prime Minister himself about it. He was His Majesty's Deputy Lieutenant here. In my opinion there is no sense in killing an unfortunate soldier or an unfortunate policeman while the judges and the higher-ups of the administration go free. And you could be sure that if there was one execution or one unofficial murder during the time we held him he would have hanged.

He was well treated and he got the same treatment as our own lads. His guard was told that if the British found them they were to shoot Bandon first and then try to shoot their own way out of it if they could. They used to play cards with him, a 110 for a halfpenny or a penny or something, and sometimes there'd be an argument, you know, someone standing up and saying, 'You reneged!' and Bandon would chip in, 'Sssh, sssh . . . the military might come.' He was the best scout they had.

The Earl of Middleton was a first cousin of his and the Earl of Middleton was the head of the southern Unionists. You had all these implications and complications, and the fact that we were holding him was, I think, one of the things that brought on the truce. At that time my wife – we weren't married then, she was in the Cumann na mBan – she sent down a note, 'Is he dead or alive?' So I said, 'Tell them in Dublin to start worrying about our own men and not this bloody earl.' So she said, 'I've got an order from Collins. De Valera wants Bandon because he's having a meeting with the Earl of Middleton.' I said, 'He's alive and well, and he's getting the same treatment as the chaps who are holding him.' It's extraordinary how the ruling class get together at such times. There's no principles involved then. He was released unharmed of course after the truce.

8

I speak from a full heart when I pray that my coming to Ireland today may prove to be the first step towards an end of strife amongst her peoples, whatever their race or creed. In that hope I appeal to all Irishmen to pause, to stretch out the hand of forbearance and conciliation, to forgive and forget and to join in making for the land which they love a new era of peace, contentment and goodwill.

King George V in Belfast, 22 June 1921

Amid all the vengeful Unionists and militarists surrounding Lloyd George were two men who had a more conciliatory view of Ireland. These were Tom Jones, the Cabinet's Principal Assistant Secretary, and A. W. Cope, Assistant Under-Secretary at Dublin Castle. They remained active behind the scenes, cajoling Lloyd George towards a truce and negotiations. Lloyd George remained as wary as ever, allowing them a degree of slack while presenting an uncompromising face to the public – he would have 'no truce with murder', he said.

But the British public was growing increasingly nervous about such rhetoric as the press continued to report, with growing horror, the events taking place in Ireland. The British Labour Party repeatedly advocated a British withdrawal and self-government for all of Ireland under one assembly. Also, a small sensation was created when Brigadier General Crozier resigned his command as head of the Auxiliaries over the gross indiscipline of his own men and the backing they received from the government, who refused to stop them. American public opinion was of course as restive as ever.

A new period of visits from unofficial peace emissaries thus

began with the arrival in Dublin of Lord Derby on 21 April
for talks with de Valera.

SEAN HARLING: Throughout that whole time there were a
number of very distinguished people who were wanting to
have interviews with the President. One of these was Lord
Derby. He'd been sent over on a peace-feeling mission. So
all these interviews used to come through Mick Collins. He
told me to arrange this interview, and said that Lord Derby
was staying in the Gresham Hotel under the name 'Mr
Edwards'. So after Dev agreed to meet him I went along to
the Gresham and I met Charlie Price, who was working
there. Charlie was the brother of Tom Barry's wife, and he
told me what room Lord Derby was in, and I found out he
was staying there with a Protestant clergyman who'd come
over from England.

So I went up and knocked and the clergyman answered
the door and I said, 'I'm from the President of the Republic'
– those were the words I always used – 'and I've called to
see Mr Edwards.' So he said, 'Any business you have with
Mr Edwards has to go through me.' So I told him that those
weren't my instructions, and I turned on my heel to walk
away.

Then a bigger man stuck his head out and said, 'I'm Mr
Edwards, won't you come in?' So I told him that the President had agreed to meet him and he said, 'What have I to
do?' So I told him I'd call back for him at seven o'clock and
take him to the President.

The next thing I had to do was arrange for a safe house,
and I picked O'Mara's – that was the bacon curer O'Mara
from Limerick who had a beautiful house in Fitzwilliam
Square. I went along to the housekeeper and told her I'd be
using the house that night. Then I sent Batty Hyland, one
of Mick's drivers, out to get the President and I went off to
the Gresham.

Now earlier I had told Dev about this clergyman and he
said to me, 'Whatever you do, don't have him with you

tonight.' I didn't know how I was going to get shut of him, so when I was coming down into the hall with Lord Derby and the clergyman I said to Charlie Price, 'Charlie, see if you can get rid of this minister.' So as we went past Charlie tips the minister on the shoulder and tells him he's wanted over at the reception desk, and when he walked over I whipped Lord Derby into the car and we were away. So Lord Derby looked around behind him and he says to me, 'That was very cute of you.'

So we went on to O'Mara's then, and he saw the President, and after the interview I took him back to the Gresham. He was a very nice man, you know, and he thanked me very much for the courtesy of the whole thing.

Lord Derby apparently discussed with de Valera the idea of Dominion Home Rule for Ireland, which was met with no enthusiasm whatsoever. Abandoning the horn-rimmed spectacles which he thought would camouflage him, he returned home to London. De Valera reported that he had 'talked to [Lord Derby] as he would to a press man'.

De Valera's next diplomatic session came a fortnight later with the northern Unionist leader Sir James Craig.

SEAN HARLING: At one stage Sir James Craig came to Dublin to see Dev, and Mick told me to make the arrangements. Before I left he said, 'Tell Dev that I think he should see him.' It used to make me laugh the way he'd say that, and whenever these things came up Dev would say, 'What does Mick think?'

After Dev agreed to see him I went around to Lord Justice O'Connor's in Pembroke Road, where Sir James was staying, and I knocked on the door and I said, 'I'm from the President of the Irish Republic.' Well, this was shocking of course, so he says, 'Won't you come in?' So I was put sitting down in this room and after a while Sir James came in. I told him then that I'd pick him up at ten o'clock the next morning.

The next morning then Batty Hyland went out to pick up Dev to take him to the rendezvous, which was a solicitor's house in Sutton, and Batty's brother Joe and myself picked up Sir James. We drove on over Butt Bridge and as we got to Clontarf, Sir James was sitting beside me and he says, 'Would it be indiscreet if I asked you where we are now?' So I says, 'Not at all, sir, you're in Clontarf.' 'Oh,' he says, 'this is where King Brian fought the Danes in 1014.'

We went on then and they had their meeting. Nothing ever came of it, but later that night I was in Amiens Street Station – that's Connolly Station now – and a driver on the Belfast train called me over and he showed me a copy of the *Belfast Newsletter*. The headline on it was, 'Sir James in the Camp of the Enemy'.

Cope, the Assistant Under-Secretary at Dublin Castle, had apparently told each man that the other was eager for a conference but, following an exchange of irreconcilable viewpoints, the meeting ended without achieving anything in the way of *entente*.

Meanwhile, the elections promised under the Better Government for Ireland Bill were to take place for the 'Northern' and 'Southern' parliaments in late May. De Valera determined to use the election machinery to elect a new Dail, and its existing candidates were returned unopposed. In the North, where B Specials were brought out to 'keep order', Unionists were given a sizeable majority – though Fermanagh and Tyrone, as ever, went nationalist. Yet another Unionist lesson to Catholic malcontents was delivered in early June with a five-day pogrom in which six men were killed by B Specials, eleven were shot dead during riots and 150 people were driven from their homes.

If nothing else, these elections provided the British with another impetus for peace, on two counts. The first was that they established, however barbarically, the existence of the Northern state, which would make any negotiation on unity far more difficult for the republicans. The other was that the act specified that if either parliament did not meet, then the area which it represented would be designated a crown colony; this signalled the unpalatable prospect of martial law for the entire twenty-six counties, the tying down of an enormous number of troops and more international embarrassment.

Lloyd George's hardliners, however, remained shrill in their demands for an all-out summer offensive. Churchill's solution was:

A hundred thousand new special troops and police must be raised, thousands of motor cars must be armoured and equipped; the three Southern Provinces of Ireland must be closely laced with cordons of blockhouses and barbed wire; a systematic rummaging and questioning of every individual must be put in force.

The military were meanwhile preparing themselves for a long engagement. Their strategists had not been idle and, correctly assessing that the IRA's strength lay in its mobility, adaptability and support from the people, they decided to emulate it by forming their own experimental flying columns – relatively small units of well-trained, highly mobile and lightly armed and dressed commandos. Reprisals were to stop and 'column' members were instructed to behave with maximum civility to the populace as they chased its defenders around the hills.

Peace, nevertheless, was more politically expedient for Lloyd George's government. He was precariously placed, as both Churchill and Austen Chamberlain were conspiring to get rid of him. Also, delegates from all over the Empire were assembling in London in June for an Imperial conference, and the imposition of martial law over three-quarters of Ireland would be not only an embarrassment, but also acutely disquieting to the delegates. General Smuts, the erstwhile Boer commander, was in London at this time trying to exert a liberal influence at the conference. He too turned his hand to Ireland, trying to convince de Valera to accept a solution on similar lines to the Boers' own settlement with Britain. He arrived in Dublin on 5 July, and Sean Harling arranged the meeting.

SEAN HARLING: The most interesting of the meetings I had with any of the people who had come to see Dev was with General Smuts from South Africa. It was very close to the time of the truce. I went along to the Shelbourne Hotel where he was staying and when he saw me I think he got a bit of a shock, because he paused, and he said, 'I'd rather not discuss the business you're here for for a few moments.' Then he said, 'Would you mind if I were to ask you if you're an officer in the Irish Republican Army?' It was because I looked so young, you see. So I said I was, and he said, 'I want to tell you a story about something that happened to me during the Boer War. I was encamped in a place near Bloemfontein in the Orange Free State and a young man about your own age ran into the camp this one evening and told me that I was in danger of being arrested. He said that he was working in a restaurant twenty miles away and four British officers came in for a meal. While he was clearing off the table he heard one of them say, "We'll get Smuts tonight." Then the boy said to me, "I knew you were out here so I left off my white coat and came out to warn you that you were in danger of being captured." This boy was very sick and my medical officer examined him and found that he was very far gone with consumption. As I broke camp we took the boy with us. He only lived for about four days. We buried him with full military honours and there's now a beautiful statue erected in his memory. You'll see it when you come out,' he said, 'which I am sure you will do.' But I never did, I just took him over to see the President at Dr Farnan's and then took him back to the Shelbourne.

De Valera remained unmoved by Smuts's ideas, which he had in any case already dismissed; but Smuts nevertheless had a significant influence in the peace when it finally came. Lloyd

George's opportunity for a public peace offer to de Valera came when King George V, who had always agonized over the actions of his forces in Ireland, sailed to Belfast to open the Northern parliament on 22 June. It is said he was not content with the first speech which was provided for him, and he sent for Smuts to help him rewrite it in a more conciliatory tone. The result was a heartfelt, if imprecise, plea for peace among 'my subjects'. Lloyd George determined to use this speech as the context for an opening to negotiations; it was, after all, laden with Imperial pomp and connected with a further solidification of the northern state.

But the plans were very nearly jeopardized by the arrest, apparently accidental, of President de Valera on the night of 22 June.

SEAN HARLING: The night de Valera was arrested I went along to Ormond Quay to call on Cathal Brugha, like I did to all the ministers to see would they have any documents for me to bring out to the President. Now on this night Cathal says to me, 'Sean, I've a very dangerous document here. I want to discuss it at Saturday night's Cabinet meeting. Make sure it doesn't fall into anybody's hands.' Well, it did fall into British hands that night, and what it said was, 'Intensify the campaign' – that was the head of it, and it had proposals for not allowing British soldiers to walk anywhere, armed or unarmed. So I took this out to Dev.

Now out where Dev was living at Glenvar, Batt O'Connor had built a rockery outside under the conservatory window. He'd cemented the rocks together so you could lift them up and hide anything in there, and what we used to do was put all the government documents in a deed box at about ten o'clock every night and then hide it in the rockery. That was curfew time, and it was just around then that I saw a lorry swing in the gate and soldiers jump out of it and start to advance on the house with their rifles. I went in to warn the President, but by the time I got to the hall there were already soldiers in the house, so I just went out by the conservatory and through the orchard. I passed a British soldier there, but for some reason he didn't seem to mind me at all.

I didn't find out until the next morning what had happened at the house, but what it was was this. De Valera was living there posing as a retired British officer, a Captain Hayden, and he had discharge papers and everything. He was supposed to have been discharged on the grounds of ill health. So when the raiding party arrived, Dev and the officer in charge started having this friendly chat while the rest of them went around looking through the house. After a while the sergeant came down to report to the captain that everything was in order, and he looked down on the floor and saw the deed box with this document from Cathal Brugha sitting right on the top of it. So he passed it over to the captain who looked at it and said, 'These are very seditious documents, Mr Hayden.' Kathleen O'Connell jumped up and said, 'They're mine,' and Dev said they were his, and the officer said, 'We won't argue about them. The two of you had better come along.' So that's how they were arrested.

But in the meantime I had got out through the orchard into Professor MacNeill's garden – that was Eoin MacNeill – and then out his front gate. I was in a very difficult position because it was after curfew and I could have been picked up by any British patrol that might be passing. But I saw a light on in an old tram depot there, the Dublin United Tram Depot, and I went in there and asked the nightwatchman if I could stay the night in one of the trams as I'd been curfewed. So he said he was off at eleven o'clock, and as he only lived in one of the tram cottages at the back he said I could stay the night there. I was pretending all the time that I was from Dublin and that I'd just been caught out, but he must have known me because as soon as he got into his house he stood at the foot of the stairs and called up, 'Nick! There's a friend of yours here.' And wasn't he the father-in-law of Nicholas Kelly, the OC for the IRA in Blackrock.

So they made up a bed for me on the sofa, but I didn't sleep a wink all night; there was a grandfather's clock bonging away all night and I was worrying like hell about what was happening up at Glenvar. The minute five o'clock came – that was curfew over – I got up and went straight over to Glenvar. When I got up to the house, Maeve McGarry the housekeeper was there, whinging up and down the hall, 'Oh, the Chief is gone, the Chief is gone,' you see, and 'They took Kathleen too.' She gave me all the details then, so I got on me bike and cycled over to Batt O'Connor's in Brendan Road in Donnybrook to find out where Mick was so I could tell him about this. He told me Mick was just staying a few doors away, at number 6 Brendan Road, in a house owned by Dail Eireann. So we went over there, but Mick already knew about it. He told me that Dev was being held in Portobello Barracks, and he gave me the address of a place just opposite there where I was to stay and keep an eye on things and report any developments to him.

I wasn't at this place very long at all before this fellow from the Board of Works came into the house where I was watching. He had come from the barracks. He was working for Mick and he says to me, 'Tell the Big Fellow' – that was Collins – 'that the Long Fellow' – that was Dev – 'is having a posh time in officers' quarters.' He meant that Dev was getting the royal treatment inside in the barracks. A little while after that the same fellow came over and said Dev was being released. Well that took me off me feet altogether. I couldn't believe they were going to release him, you know. But really what happened is that he was arrested by mistake, because just around then a letter was being prepared to be sent over to him from Lloyd George looking for peace talks. Cope was all in the air and saying that Dev had to be released right away. Old King George was very anxious for the whole thing to be settled and he was putting

232

great pressure on Lloyd George. So he had to be released then.

Apparently when Dev was on a tour of Australia some years later he was contacted by the sergeant who arrested him and he said it was only an investigation raid and he'd been picked up by accident, but I was after being told by Nicholas Kelly that what had happened was that they had raided the mails that day, and as they were driving along in their car they emptied out the mails and threw the sack over the wall into the grounds of Glenvar. Some policeman on the road had apparently seen this and reported it, and that's why the house came under suspicion and was raided.

Lloyd George's letter reached de Valera on 25 June. Sean Harling had picked it up at the Mansion House and brought it out to Blackrock. He met de Valera on his way to the railway station; when de Valera read the letter he said to Sean Harling, 'It looks as if we'll be in the Viceregal Lodge soon.'

De Valera made his reply and established his headquarters in the Dublin Mansion House, to which General Macready was summoned on 8 July to discuss the terms of a truce. Macready walked warily through the enthusiastic crowds carrying a concealed gun, but was unharmed and the following day concluded the arrangements, which specified the lifting of the curfew and the end to all hostile actions, though not to drilling and training. The truce came into effect on 11 July 1921.

It was a momentous occasion for Ireland, and the country was ecstatic at the end to the terror and above all at this acknowledgement of its underground government. Lloyd George had been shifted by the IRA a considerable distance from earlier days when he had claimed to have 'murder by the throat', was insisting on unconditional surrender and dismissing Dominion Home Rule as 'all pure nonsense'. There were bonfires, the flying of the tricolour and endless singing of patriotic songs to celebrate this fact.

BRIGHID LYONS THORNTON: We were all happy and excited with the truce. We went mad. The hoardings were torn down in O'Connell Street and we all roamed the streets. The curfew was lifted, the lid was off and we all enjoyed ourselves. It was like the Mardi Gras.

SEAN KAVANAGH: I was in Mountjoy with a few hundred other chaps when I heard about the truce. That was really the victory of the whole thing. Mulcahy always maintained that, that the truce was the most significant thing in the war against the British at that time because it was they that asked for it, not us. They had called us murder gangs, and now they wanted to treat with us as a legitimate army and government. I don't think we could have carried on much longer without it. It gave us a kind of breathing space to train more Volunteers and purchase more arms for a resumption of hostilities, if necessary.

PART FIVE

They'll come right in the end

11 July 1921 to March 1923

'Liam Mellows was looking after me and about two or three other women, and I said to Liam, "How long will this fight last?" "It will last a long time," he said. "Will it last five years?" "Oh no," he said, "it will last much more than that. But they'll come right in the end." '

Maire Comerford

1

The end of this phase of the great Irish adventure was far more sudden than its period of development. Though few in Ireland could have perceived it during the euphoric summer of 1921 – with bands playing, curfew lifted, national pride at its zenith, Volunteers regaled as titans and the British back in their barracks – the momentum the country had acquired during the war years was already dissipating itself. By the winter it had become everything it had not been in the immediate past: undisciplined, fissiparous, quarrelsome and vainglorious. Into the vacuum came all the mean provincialism and conservatism which Ireland had previously known during the worst periods of British rule. By the summer of 1922, it had buried itself in the particularly gory squalor of civil war.

2

It was by no means pleasant to be obliged in the course of duty to associate with men whose methods, apart from their devotion to their cause, can only be characterized as murder and assassination by those who hold that even the act of slaying one's fellow creatures should be marked by some adherence to the chivalry of bygone days.

Sir Nevil Macready

The terms of the truce had implied parity between Ireland and Britain. Dail Eireann and 'that band of murderers', the IRA, were acknowledged, if not officially, then at least for the purpose of liaison work and negotiations. The Irish, not surprisingly, celebrated it as if it were a victory. For the politicians at Westminster, however, the truce was never more than an expediency, nor could British officers serving in Ireland disguise their repugnance at the prospect of negotiating with 'gunmen'.

TOM BARRY: I was standing on a roadside in west Cork and somebody came along and said, 'There's a truce with the British.' I'd been hearing rumours about this for the past twelve months and I didn't believe it, but this fellow went off and got a newspaper which said that de Valera was meeting Macready, the British Commander in Chief, so I had to believe it then. I thought the terms of it were very good for a crowd who'd been called a 'murder gang' up to then. It was the first time I saw us referred to as the Irish Army.

Just before the truce there'd been a change in the command structure. GHQ in Dublin had instituted divisions, and I was named Deputy Divisional Commander for Cork, Kerry and Waterford. Then when the truce came I was appointed Chief Liaison Officer for the Martial Law Area. There were only eight counties on the map under martial law at the time. They were thought to be a special problem. I was glad to see that we were considered to be a problem to the British.

I was told by headquarters to go into Cork and select a hotel to use as my office for the liaison work, so I said, 'What hotel do you want me to get?' 'Go to the Imperial.' 'Oh no,' I said. 'We'll go to a small hotel. We're the representatives of people who don't use these posh places.' I could already see the rot setting in, you see, these fellows relaxing into these roles that were too big for them. So I went into Turner's Hotel, which was a small family hotel, and I had two rooms, one I could use as an office and the other to sleep in. A phone was put in immediately of course, and I had a guard on me in case I might be assassinated.

There was an invitation sent down from Dublin then for me to meet General Strickland at his headquarters in Cork. So I was driven over to see him in an old Ford Tin Lizzy we'd captured, and I was met at the gate by these two British officers. One was a major and the other a captain, and they took me over to what is now an Irish army mess; it was the General Officer Commanding's headquarters at the time.

So the two officers went off, and when they came back they said, 'The general is now ready to see you as Mr de Valera's representative.' So I said, 'Wait a while. I'm not Mr de Valera's representative, nor Mr Collins's representative. I'm representing the Irish Republican Army, which has been recognized by the terms of the truce.' The truce was a first-class thing, you know. It gave us rights which we wanted and were entitled to. So they went inside again for a while, and when they came out the Major says to me, 'I'm afraid the general can't receive you. He's been in touch with headquarters and he can't receive you except as Mr de

Valera's representative.' So I said, 'That's fine with me. I didn't want to see him in the first place. It was him requested the meeting.' It was a deliberate thing on their part to insist that we weren't an army. Now I had at least a hundred bloody British to my personal account in west Cork, and I wasn't about to be looked upon as some bloody henchman for de Valera or anybody else. I was a soldier fighting in a war, and when the truce came I was appointed by the government of the Republic to represent its army. But the implication of this thing was that I'd committed a hundred 'murders', as they would have called them.

So I went back to my office, and I was determined not to get sidetracked on this thing. I instructed the guard I had that if any British officers came along to see me they were to repeat my exact words, and I made the guard repeat them for me: 'General Barry will be glad to meet you if you are meeting him as an officer of the Irish Republican Army, and not as Mr de Valera's representative, Mr Collins's representative or Mr X's representative.'

So the same two British officers I'd met before came along about two hours later and when they heard this they were a bit flabbergasted, I suppose, but they knew I was right. I'd talked to them earlier about this and they were two decent officers, they were quite understanding, and they couldn't understand why their own people were making such a fuss about it. I never saw Strickland at all in the end.

I rang Mick after it to tell him what had happened, and he was quite silent about it. I was rocking the boat apparently. He came down to west Cork then. He saw his homestead, which the British had burned down, and when I mentioned to him again about the Strickland business he said, 'There's trouble over that.' But he told me not to worry about it, and a few days later I got a message that I was to report to Dublin. I was to meet General Macready, the commander in chief, the following day.

So I went to Dublin and I got a bed in Vaughan's Hotel, which Collins used to use, and in the morning I had a bath and a shave and I got into my best suit. After I finished breakfast I was having a smoke and in came Collins with this fellow called Ned Duggan. I'd never heard of him before. He was some kind of a bloody minister or something, and he was a lawyer. Collins introduced us; he said, 'This is Ned Duggan. He's the Chief Liaison Officer for all Ireland.' We had no partition then.

So I looked at him, anyway. He was dressed in a black coat, waxed moustache, black homburg hat, striped pants and spats. And he was supposed to be an IRA man. He was no more an IRA man than I was an atom bomber. He was carrying a briefcase and he shook hands with me, and I said, 'Christ almighty, my best suit is only in the ha'penny place.' This was one thing our country badly needed a lesson in, this aping of the British or the Germans or the Americans. A small country like us. One of the reasons why we were so successful, or at least came near success, in 1920 and '21 was that the facts of life were driven into our men: nobody was to get above their status or have any views about being anything important in the world. I could see the way the headquarters was carrying on in Dublin – big carpeted suites of rooms in the Gresham Hotel and bottles of whiskey and brandy all around. I went in and told them they should be ashamed of themselves.

But anyway, I set off with Duggan in this posh car to see Macready and we chatted a bit on the way. Duggan said, 'I hope we won't be too long with this man, I've other business to attend to.' So I said 'The quicker we get away from him the better, because I don't like this job at all.' I had protested earlier that I wasn't the right man for liaison work, because I hated these British officers and they hated me. Liaison work shouldn't have been given to such an active person as I was. But I suppose they felt that as my name stood for something in Cork that I could at least control the men.

We got there then and were shown in, and there were officers standing around deliberately smoking and sniggering at Duggan, ignoring us. It was a deliberate set-up, and I said to Duggan, 'There's something wrong here. You're a minister and they should have been standing to attention at least when you're passing.' But he didn't even seem to know what I meant.

So then we were brought in to 'the presence', Macready's office. There were four or five officers standing around, some of them in spurs. Whatever they were doing in spurs on that carpet I don't know, but I knew they would be that type. Macready stood up and shook hands with Duggan, whom he had met before. He took no notice of me. I said to myself, There's going to be high jinks here in a bit. So Macready started in then. 'Well, Mr Duggan, this black-guardism by you Irish chaps, it'll have to stop – assaulting the troops. . . .' Christ, he started this long diatribe then about all the things we were doing to endanger the truce. And every time he said that such and such a thing would have to stop, Duggan's reply was, 'Yes, general, it will be done. . . . Yes, general, it will be done. . . .'

And then Macready said, 'Particularly, keep your men off the streets. This truce mightn't last long, and we don't want to be the cause of breaking it, but we'll have to take action.' 'Oh, general, don't worry, it will be done,' says Duggan.

Then Macready mentioned some incident in Tipperary where he said some British soldier had been beaten up. But I knew about that case myself, and I knew it was the soldiers who were responsible. They'd been out and got drunk and went looking for trouble. Our own fellows weren't always blameless, but they were angels compared to the others. Sometimes we had to take action against some of our own, and we'd fire them out of the IRA, tell them to get out of the country, that they were a disgrace for starting rows and so on. But I'd say four out of five cases were started by the British. So anyway, this thing went on, and it was 'Yes, general' all the time from Duggan and, Christ, I was starting to boil.

Then Macready turned to me after a quarter of an hour of giving instructions to Duggan, and he says, 'Now, Barry, you've heard what's to be done' – and there were no titles for me, no 'Mister', no 'Commandant'. I was a general actually at the time. So I laughed and said, 'I'm listening, Macready.' He was one of these overfed, bloated . . . one of these bullies. And I said, 'And I'm listening to Mr "Yes, general, it will be done" Duggan. Well you know, Macready,' I said, 'and Duggan, it *won't* be done. None of these things will take place, and I'll see that they won't, even if we make bits of the truce. As far as I can see from the behaviour of you here, the sooner we get to grips again and fight it out the better.' It was disgraceful to hear our Irish troops, as we were at the time, the troops of the elected government, referred to as if it was we were the army of occupation, not these bloody British scuts.

So Macready was turning blue by this time, and I don't know what way Duggan was. Then I remembered a story I heard about a speech Lord French made when he was leaving Ireland. French despised Macready. So I made my way to the door and I turned around and said, 'After all your crude and insulting behaviour, Macready, I can well understand what Lord French meant when he said at his farewell dinner, when the wine was flowing, that the one big regret he had was leaving behind such decent men as his staff to a flatfooted bastard of a London policeman.' And that's what Macready was of course. He'd been Commissioner of the London police. He'd been given that job after the war because the British government were afraid there might be a revolution and he was enough of a bully to put a stop to it.

So I went out and I told our driver to take me back to Collins, and I told him the whole story then, even the bit about calling Macready a 'flatfooted bastard of a London policeman', as French had dubbed him. 'You didn't,' he said. And I said, 'I did.' 'Where's Duggan?' says he. 'I don't know,' I said. 'I hope to Christ he's gone into the bloody Liffey. I left him behind with Macready. He seemed to be getting on very well there.' So that was my first and only meeting with British officers.

The British remained wary of flagrantly violating the terms of the truce, and their men rarely did anything more serious than indulge themselves in the occasional drunken brawl. But, not surprisingly perhaps, it was a different matter for that section of the British forces which was most a law unto itself – the secret service. They simply disregarded it, as David Neligan discovered.

DAVID NELIGAN: A curious thing happened during the truce. This major said to me that the chief of the British secret service wanted to see me at the Castle. So I wended my way down to my old headquarters, to this office where there was a little man named Count Sevigné – Anglo-French, a small man with a narrow face and starey eyes. He committed suicide later in London. I read it in the paper. Suicide is the secret service man's occupational disease, poor devil. So anyway, he says to me, 'You're Neligan.' I didn't know what was coming of course. So he wrote down my description: 'Twenty-two years old, about 6 feet 1½ inches, long pale face' – it was pale right enough, because I didn't know what he was going to do. So then he says, 'Neligan, we're sending you to London tomorrow morning. Here's the letter of introduction. A woman will meet you at Holyhead.' Right cloak-and-dagger stuff.

So I went all over town looking for the gang, Tobin or the rest of them, but they were all drinking their bloody heads off and they weren't frequenting the usual joints at all. There was a terrible decline at that period. I was desperate to find out what was in this letter, and what this trip to London was all about. So I thought that the only thing for it was to go to the Gresham Hotel, which was the liaison headquarters. It was a dangerous place for me to be seen because the place was crawling with British secret service men. All of us in the secret service had been told to carry on as usual through the truce, so long as we didn't get caught.

So Emmet Dalton was the liaison officer and I went up to his office. My hearing was much better then than it is now, and I thought I heard an English accent inside this joint, and I listened carefully. Christ, I said to myself, that's Cope – that was Lloyd George's man in the Castle. So the door shot open and Cope came out saying 'Goodbye, captain,' to Dalton, and I just had time to dive into a bedroom so he wouldn't see me. 'Where in hell did you come out of?' says Dalton. 'Did you see Cope?' 'I did,' I said. 'But listen, Emmet, I have a letter I'm supposed to take to London and I need to have it opened.'

So the letter was sent off straight away to Pat Moynihan, who was able to do a great job on letters and seals and so forth. But he could have saved himself the trouble, because once he got it opened he found that it was in cipher and we hadn't the key.

So I went across to Holyhead and met this woman and she told me to go to Faulkner's Hotel in Charing Cross, where I'd meet another man. So I met this big Englishman there named Woolley. He was a fine old fellow. We had some peculiar way we had to introduce ourselves, and we talked for a while in a desultory manner. Then he said, 'Neligan, you see those two birds back there?' There were two nice-looking girls sitting there. So I said I did. 'Well,' says he, 'do you see the one on the right?' 'Yes,' says I. 'Well, I have her for the weekend and the other one is yours.'

I didn't know what to do then, but I said, 'Listen Woolley, back at my hotel there's a raging jealous fight. I daren't stop off anywhere else.' 'Don't say another word, old boy, I'm in the same boat myself.' I had to make out I had another woman, otherwise I don't think he would have believed me. I was afraid to have anything to do with it. It wasn't just that I was too virtuous, mind you, but I thought it might be a trap. It wasn't, actually. He was just laying on the hospitality. So I stopped there for a week or a fortnight, I forget which, meeting Tobin by night and Woolley by day, and to this day I never discovered what I was sent over for.

One of the sights I saw when I was there was all the wretched ex-officers begging in the streets. They had their medals pinned on to barrel organs, or they were selling matches and toys along the gutter. This was Lloyd George's 'land fit for heroes'. It was no wonder so many of them went over to Ireland to join the Auxies.

The IRA, like the British secret service, was aware of the fragility of the peace, and tried to maintain some semblance of war-readiness. Reorganizing, drilling, rearming and intelligence work went on, and Volunteers were exhorted by local commandants to prepare themselves for a resumption of the unequal contest. But a peacetime guerrilla army – however tenuous the peace – is an anomaly: it depends on the tensions and heightened awareness produced by extreme danger; coming down from the privations of life in the hills and back streets produces a sense of relief from which it is almost impossible to recover. Here and there too could be discerned an inflated sense of importance among some Volunteers who, leather-gaitered, strutted about their home towns, brandishing their guns and commandeering cars. There was talk of a 're-pentant' England, an England 'brought to her knees', whose mighty army had been 'driven from our shores'. Most Volunteers did what they could to stem the premature and un-realistic celebrations, but the morale, alertness and fundamental pragmatism of the IRA were nevertheless on the wane.

Also, the anonymity on which they had always depended was now ending. Collins was attending public meetings, making speeches and having meetings with Castle officials. A resumption of war on the old lines was quickly becoming impossible.

TOM BARRY: The truce went on for six long months, and I
feel it was deliberately calculated by the British to drag it
out as long as they could. They were used to dealing with
subject races, and they knew very well that a long truce is
always bad for the weaker force. They knew that our morale
and effectiveness were bound to deteriorate over a long
period. All the British forces in Ireland, and all the other
places all over the world which they were occupying at that
period, they were all housed in barracks, they were paid,
dressed and fed. But what was our guerrilla force going to
do in that six long months? I was all right because with my
liaison work my hotel bill was being paid by Dublin, so I
didn't have to bother. But the rest of my men had to bother.
They had to live and eat and be clothed and they might
have dependants to look after. No one was paying them.
When a man was an active-service IRA man, he was able
to live in the country with us because the people always
looked after us. But this didn't happen during the truce. He
might be the oldest of a family of six or seven, or the son
of a labourer or small farmer, and when he went home
somebody might be hungry and he'd have to get to work.
A lot of them just graduated out of the area to look for work
elsewhere. They couldn't afford to stay around training and
maintaining a state of readiness. I would estimate that by
the time the Treaty was signed there was at least a 30 per
cent deterioration in our effectiveness and our structure and
our morale. And this was a carefully calculated policy by
the British.

Far more subtle calculations were evident in Lloyd George's
diplomatic exertions with de Valera. De Valera had sailed to
England with a distinguished party of his ministers and
advisers the day after the implementation of the truce and met
Lloyd George alone in Downing Street on 14 July 1921. The
Welsh Prime Minister of Britain greeted the austere Spanish-
Irish-American as a fellow Celt and seated him opposite a large
wall map decorated principally in the red of the British Em-

pire. He then extemporized on the wonders of this Empire and its capacities to transform itself: would not Pitt, Palmerston and Gladstone be surprised to discover that, during that very week and around that very Cabinet table, Dominion premiers were meeting the British Prime Minister *on equal terms* in an Imperial Conference? One chair only remains vacant, he said, and when de Valera refused to bite, he declared that it was waiting for Ireland. De Valera remained unmoved, silent and, according to Lloyd George, inscrutable throughout these beguiling manoeuvres – the wall map and vacant chair being to him merely signs of a familiar British acquisitiveness.

Such were the preliminaries to the proposals and counter-proposals and voluminous correspondence which passed between the two statesmen during that summer and autumn. These were aspects of a game new to Ireland, struggling to emerge into statehood, diplomacy and new national symbols, but which Britain played with long experience and skill. Lloyd George had to play it hard because he knew he was arguing not only with Ireland but also with India, Egypt and all the other red splashes on the Imperial map, for they too would soon be queueing up for independence. Lloyd George's strategy in his exchanges with de Valera was to give away nothing to Ireland, but to do so in a language of maximum magnanimity. On his side he had the most powerful press in the world, inexhaustible funds, a magnificent army with the most sophisticated weaponry, and a team of the world's most able diplomats and constitutional lawyers. The Crown he represented was still proclaimed to be a symbol of benevolence and civilization uniting an enormous area of the earth's surface. De Valera, for his part, had only an exhausted army, a populace habituating itself to the relief of peace, and a compelling moral argument. He tried to hold on to his Republic but, against such odds, he could not hold it very long.

Lloyd George's opening offer, delivered in time for his fourth and last meeting with de Valera on 21 July 1921, was a constricted, almost punitive form of Dominion Home Rule. It specified that Ireland was to come into the Empire, that

Britain was to have unreserved control over the Irish seas as well as rights of recruiting in Ireland, that Ireland was to assume part of the War Debt and the burden of Imperial defence, and that partition was to be maintained at the Unionists' pleasure. De Valera quickly rejected these terms, despite a dire threat of war from Lloyd George, and the two men settled down to conduct a protracted correspondence from their respective capitals.

In this correspondence, concerned solely with finding a basis to *begin* discussions, de Valera, in concise and moderate terms, tried to hold his own against Lloyd George's Imperial demands. Ireland, said de Valera, had sacrificed everything to defend the sovereignty which had been proclaimed in 1916 and confirmed at subsequent elections, and only on that basis could it negotiate. Lloyd George replied, 'We can discuss no settlement which involves a refusal on the part of Ireland to accept our invitation to free, equal and loyal partnership in the British Commonwealth under our Sovereign.' An explicitly free and voluntary partnership was thus insisted on at the point of an implicit gun. Meticulously phrased documents in this vein passed back and forth until a formula was finally agreed which would allow a conference to open in London on 11 October 1921 'with a view to ascertaining how the association of Ireland with the community of nations known as the British Empire may best be reconciled with Irish national aspirations'. De Valera believed that this would permit discussions to begin without prior conditions on either side.

But much had already been bargained away, even if only implicitly. The Republic itself, hitherto sacrosanct, disappeared into something called 'external association' – an ingenious but then rather vague concoction dreamed up by de Valera as he was tying his bootlaces one morning. It was designed to reassure Unionists and meet Britain in a spirit of neighbourly compromise. It meant that Ireland would agree to *associate* itself with the Empire but would not be an integral part of it. De Valera illustrated the notion to interested parties by taking out his compass and drawing a number of circles representing dominions within a larger circle representing the Empire with an additional circle – Ireland – tangential to it. The Crown was to be acknowledged as the head of the states – the British Empire – with which Ireland was to be associated, and of the association itself, but not of Ireland. To de Valera it was fair, generous and, virtually, his last word; to Lloyd George it represented a fissure in the republican edifice into which he would drive his wedge. Most important of all, to the British public, who read the correspondence in the daily press and to whom the politicians would be addressing themselves, it appeared that Ireland was willing somehow to reconcile itself to the Empire.

3

When Englishmen set to work to wipe the tear out of Ireland's eye, they always buy the pocket handkerchief at Ireland's expense.

Colonel Saunderson, Ulster Unionist leader

The delegates selected by de Valera to parley with the British diplomats within these ever more limiting confines were Arthur Griffith, Michael Collins, Robert Barton, George Gavan Duffy and Eamon Duggan. Their head secretary was Erskine Childers, and others in the party included John Chartres, Fionan Lynch, Dermot O'Hegarty and Desmond Fitzgerald. It had been commonly assumed that de Valera would head the delegation, but the President himself thought not: as head of state and government he should remain at home, a moderating influence on the extremists, a symbol of Ireland's sovereignty to the British and a rock of stability to the people. There were also, it seems, other considerations.

SEAN HARLING: I remember Dev saying during the truce that he wasn't going to make the same mistake as President Wilson. He said that if President Wilson hadn't taken part in the Versailles treaty negotiations, if he had kept out of it and had sent men under him to carry that out, he would have come out of it better off. He said that for that reason alone he wouldn't go to London.

Of those who did go, Duffy, a former Sinn Fein diplomat, and Duggan, the Chief Liaison Officer who accompanied Tom Barry on his visit to General Macready, were lawyers; Barton, at that time Minister of Economic Affairs, was an Anglo-Irish

251

former British officer, former public school boy, thought to have an intimate understanding of the English mind; Griffith, the head of the delegation, was a reluctant war-maker never entirely at home with the concept of the Republic and was chosen to represent the moderate wing; Collins was chosen for his personal persuasiveness, his hold over the harder men in the IRA, and his administrative ability and grasp of detail. Collins resisted the appointment to the end, but relented under personal pressure from de Valera.

The delegates were sent on their way under an ambiguous directive; indeed, their credentials and instructions represented one of the many empty formulae of that period designed to accommodate varying viewpoints but which, when later subject to embittered scrutiny, exploded into civil war. They had powers to 'negotiate and conclude' a treaty, but must first of all submit it to Dublin for approval; they were allowed 'free range' of discussion, but were liable to be rebuked for ranging too far. When they 'concluded' without 'submitting', they came to be called traitors.

Sean Harling was there when de Valera issued their credentials.

SEAN HARLING: Dev was out in his study in Glenvar and he said to Kathleen O'Connell that he wanted to prepare some documents. I can remember him pacing up and down as he usually did when he dictated letters – he couldn't seem to sit down – and he started off, 'I hereby appoint Art O Griobhtha [Arthur Griffith] as Envoy Extraordinary and Envoy Plenipotentiary from the elected Government of the Republic of Ireland. . . .' And he finished that and said to her to make three copies. Then he started again. 'I hereby appoint Mícheál O Coileáin [Michael Collins] as Envoy Extraordinary and Envoy Plenipotentiary of the elected Government of the Republic of Ireland. . . .' And he did the same for Duggan and Barton and the rest. I was in the study when he did this and I'll never forget the wording of it even though I didn't know what it meant at the time. I had to go into town afterwards and give the letters to all the delegates individually.

Mick didn't want to go at all. He saw himself as a soldier and didn't think he was the right type of person for negotiations. But the Cabinet made the decision and he had to go then. But he also said that if he was being sent to negotiate the treaty then he would have to be given the power along with the rest of them to conclude it. That was at the Cabinet meeting and I was there.

On the morning of 11 October 1921, the Irish team met their formidable British counterparts: Lloyd George, Winston Churchill, Lord Birkenhead (once the notorious F. E. Smith, Sir Edward Carson's chief English co-conspirator in 1912), Austen Chamberlain, Sir Laming Worthington-Evans (Secretary for War), Sir Hamar Greenwood and the Attorney-General, Sir Gordon Hewart.

At this stage the Irish still had in their favour a good measure of world opinion and the fact that three-quarters of their people had voted for a sovereign, independent Republic. The suffering they had endured to maintain it had won enormous sympathy and admiration. This gave them a certain moral force and they would have to be clearly unreasonable in their proposals for the British public to tolerate their government's resuming hostilities against the Irish. The Irish proposals, as it turned out, were eminently reasonable. They displayed statesmanship and imaginative sympathy; above all, they were plausible. They acknowledged the wishes of the Irish people in the form of a sovereign parliament and fiscal autonomy. They reassured Britain on Imperial security by a pledge of neutrality and agreements on joint defence. And they offered to the Unionists in the North a link with the Crown through the concept of external association and, if necessary, control over their own destinies in the form of their own parliament under the Better Government for Ireland Act, except that it would be subordinate to Dublin rather than to Westminster.

The British, however, had no interest in any Irish proposals, only in a response to their July offer to de Valera, thus quickly moving matters onto their ground and plunging the discussion into quibbles within the framework of Dominion Home Rule. This set the tone for the conference: rights and principles giving way to legalistic formulae, reasoned debate losing out to tactics, usually of deception, the moral force of history dissipating itself amid minutiae and sub-clauses. When the Irish tried to draw back the discussion to broad principles they were met with either evasion or blank refusal to consider them.

There were two issues before the conference: the unity of Ireland and its constitutional relationship with the Crown. Though to the Irish people recognition of the Crown, of course, rankled, by far the most important issue to them was the unity of Ireland. For this, and for this only, might they be willing to resume war; for their part the English people, so long as there were certain guarantees of autonomy for Ulster Unionists under a Dublin parliament, would be unlikely to deny the justice of Irish unity. Therefore, if negotiations appeared to be breaking down, the Irish delegates were to force the break on the issue of Ulster, for only on this issue could they expect to maintain popular support. For their part, the English delegates were to force the break, if it came, on the Crown, for a highly principled stand by the Irish on this issue could be made to appear unreasonable.

The complex manner in which Ireland lost so much ground on both Irish unity and on the Crown makes sorry reading. Lloyd George first of all succeeded in blurring the distinction between the two issues by making the settlement of one conditional upon concession on the other, and then won the battle over whether he or the Irish should concede first. He then employed all his skills of bluffing, threatening and dividing. As an expedient he suggested private meetings between smaller groups of delegates, thus splitting the Irish delegation and making less likely the disadvantageous arguments on broad principles that were likely to occur in full plenary sessions. Then Lloyd George's tactic – and it was the one through which he won his victory – was to focus his attention on Griffith, the head of the delegation, and draw him imperceptibly into British party politics.

Lloyd George confided privately to Griffith that he was facing a motion of censure in the House of Commons over his Irish negotiations; he was sticking his neck out for Ireland – could not Griffith see his way to helping him out in his lonely battle by giving some assurances on the Crown and Imperial security? He could at least then indicate to diehard Unionists that some progress was being made, but if he had nothing to show he stood to lose the vote. Did Griffith know what that meant? – the unleashing of a Tory-inspired terror on Ireland. . . . With this battle won, Lloyd George assured Griffith that he would go all out for Irish unity, even to the point where he would resign if he met with intransigence. Griffith, who was personally never very disturbed by the concept of the monarchy, drafted a most accommodating letter on Irish recognition of the Crown. Barton and Duffy, when shown the draft, were horrified and Griffith somewhat ill-temperedly agreed to draw back towards external association. But even the compromise formula of external association was being chipped away at. Ireland was edging closer to the Empire, and the Crown was being pushed back towards Ireland. Lloyd George confidently informed his Cabinet that the Irish 'had pulled down the Republican flag and adopted the flag of Empire', having easily crushed the censure motion in the Commons.

Lloyd George then went a round with Sir James Craig, though Craig, unlike the Dail's representatives, was treated with soft persuasion rather than ruses and threats. The autonomy of Craig's territory in the North would be guaranteed under a Dublin parliament, said Lloyd George, and what is more, his taxes would be lower. Craig, however, saw no reason to shift from the 1920 agreement. Lloyd George then found himself in a corner – wedged in by the Irish delegates' insistence on unity, Craig's refusal to consider it and his own promise to resign if he failed to achieve a united Ireland. He quickly concocted a new scheme to extricate himself. The Treaty, he

told the Irish delegates, would specify a united Ireland, but
the members of the Northern parliament would have a right
to vote the North out within a year of ratification. If they did,
however, they would have to submit their territory to a Boundary Commission which would limit it according to the wishes
of the people. The implication was that Fermanagh, Tyrone
and large sections of Derry, Down and Armagh would be
handed over to the Dail, with the remaining fragment too
small to be viable. Neither Collins nor Griffith were at all
enthusiastic, but Lloyd George then explained his new dilemma to Griffith. There was to be a Conservative Party conference in Liverpool; Bonar Law was likely to disrupt it by
claiming that Lloyd George was demolishing the Union in his
Irish negotiations. If Bonar Law's inflammatory rhetoric was
successful, Lloyd George's coalition government was in danger
of falling. Birkenhead and Chamberlain, both Tories, were
willing to quell the revolt by presenting the Boundary Commission idea, but they needed Griffith's assurance that he
would not undo their effort by repudiating it. To Griffith it
was merely another internal British matter which committed
him to nothing, except silence. A document was drawn up,
Griffith gave his assent and then promptly forgot all about it.
He had no idea that he had just given away the unity of
Ireland.

Matters had now assumed a familiar form. There was Lloyd
George, intimating contrary notions to opposing parties, per-
forming a vanishing act on the most contentious issue (Ulster
again) by deferring it to later consideration, all the while
accompanying his declarations of his own high principles with
threats to resign. Amid all this busy activity he was carefully
laying the ground for his escape route.

Negotiations thereafter were not untroubled – they nearly
broke down on 22 November and there were trips back to
Dublin followed by fresh Irish proposals – but they held
together into the first week of December. The Irish had apparently been instructed at a Cabinet meeting on 3 December to
hold firm on their commitment to unity, not to accept an oath

of allegiance and at the same time not to break on the Crown – though the delegates returning to London drew differing conclusions from this meeting. These terms, of course, were what they had been endeavouring to win for nearly two months, with little success. Griffith nevertheless kept trying, arguing tenaciously with the British for a further modification on external association. He was met with instant refusal. Duffy pleaded simply, 'Our difficulty is to come into the Empire, looking at what has happened in the past,' to which the British threw up their hands and replied that war was now the only option. Tom Jones, the Cabinet's principal assistant secretary, remained active, however, and the two sides decided to give it one more day.

The following day, 5 December, was to be the conference's last as Lloyd George had promised results to Craig by 6 December. When they met again on 5 December, Griffith said that he was willing to enter the Empire in return for a united Ireland, but he must have assurances that Craig would agree. Lloyd George, who had now been holding his ace for several days, sprang forward, brandishing the Boundary Commission document to which Griffith had earlier, in all innocence, given his assent. Lloyd George asked Griffith if he now meant to go back on his word. It was an eleventh-hour ploy, and it worked to full effect. 'I have never let a man down in my life,' said Griffith, trembling with indignation, 'and I never will.' The chance of breaking the negotiations on the issue of Ulster had passed.

Lloyd George had hit his stride. With the air of one pawning an heirloom, he offered up total fiscal autonomy, even to the point where the Irish were granted the right to impose protective tariffs against Britain. Earlier there had been some tinkering with the oath to make it slightly less repugnant to the Irish. With these concessions, along with the Boundary Commission proposal that would leave the door open to eventual unity, it did not appear to be such a bad agreement. Lloyd George then pressed his advantage with an absurd but menacing touch of melodrama. He had two letters, he said, one of which would have to go to Craig that night. There was a messenger and special train waiting to go to Holyhead, where a destroyer was docked which would take the messenger to Craig in Belfast. One letter said that there was a settlement, the other that negotiations had broken down; one meant peace and the other war. Griffith had pleaded for time to return to Dublin, but Lloyd George refused. Holding up the letter which said that negotiations had broken down over Sinn Fein's refusal to come into the Empire, he made his now famous threat: 'If I send this letter it is war, and war within three days. Which letter am I to send?' It was surely a colossal bluff, for the British public would not have tolerated a return to the murderous terror in Ireland, but Lloyd George had thrown his all into the threat and the Irish delegates believed him. Burdened by memories of hangings and barrackyard killings, their nerves strained to the limit, the Irish delegates retired to consider their position. Churchill later wrote of Collins as he left the negotiating table: 'Michael Collins rose, looking as though he were going to shoot someone, preferably himself. In all my life I never saw so much passion and suffering in restraint.'

One by one they joined Griffith in his readiness to sign, first Collins and Duggan and then, under severe pressure, Barton and Duffy. The delegation then returned to Downing Street and, following some further amendments, the two sides finally signed the Treaty at 2.10 a.m. on 6 December. Later that day Collins wrote to a friend, 'When you have sweated, toiled, had mad dreams, hopeless nightmares, you find yourself in London's streets, cold and dank in the night air. Think – what have I got for Ireland? Something which she has wanted for these past seven hundred years. Will anyone be satisfied at the bargain? Will anyone? I tell you this – early this morning I signed my death warrant. I thought at the time how odd, how ridiculous – a bullet may just as well have done the job five years ago.'

The Irish delegates caught the boat train from Euston Station that morning. David Neligan was ordered to Dublin from his mysterious mission at the same time.

DAVID NELIGAN: I got a telegram to get back to Dublin when the Treaty was signed, though I hadn't heard about that yet. There was a fabulous crowd at Euston Station, and I asked a London bobby what it was all about. 'Oh, it's them "Shin Finers",' as he called them. 'Seems we've made peace with them.' And he was right, because when I got on the train I could see Collins, Griffith and the rest of them. I saw Collins on the boat too. He looked very pale and not too well at all. He'd been up all night the night before. He didn't come near me because he was talking to Cope, but I spoke to Liam Tobin. He said, 'We have to face our diehards now.' That was the first time I heard that word allocated to a certain section of Irish politicians.

The Treaty was not a reasoned compromise between two strongly held ideals, nor the validation of one such ideal over another; it was a trick, effected under the spectre of force, and the appalling truth is that Lloyd George privately celebrated it as such. It nevertheless had a number of tangible results, some of them advantageous to Ireland. The British army, administration and judicial structure which had plagued Ireland for centuries were departing at least from twenty-six of Ireland's thirty-two counties; these functions were for the first time to be performed by Irishmen, elected by the people or appointed by their representatives. Dublin Castle, symbol of privilege and tyranny, was to be vacated and Ireland's own flag was to fly from its roof. And Ireland, even if only through a legal fiction (and was not the Oath another kind of legal fiction?) was to have constitutional equality with Britain.

But the Treaty also represented the signing away of the Republic, the national symbol which men had died for. It preserved, however obscurely, the Crown in Ireland and Ireland in the Empire. And it perpetuated the division of the country – though this remained an open question because of

259

the Boundary Commission. The Treaty offered none of the psychological release which the people desperately required and which could only have come through an Ireland united and free. Worst of all, it marked the end of the revolutionary momentum which the country had acquired – the clear visions, the imaginative social experiments, the magnificent confidence – and replaced it with mere divisiveness and prosaic power games. Ireland, for all its previous assertiveness, suddenly became a place that might have been if. . . . – if the delegates had returned to Dublin before signing . . . if they had held out over unity . . . if they had called Lloyd George's bluff . . . if de Valera had not stayed behind . . . if the truce had not lasted so long, etc. Speculation on the future of Ireland had been ambitious, vigorous and practical; it now became idle and dreamy, growing ever more listless as the years passed.

This, then, was the document which the delegates brought back to Ireland. It was seen in many different lights. None but the most naïve saw it as a final solution, but many saw it as a just beginning; to others, of course, it was a betrayal.

MAIRE COMERFORD: The young men who had been returned to Dail Eireann had no experience of the world of politics, none at all. Most of them had never before been in a parliament in their lives. They had to take up the thread of politics, and when the truce came and negotiations with Britain were called for, the people they had to face was the team that defeated the world at the Versailles conference. That conference brought Britain – although severely depleted from that war, owing debts to everyone and having been saved by America – it brought England out on top through the skill of the negotiators. This was the Lloyd George team which we had to face at the time in London for our own Treaty negotiations. The whole world found out afterwards that whatever rules there are in war there are no rules whatsoever in diplomacy. It's a blackguards' game: there's no honour, no straightness, no morals. The party sent over to England to negotiate were very brave men, who undertook a very brave mission, but what hope had they against the skilled diplomats of England? You can see from the minutes of the Dail that they were called a peace mission. What chance did you have of winning against Lloyd George by calling yourself a peace mission?

Above all our delegates had to keep the nation steadfast in its demands, demanding freedom and making every possible demonstration to put that demand across the world, making the cause felt. The soldiers of the IRA had defended a government, Dail Eireann, which had been put there by the will of the people, which must stay there, which must be defended, which no one must betray, and from which there is no retreat whatsoever. But our poor politicians got into a receding tide as idealism faded all over the world. They were sucked away into bargaining, into diplomacy, and eventually they were sucked into counter-revolution, as I see it. They brought home, under threat of war, this Treaty, which betrayed Dail Eireann and committed us to enter the British Commonwealth. This was very easy to put over in Ireland, because there had been a great deal of propaganda following the emergence of the British dominions; they were presented to us as independent nations who could leave the Commonwealth if they wanted to. For people who were fighting a war of survival against the British Empire – very small numbers with very few resources – it seemed a lot easier to tell a few lies and take a few oaths and go into the British Commonwealth than to continue with the fight. This solution was put before the electorate by people who were the heroes of Ireland. Michael Collins only survived long enough to do this. He was too fine a man to survive long with the counter-revolutionaries that came after him. And this was called the birth of democracy in our country, when in fact it was a most outrageous denial of the expressed wishes of the people.

JOHN L. O'SULLIVAN: I was of the opinion that this Treaty

261

could finish the bitterness between Britain and Ireland, if we worked on it and stood by it. I believed that we could use it as a foundation to get better relations, that the British might feel more lenient towards us and help us. At that time, of course, the British hadn't left. There was the army, the RIC, the Black and Tans and the Auxiliaries and all the others they had brought against us, and when they did leave we at least felt that we had something solid gained. As well as that, we saw we'd have our own local government, our own judicial system, that we'd nearly have control of running our own country. The only thing that I have against it is the cutting off of the North. That raised its head at the time and it is still doing it today. That was a very dangerous time, when the nation was deciding which road it would travel.

And I felt too – a lot of us did – that we trusted Michael Collins. He was the man we trusted above all the others during the long struggle for independence. The officers who went up to Dublin from the Southern Command always approached him for anything. He was the man everybody went to when they were in trouble. That was the general view of the people I was in prison with, that they accepted his views and thought we could use the Treaty as a stepping stone, as he called it, to full freedom. The people had stood a terrific campaign, they had resisted hunger, raiding, loss of family, loss of property, loss of everything they had, and Collins felt that if they got a breathing space we could build the country up economically and try to get better relations with our people in the North. We thought we could persuade our people there that we could live together happily, no matter what religion, no matter what class or creed, and that we had a lot better chance of surviving and prospering together.

Of course a lot of people down in this part of the country were against it. A lot of them had lost their brothers and sons and near relatives, and you could understand why they were very anti-British and wanted to keep up the fight.

BRIGHID LYONS THORNTON: I remember being over at Mrs Tom Clarke's house when the Treaty negotiations were going on, and all the extremists were over there and they were very excited and they said we were going to get everything except the name 'Republic'. This is what they had heard. But then when I finally saw the provisions of the Treaty I was shattered. It was terrible, an awful blow. It was a bad time because my aunt was ill and I wasn't too well either, but the terms really disgusted me. I didn't think we should have to pay any tribute to the King of England, and what really knocked me was having to pay pensions to the RIC. I know it was one of the smaller things, but I really thought that was terrible after the way they'd been so hostile to us. I thought that this wasn't the Republic we'd fought so hard for.

But then I began to think, What is the alternative? During the truce the Auxiliaries and the RIC and the rest of them had fraternized with the IRA, they had drunk with them and gone around the towns with them and they knew that we hadn't any resources. All through the previous years we'd had the support of the people, both young and old. It was the support that kept us going, not the guns or the grenades. The people really had to bear the brunt of the suffering – old people, people living away out in the country who were cut off from companionship. They used to have to wait every night for the lorries to come and for the eldest boy to be dragged out onto the road and shot. If there was any hope of peace you couldn't blame them for taking it. I'll always maintain that we couldn't have gone on with the fight.

And then, too, I began to think it wasn't too bad after all. At least the British were leaving. I remember going down to Dame Street the day the British left the Castle. Now that was always the mythical symbol of the British Empire to us, and here they were leaving it and Collins was taking it over. We were very pleased and proud to see it, and I thought the Treaty was at least a great measure of freedom and we could build on it and go on in the future.

I remember meeting some students after it and they said that there was going to be a split over the Treaty. Well that just lapped me altogether. I thought that if we had another split that we just wouldn't survive. I know that wasn't a particularly deep thought, but it was in my mind anyway. And then as time went on we were meeting people and hearing of who went this way and who went that way. It was all very harrowing. Some of your greatest friends were against you.

JOSEPH SWEENEY: I was at home in Burtonport when the morning train came in with the newspapers giving the details of the Treaty, and it was there that I first read the whole text of it. I was rather stunned in a way, because one side of me said, 'To hell with this, this is not what we were fighting for.' But another side of me warned me to be careful and not to make any hasty decisions. There was also confusion in my mind because of the fact that I was a member of the Irish Republican Brotherhood and I had taken a pretty strict oath to fight for a Republic. So I thought that in the circumstances I had better get to Dublin to find out where I stood. Accordingly I came to Dublin to seek out Collins. I went along to the Wicklow Hotel, where I hoped he would be having his lunch as usual, and as it happened I met him coming out. I must say I never saw him look so depressed. He had the appearance of a man who was completely fed up with everything. I didn't like to bother him because apart from everything else he was besieged on all sides by people who wanted to know what was going on, and a lot of fellows who were looking for jobs, the sort of self-seekers that follow in the wake of an agreement like this.

So Eoin O'Duffy was there with Collins and I called him aside and I said, 'You're an IRB man,' I said, 'what's the position with regard to the IRB and the Treaty?' He said,

'You're free to do as your conscience dictates.' 'Is that definite?' I said. 'Yes,' he said, 'the Head Centre has given permission for everyone to make up their own minds.' Now the IRB was composed of cells or circles, as they called them, and each circle had a head, and the heads of these circles would meet – it was mostly done on a county basis – and then there was a Head Circle, which was the centre of the whole organization. It was done in this way to preserve secrecy. Now of course the Head Centre was at the top of this structure. So I said to O'Duffy, 'Who is the Head Centre?' 'There he is in front of you,' he said, 'Michael Collins.'

So having heard this I went back to Donegal and we had a meeting of the people who had first selected me as a TD candidate and who ran the political machine there, and we had quite a discussion about the merits and demerits of the Treaty. At the end of it all it was decided that I was to vote for the acceptance of the Treaty at the Dail debates.

MARTIN WALTON: I was in the hospital in Ballykinlar internment camp when we got the news of the Treaty. My left lung had given way on me. Outside I could hear them banging kettles and tins and that, celebrating their coming release. Of course the average man was delighted to get out. Internment is a different thing and takes an entirely different effect on a man from a set sentence. At least with an ordinary sentence you can count the days to when you'll be out, but with internment there's no end, no beginning. The ordinary Joe Soap who knew anything about history would have regarded this as another 1798, that we'd all be hanged, killed, that if we got out alive at all we'd be dead lucky.

I thought myself it was a wonderful achievement. The only snag I could see in it was partition. I couldn't see any future in that. I believed that every day it lasted the ditch would grow deeper and deeper. But we thought the Boundary Commission that was promised might solve it, but of course that wasn't the case. That part of the settlement tied in with what the great Fenian John Devoy had said: every concession we got from England had to be wrung from her, and every agreement she made with us was halting and incomplete. That applied to the Treaty too.

TOM BARRY: It wasn't a treaty at all, it was an imposition on the Irish people. Amid all the writing and the signatures and all the rest of it, there were certain facts which stood out. One was that Ireland was partitioned; six of our counties were to remain part of British territory, and if that wasn't bad enough you had two more, Cork and Donegal, with British garrisons. That outed the Treaty for me and a lot of other people. Another thing was an oath of allegiance to a foreign king, and that oath of allegiance made us a subject people. We had been killing Britishers and they were killing us because we were saying, 'We are no longer a subject race of anyone, of any king or queen or any other foreigner. The days of our subjugation are finished.' And on top of that you had a governor general appointed by the British and you had a constitution drawn up by the British imposed on us under threat of force. Redmond could probably have got that for us without a drop of blood being spilt.

4

Our love of disputation sometimes makes us indecent – as when we argue over a dead man's coffin whether he was a Nationalist or not.

Patrick Pearse

Eamon de Valera was outraged by the settlement – by its poor terms but above all by the delegates' failure to consult with Dublin before signing. With the imperious air of one carpeting wayward subordinates, he summoned them to a Cabinet meeting to explain themselves. Afterwards, he publicly disowned the Treaty, declaring that he could not bring himself to recommend it to the people.

This was the first public display of a split in the republican ranks, of the agonizing six-month drift towards civil war. Ireland now entered the by now familiar post-revolutionary period of anti-climax and divisiveness. Irish revolutionaries had united around the single policy of change: differences over political theory had been suppressed and deferred in the interest of presenting a united front. The change brought by the Treaty was not sufficiently fast or unambiguous, and the result was a period of mutual accusation, often tinged with reluctance. Contrary visions and political theories emerged, clashed and then exhausted themselves while the country, without concerted leadership, lapsed further into chaos. The British pointed to these disputes with immense satisfaction as some vindication of their previous role, their 'civilizing' qualities. But the British were not required to bring a nation, with all its symbols, institutions and working practices, into being in an instant. This is the task that faced Ireland, and it had to be

267

accomplished by men who had grown accustomed to settling differences with guns.

The Treaty had to be ratified by the Dail, and on this de Valera staked all his hopes. The debates opened on 14 December 1921 and proceeded, under the cloud of Lloyd George's threatened war, with much personal acrimony and personal pleading, all the way to 7 January 1922.

Opponents of the Treaty spoke of ideals – of the Republic betrayed, of the debt to the past. All the women members of the Dail – Mrs Pearse, mother of Patrick and Willie, Mrs Clarke, widow of Tom, Mary MacSwiney, sister of Terence, and Mrs O'Callaghan, widow of the Lord Mayor of Limerick who had been murdered by the Black and Tans – were vehemently opposed to it, citing the debt to their personal dead. Liam Mellows, a young IRA commandant, gave a stirring speech against the Treaty as merely a continuance of the national humiliation. Countess Markievicz, one of the few holding on to the fusion between republicanism and socialism, resurrected the ghost of Connolly in opposition to the Treaty.

De Valera was more circumspect than these. He countered the Treaty by reintroducing external association in the form of something called Document Number Two, number one being the Treaty itself. He believed that if the Treaty were defeated and his Document Number Two accepted as the alternative, then Britain would not risk a war on what were really minor concessions. His proposal was withdrawn from consideration on a technicality, but it nevertheless hung in the air for many years as de Valera's solution to the impasse.

JOSEPH SWEENEY: When the Treaty debates were in progress I made it known very early in the proceedings that I had made up my mind to vote for the Treaty. Consequently, two of my fellow TDs from Donegal came to me and said that Dev wanted to talk to me about the Treaty. But I said I didn't want to talk to him, that I had formed my own opinion and I would not meet him. They came to me again a second time, but I refused then also.

Then one day I happened to walk into Dev in a corridor when the debates were going on, and he took up a rather schoolmasterly attitude towards me, and said, 'I hear you're voting for the Treaty.' 'That's right,' I said. 'Why?' he said. I said, 'Because I don't believe the difference between your Document Number Two and the Treaty is sufficiently great to plunge the country back into war again.' 'Who told you there was going to be a war?' he said. I told him that I didn't consider Lloyd George's threat of war to be an idle one. 'Document Number Two doesn't enter the question,' he said. 'Oh yes it does,' I said, 'because you introduced it into the debate; consequently it is on the records and is a live issue. Furthermore I hear you have a Document Number Three, and I don't think it's worth it to plunge the country into argument over such small differences.' I turned on my heel then and walked off.

I met a few others at the time too. Margaret Pearse, that was Pearse's sister, attacked me for my position, and so did Sean MacBride, who was even younger than I was, but I held to it because I thought it was the only sensible thing to do at the time.

Collins, ever the pragmatist, saw the Treaty as a major transference of power, a base from which to evolve – a 'stepping stone', as it came to be called – and he seemed desperately anxious to get on with the work. Amid all the invocations, during the debates, of Ireland's dead generations, Collins said, '[Our history] has not been a struggle for the ideal of freedom for 750 years symbolized in the name 'Republic'. It has been a story of slow, steady economic encroachment by England. . . . Nobody notices, but that is the thing that has destroyed our Gaelic civilization.'

TOM BARRY: I would say that the reason Collins signed the Treaty was that he was of the opinion that Lloyd George would have wiped us off the face of the earth if he didn't sign. I would say too that he hadn't finished with the English, and that he could foresee more armed action in four or five years' time. I can imagine Collins's brain working at full speed. Now I didn't know Collins's private thoughts any more than he knew my private thoughts, and I doubt whether anyone did because Mick was an enigma. But I would say that what he had in mind was to build and extend a proper army, to have our own uniforms of a recognized state and become a member of the League of Nations and build up strength here, so after four or five years we'd be in a position in the world where it would be very difficult for the British to stay in *any* part of our country. He said it himself in the Dail, he said, 'This is not freedom, but it will give us a chance to achieve freedom.'

As the Dail preoccupied itself with these considerations, the people of Ireland were coming to accept the Treaty as a *fait accompli*. They dreaded a return to war, and had had dinned into them from every pulpit and leader column in Ireland the Christmas message that the signing of the Treaty was a great day for Ireland.

TOM BARRY: When the Treaty came out the whole press of the country went mad backing it, so we decided that there was another side to it and I drafted half a page notice pointing out the disadvantages of the Treaty. I wanted it to appear as an advertisement in the *Cork Examiner*. But the *Examiner* refused to take this ad and I visited them a few hours later with half a dozen armed men and I said, 'Publish this or you can pay for it.' Actually Collins mentioned this in the Dail debates, about the crowd in Cork that went into the *Examiner* and forced them at the point of a gun to publish something they didn't want to publish. Of course from his point of view he was right, and I accept that it was irregular. But it was something that had to be done. Somebody had to let these facts be known.

Collins was disconcerted at the way the sides were shaping

up. He looked around him and saw against him some of the men he most admired – hard fighting men like Tom Barry – while on his side were every reactionary and supporter of the Establishment in the country. 'I wish we had the bishops against us,' he said ruefully.

Collins tried to preserve a workable structure by proposing to the anti-Treaty faction that they abstain on the vote, thus allowing the Treaty to go through without their consent. They could then take their seats in the new Dail, the pro-Treaty faction having absorbed all the moral opprobrium of compromise while they reserved for themselves the purity of republican opposition. De Valera, however, would not consent. He did not want the Treaty at all and he believed he would win the vote.

The vote was taken on 7 January 1922, with the result that the Treaty was passed by 64 votes to 57.

SEAN HARLING: Just before the vote on the Treaty was taken Liam Mellows came to me and he gave me a flag and he said, 'Sean, as soon as the vote is taken, if it's in favour of the Treaty, go over to O'Connell Street and hoist this flag over the GPO.' It was just about turning dark then and when the vote was taken and went for the Treaty, I did what he said. I went over to the GPO with another lad and we hoisted up the flag. What it was was a republican flag with a small Union Jack stitched into the corner. That was his idea of the meaning of the Treaty.

There were terrible disagreements, of course. Arthur Griffith had said that with the Treaty they were able to march into the British Empire with their heads up, and when he said this someone shouted out, 'Mind you don't trip over the effin' mat.' It was a very rough time. When the vote was taken Dev just dropped down and started to cry. He really genuinely cried.

The Dail now faced the unsavoury task of disestablishing the Republic – a constitutional as well as a moral dilemma –

271

and replacing it with the Free State specified under the Treaty. De Valera resigned the presidency, but his supporters hit on a final manoeuvre which might yet salvage the Republic: a motion to re-elect de Valera. If he won he would be mandated to repudiate the Treaty. The vote was taken and he lost by 60 votes to 58. Collins nominated Griffith to take his place, but de Valera protested against the notion of a President of the Republic pledged, through his adherence to the Treaty, to disestablish the Republic over which he presided, and he led his followers from the Dail. Collins was then appointed to the chairmanship of the Provisional Government, charged with running the country until elections could be held to replace the Republic with the Free State. The status of this Provisional Government, which set up the machinery of state, was of dubious legality at best, but it was by no means the only flexible arrangement of the time.

Collins then plunged into a period of the most intense activity, some of it suitably statesmanlike and some of it more in the spirit of his former improvisations during the war – what his friends called 'irregular' and his enemies called 'illegal'. He had first of all to set up his own effective ministries, and with them to take over the apparatus of administration from the British. He had to establish a functioning judiciary, police force and army and draft a constitution for the new state. He also tried to articulate the aims of this new state to the world through a number of press interviews and even a series of articles in a New York paper. He tried to heal rifts in both the Dail and the IRA through various pacts and stratagems. He made repeated trips to London to confer with the British and also liaised with Sir James Craig.

His problems were interrelated, and had to be solved simultaneously: he could not placate the British without driving de Valera further from him; he could not entice de Valera without bringing down the wrath of the British, and he could make no steps towards a settlement on partition without unity in his own ranks. All of these forces were moving out of control at an increasing rate. The IRA, for instance, was disintegrating. Like the Dail, it was split fairly evenly over the Treaty, and as the British evacuated barracks all over the country and were replaced by local IRA units, they became pro- or anti-Treaty bases, often according to the sentiments of their local commandants. Shots were occasionally exchanged, banks and post offices raided and arms commandeered. In March, pro- and anti-Treaty forces, the latter under the command of Ernie O'Malley and Tom Barry, converged on Limerick and a serious clash was only narrowly averted through the intervention of Liam Lynch.

SEAN HARLING: At one stage during the Treaty debates there was a telegram delivered at the door to me addressed to M. P. Collivet, who was a TD for Limerick. So I went along to give it to him, you know, and he opened it and he said, 'Irregular forces advancing on Limerick. Please advise.' That was what the telegram said. So Paudeen O'Keefe, who was a TD from Cork, he was sitting beside him and he got up and said in a very broad Cork accent to Eoin MacNeill, who was in the chair, 'Point of order, point of order! We have a Treaty here and the whole city of Limerick is in "chowce" ' – that's the way he pronounced it: 'chowce'. There was a great laugh went up then, and later on when I was with Dev in the car going home I asked him what the laughing was all about, and he said to me, 'Sean, the word is chaos.' Funny enough, I didn't know that word then, but it was a very good description of the state of the country at the time.

Collins had in the meantime entered into a pact with Sir James Craig whereby Collins agreed to end the boycott on Belfast instigated earlier in response to the pogroms against Catholics in the North. Craig, for his part, undertook to protect the nationalists within his own jurisdiction and secure the re-employment of Catholic workers driven from the Belfast shipyards. The pogroms nevertheless continued; they had even, through the swelling ranks of the Special Constabulary, become institutionalized. These riots were, as ever, ascribed to 'Unionist fears', but at their root could be found Lloyd George's duplicity over the Boundary Commission. He had led Craig and Collins to believe precisely what he knew they wanted to believe, just as he had done with Carson and Redmond in 1917. Craig had been told that there might be some minor adjustments in the border, and that if anything his government was likely to gain territory. Collins, of course, had been told that the Boundary Commission was simply a device to effect Irish unity. When Collins made known that he expected the transference of Fermanagh, Tyrone and large areas of other counties to Dail jurisdiction, the Unionists entrenched themselves behind the slogan 'Never give an inch'. It was then, as it is now, a question of the right to govern.

Sir Edward Carson had made a conciliatory pre-Treaty speech in which he asserted that, with Ireland in the Empire, the North and South could freely join hands in a united country. Ireland was now in the Empire, however reluctantly. But the regime which Carson had founded in the North was in open war with its nationalist citizens. A new Special Powers Act was put through the Northern parliament; this permitted flogging and death sentences as penalties for arms offences. A and B Specials, armed and uniformed by the British, were leading mobs through nationalist areas, burning and murdering as they went. Sir Henry Wilson was taken on to advise on 'defence'. Thousands of Catholic refugees were evacuating the North for the dubious safety of Dublin and other southern towns.

To Collins the matter of the North became a desperate obsession, and his actions took on an ambivalence with regard to the strict procedure of the law. He registered vehement protests with both Craig and the British Cabinet, but he also arranged with Liam Lynch, the commandant now leading the anti-Treaty section of the IRA, for the transference of arms to Northern IRA units, whatever their attitudes to the Treaty. These were charged with defending Catholics against pogroms and, it should be added, with protecting Protestants living in

Catholic areas against reprisals. Some Volunteers, mesmerizing themselves with hopes for a way out of the impasse in the IRA, entertained the idea that Collins would break the Treaty, unite the IRA and march on the North. But there were no such grand or simple options open to him. He was just acting out of a sense of anguish.

Both Martin Walton and Joseph Sweeney became involved in these plans.

MARTIN WALTON: I was a member of a party that was preparing to go to the North with a consignment of arms. They were mostly guns that we'd got from the British. All the identification numbers were filed off them. This was just before the Civil War started. I don't think anybody of any consequence at that time wanted partition, even Craig. It was only a rotten little crowd who got a taste of power and wanted to hold onto it. They were subsidized by the British government and they still are. I don't know how many of us were to go up there, but I knew over a hundred men myself. But the guns never got there. The bloody Civil War here messed everything up.

JOSEPH SWEENEY: Collins sent an emissary to say that he was sending arms to Donegal, and that they were to be handed over to certain persons – he didn't tell me who they were – who would come with credentials to my headquarters. Once we got them we had fellows working for two days with hammers and chisels doing away with the serials on the rifles. Eventually I met Charlie Haughey's* father in Greencastle, in the hills above Omagh, and he presented the credentials. About 400 rifles in all were taken to the Northern Volunteers by Dan McKenna and Johnny Haughey.

The split in the IRA, meanwhile, was becoming a chasm.

---

*Charlie Haughey became the Irish Taoiseach, or Prime Minister, in 1980. He himself was charged in 1970 with illegally running guns to Northern IRA units to help protect Catholics against pogroms.

Anti-Treaty Volunteers met in Dublin and formed a Republican Executive which repudiated any allegiance to the Minister of Defence or the Chief of Staff and pledged itself to preserve the Republic by resisting any regime which would disestablish it. Their spokesman was Rory O'Connor, and leading members included Liam Lynch, Liam Mellows and Ernie O'Malley. On the night of 13 April 1922, this Republican Executive quietly occupied the Four Courts in Dublin and established their military headquarters there. Apart from Craig's regime in the North and the Crown (which claimed to rule impassively over all), there were now several contending forces seeking allegiance in Ireland: the Provisional Government, the still-existing Dail Eireann, moderate anti-Treatyites who looked to de Valera (still clutching Document Number Two), the Republican Executive in the Four Courts and various joint committees which strained their nerves for a formula of unity. Collins cast lines in all directions in an effort to pull the disparate forces together.

Collins declined to move against the men in the Four Courts, and the British grew increasingly nervous about his reliability over the Treaty. A. W. Cope, still in Dublin Castle, gathered information wherever he could. At one stage he sent for David Neligan.

DAVID NELIGAN: Mick Collins sent me into Oriel House, a kind of intelligence bureau for the new government, after the Treaty, and one day when I was there I was told I was wanted on the phone. It was Cope, and he wanted to see me. So I went along to the Castle and Cope said, 'Neligan, aren't you one of our fellows?' 'Yes, sir,' says I, 'it was yourself that got me transferred from the police into the secret service.' 'I remember that very well,' he said, 'but now I hear you're working for the Provisional Government. How did you get in with that crowd?' 'Well, sir,' says I, 'I saw an advertisement in the *Evening Herald* that there was a meeting of resigned and dismissed police at the Mansion House. At the meeting some of the policemen asked if they would be given their pensions, and the Provisional Government said they couldn't do that, but if they wanted a job they could apply to Oriel House. So I applied and got in.' That was a lie of course, because Oriel House was just for intelligence officers; no extraneous types at all. 'By Jove, that's good,' says Cope. 'If Collins only knew.'

Then he got down to the real purpose of the interview. 'Tell me, Neligan,' says he, 'is Collins in earnest about the Treaty?' This is where I wanted a crystal ball to gape into it. I hadn't seen Collins since he went back to Ireland on the mail boat, and I had no idea if he was in earnest or not. Everything was in a state of flux at the time. But I told him that Collins was in earnest about it.

'Tell me, Neligan,' says he, 'is there going to be a fight?' Here's where I wanted the crystal ball again. I said, 'Yes, sir, I can see it coming.' Then Cope said, 'Who's going to win?' 'Collins is going to win, sir. He's the ablest man they have.' But I couldn't know that, because you had people like Rory O'Connor and Liam Lynch going against him. So Cope said, 'Well I'm damned glad to hear you say it, Neligan. I think the Treaty is a good thing for this country. I'm leaving next week to go back to England.' So I said to him, 'That's fine for you, sir. How about me after risking my life for the British government?' 'Don't say another word, old boy,' says Cope. 'I'll get you your pension. And if that doesn't suit you you can come to India with us.' So I told Mick all about this, but he told me to stay where I was. But the last thing that Cope did was to transfer me to the RIC for the purpose of getting me my pension, and I'm still getting it.

The occupation of the Four Courts had the most tangible results in the North, firing Unionists into a new spate of anti-Catholic rioting. Men of all views in the Dail and IRA knew that their continued disunity left the Northern nationalists at the mercy of the Unionists and their police. A committee composed of both pro- and anti-Treaty TDs struggled

277

vainly for a basis of unity, and finally decided to use the elections that were due to give the people's verdict on the Treaty. From this committee evolved an election pact between Collins and de Valera: Sinn Fein was to stand as a panel in which the 64–57 result on the Treaty vote was to be preserved in the Dail; the Cabinet was to have five pro-Treaty members and four from the anti-Treaty side. The arrangement strained the concept of democracy and allowed no clear verdict on the Treaty, but both Collins and de Valera were above all concerned with stemming the chaos.

Craig instantly went into renewed frenzy at this fresh whiff of Irish republicanism. He publicly disowned the Boundary Commission and his inexhaustible Specials took to the streets yet again. Sir Henry Wilson railed against the pact from platforms and in government corridors, advocating the re-establishment of the Union. Lloyd George, with a cooler, more Machiavellian cast of mind, thought he detected in the pact a nefarious plot to snatch away his victory on the Treaty. If de Valera had been enticed into such a pact, he reasoned, then the lure must have been the promise of a republican constitution, with a revised oath of allegiance sufficiently toned down to allow de Valera and his supporters to participate in government. Collins in the meantime was pressing Lloyd George with singleminded purpose on Britain's responsibility for the lawlessness in the North. Was this not, Lloyd George suspected, a renewal of the Crown/Ulster controversy of the Treaty debates: was not Collins trying to establish the Republic by stealth and bring about a new break on Ulster? Lloyd George decided to defuse the Ulster question by setting up an 'impartial inquiry' – an escape route, like the Boundary Commission – and insist on the letter of the Treaty's law where the oath and the constitution were concerned. Churchill likewise insisted upon a quick election and inflexibility on the clauses of the Treaty, fulminating in the House of Commons about British troops being kept in a state of readiness in the event of the agreement being broken.

This of course doomed the pact and propelled Ireland towards civil war, but that was by no means disadvantageous to the British. It was, indeed, imperialism at its most effective – dividing and ruling, removing the popular base of the revolution and turning it against itself. Britain was again let off the hook as attention was deflected from the North; soon republican resistance would be crushed, by Irish rather than British soldiers, the border would congeal and Britain's flank would remain secure, at least for this round.

Collins had watched Churchill and Lloyd George in the House of Commons from the Strangers' Gallery and saw all hope for the pact disappear. He finally withdrew from it just prior to the election during a campaign speech in Cork. The election duly took place on 16 June 1922; the draft constitution on which the people were to vote had only been issued that morning, and the result was a large pro-Treaty majority. De Valera waited for an invitation to form a coalition which never came.

5

The British Government could not allow the Republican flag to fly in Ireland. A point might come when it would be necessary to tell Mr Collins that if he were unable to deal with the situation, the British Government would have to do so.

British Cabinet minutes, 5 April 1922

A kind of centrifugal force had now replaced leadership in Ireland. Political programmes were abundant, and so was will, but they ceased to exist in the same place. Labour articulated radical socialism and produced outlines, but deemed that to be sufficient. The Republican Executive had only sincerity and the remnants of their old momentum. De Valera achieved abstract symmetry in his formulae for unity, but the force of events broke them apart. Britain and Craig were going their own respective ways unhindered. Collins, seeing this, grew tentative and depressed, his precarious hold on his former self loosening as civil war drew nearer. He and his comrades had all in their own way imagined their perfect Republic, and Collins could now see it metamorphosing into an embittered and lacklustre little province, its north-east corner held by Orange truncheons, the rest, as he said himself, 'besmirched by our towns and villages – hideous medleys of contemptible dwellings and mean shops and squalid public houses'. His emotions, always outsized and exuberant, had become unwieldy. When he met Erskine Childers in a corridor in the Mansion House during the Treaty debates he balled up his fists and wept when told that he and Childers could not be reconciled. Later, when his friend Harry Boland lined up against him, he wrote, 'Harry – it has come to this! Of all things, it has come to this!' Life had been all inspired risk, boisterous camaraderie and purposeful work; it was now all desultory calculation, defensiveness and enmity. The country was on a miserable and protracted slide towards civil war; everyone in Ireland watched it in helpless horror. As early as January 1922, Collins wrote to Kitty Kiernan, the girl from Granard in County Longford to whom he had become engaged, 'I am really and truly having an awful time, and am rapidly becoming quite desperate. Oh Lord, it is honestly frightful.' And matters had become very much worse since January.

Thus faltering, and with his feeling of helplessness about the North growing ever more enormous, he reverted to methods which had succeeded in the past. He believed he saw the figure of Sir Henry Wilson behind the Orange mobs and Special Constabulary – as he had stood behind the policy of terror in Ireland in previous years – and accordingly Wilson was shot dead outside his home in Belgravia on 22 June by two IRA men. They were Joseph O'Sullivan and Reginald Dunne, both former members of the British army; they were quickly captured because O'Sullivan, who had lost a leg at Ypres, could only hobble and Dunne would not leave him.

JOSEPH SWEENEY: I met Mick on the day that Field-Marshal Wilson was shot in a doorway in London, and I said to him, 'Was that an official job?' 'Yes,' he said. I never went any further than that with him, but that is a thing that has been in dispute for several years. I've never said anything about it before, but I think the time has come for not holding out on these things.

Wilson's death was the catalyst which hastened the now virtually inevitable Civil War. The House of Commons shook with righteous indignation, the British public recoiled in horror at a style of killing they thought had passed with the signing of the Treaty, and the government blamed the men in the Four Courts. Lloyd George informed Collins, now conspiring to secure the freedom of O'Sullivan and Dunne from their prison in England, that he could no longer tolerate 'an arsenal in open rebellion in the heart of Dublin'. Churchill was more explicit: he said that unless the Provisional Government removed the Republican Executive, the British would regard it as a breach of the Treaty and would take 'full liberty of action in any direction that may be proper'. Collins simply scowled, 'Let Churchill come over and do his own dirty work.' Macready, however, in an odd reversal of roles, was more circumspect than the politicians; any move by the British, he advised, would simply unite the IRA against them; better let the Provisional Government do it for them.

Griffith had long been in agreement with the sentiments expressed by Lloyd George, though of course he would never openly admit it. Collins, however, prevaricated, asking for evidence connecting Wilson's death with the Four Courts. But neither he nor the Four Courts could hold out much longer in this fashion as the Irish election results had committed them both to action: Collins to the establishment of the Free State regime, the Four Courts garrison to the replacement of that regime by the Republic. Then on Monday, 26 June 1922, the same day that Churchill was making his threats in the House of Commons, a Republican officer named Leo Henderson was despatched from the Four Courts to commandeer some cars from a Dublin garage. They were to be used as part of a convoy heading north to help defend beleaguered nationalists. Henderson, in spite of the fragile truce between the two sides, was arrested by pro-Treaty troops. As a reprisal, the anti-Treatyites captured Collins's Deputy Chief of Staff, 'Ginger' O'Connell. Collins finally consented to act. At 3.40 a.m. on 28 June an ultimatum was sent into the Four Courts ordering the surrender of the Republicans within twenty minutes. Free State troops, as they may now be called, waited beside the 18-pounders loaned to them by Macready, facing the Four Courts across the River Liffey. Collins was in torment, though still hoping for a brief skirmish and then reconciliation.

MARTIN WALTON: I know that before the attack on the Four

Courts Collins asked for a roll call of the men he could depend on if they had to make an attack, and there was quite a large number, seven or eight hundred. But later on when he wanted to throw a ring around the city, a lot of those men refused to do it. They hated the idea of shooting their old comrades. There was a friend of mine whose name was Liam, and Collins came along to him and said, 'My God, Liam,' he said, and he actually had tears in his eyes, 'do you think this gives me any pleasure? Every moment is breaking my heart.' It was a heartbreaking and totally unnecessary war.

The Republicans, as expected, declined to answer the ultimatum and the shelling of the Four Courts began at 4.07 a.m.

MAIRE COMERFORD: I heard the guns the night the Four Courts was attacked. I was sleeping in Maude Gonne MacBride's house, and I must have been awakened by the guns. I got out my bike and went immediately down to the Four Courts and got in. They hadn't any real plan – no arms or ammunition to speak of. Madge Clifford was there, she was cooking. She had bags of flour there, but nothing else; she hadn't the chemical means by which you make bread rise. They had made no proper preparations for a siege.

I ran messages between the Four Courts and other Republican posts in the city. I was carrying in rifle ammunition in a handbag or in my pockets, and I was carrying out – what's that stuff you put in a bomb to make it go off? – detonators, that's it, I was carrying out detonators. Dick Barrett, I think it was, gave them to me in a Gladstone bag, and I carried them out on the carrier of my bicycle. I went along, you know, bumpety-bump along the street, which was much more dangerous than I knew, and I got to a place in York Street. I think it was number 41. There were a lot of people there sitting around a table, including Sean T. O'Kelly – I'm not sure if de Valera was there – but I came in and I said, 'Here are your detonators,' and I put my bag on the table and they all turned pale. I hadn't realized how dangerous these things were, and I suppose I could easily have gone up in smoke. It was just one of the miracles of survival.

I was there in the Four Courts for the big explosion when the shelling started. We were brought up to this great round place under the dome and told to cling onto this parapet, or whatever it was, and then when the explosion came it sort of stretched out your arms to their full length and then they came back again. Then a lot of rubbish fell down on our backs. Liam Mellows was looking after me and about two or three other women, and I said to Liam, 'How long will this fight last?' 'It will last a long time,' he said. 'Will it last five years?' 'Oh, no,' he said, 'it will last much more than that. But they'll come right in the end.'

DAVID NELIGAN: We were neither police nor soldiers at Oriel House, neither fish, flesh nor good red herring, so when the Four Courts fight started I joined Collins's army. Tom Ennis was a general in the Free State Army, and when I heard the shooting I went down to have a gape at what was going on, and I said to Tom, 'Tom, I want to join the army. Will you take me on?' 'Certainly, Dave,' he said. 'I'll make you my military secretary.' I knew as much about being a military secretary as I do about Einstein's theory, but one of the jobs I had to do at the Four Courts was to bring Tom Barry up to Mountjoy prison. He tried to get into the Four Courts dressed up as a nurse. He had a small little face under his costume. I said to him, 'Listen, Barry, don't try any tricks with me. It's not the Duke of Wellington's regiment you're dealing with now. You'll get your head blown off.' 'Don't worry,' he said, 'I won't.' He knew he was up against it. He was a desperate character, you know, and he was a column leader of genius. Collins thought the world of him. After all, he had only a handful of poor devils with rifles, and the Tans and Auxiliaries were armed to the teeth, and he mowed down two lorryloads of them at Kilmichael. By Christ, he did.

SEAN HARLING: On the morning the shelling of the Four Courts started, me father woke me up around six o'clock and he said, 'Sean, there's heavy firing in town. Listen to it.' So I got up and I heard the big gun going off. I dressed meself; I put on me breeches and the leggings of me uniform and me Sam Browne belt, and I put a civilian coat on over it and went out.

Now when a civil war breaks out, it's brother against brother, and there's no saying what way you'd go. It all depended on which crowd you got into. That was the feeling of most of the lads. They were just depressed that there was any split at all, you see. So anyway, when I went out that morning I was in the middle of the Phibsborough Road, and I went up the road instead of down. Had I gone down the road the first group I would have met would have been the Free State side, and I probably would have fought with them. Going up the road I would be going towards O'Connell Street, to the Republicans, and I would fight with them. But my mind wasn't made up as to what I would do until I found meself in the Republican group. So I took part in the Civil War as a Republican.

When I got to the Phibsborough Picture House I saw a British officer coming up on a beautiful new Red Indian motorcycle. I stepped out into the road, put up me hand and he stopped. I told him then that I was taking his motorcycle and he said, 'Would you give me a receipt for it? It's army property.' So I took out a field book, wrote out a receipt and gave it to him. Then before I left him he said, 'Thank God it's between yourselves now.'

For two and a half days Free State gunners chipped away at the walls and dome of the Four Courts, a fine eighteenth-century structure dense with invaluable archives. They were firing at very short range, but the guns were poor and the shells merely shrapnel.

JOSEPH SWEENEY: When the British realized that there was a division here over the Treaty they concentrated on fomenting it. Churchill was always impatient. He was sending all kinds of ultimata here to our government, trying to force us to attack the other side, to take the Four Courts, to do this, that and the other thing. They even handed over artillery to do the job, but they were guns with no sights and a very small amount of ammunition. I think they had the idea that we might turn it against them.

The Republicans finally surrendered their post on 30 June and Rory O'Connor, Liam Mellows, Ernie O'Malley and many others were arrested and taken to prisons which had housed several of them when they had been captured by the British only a year or two before. Throughout the siege, however, Republicans in the Dublin Brigade were taking up new posts all around the city, principally in O'Connell Street.

SEAN HARLING: I got into the Parnell Monument and met a fellow there called Sean Saunders, and he told me he was reporting to Barry's Hotel. So I went along there and I met Barney Mellows, who was Adjutant-General of the Fianna then, and he asked me to mobilize the Dublin Brigade. I went down and took over quite a number of buildings at the bottom of Parnell Street, and I burrowed from North Great George's Street, burrowed right through the shops into the bank at the corner. There was loads of money in it when I got there and, bloody fool that I was, I sent a despatch rider off to the Drumcondra Road to get the bank manager so he could bundle up the money and take it away for safety.

The new Republican posts were also burned and battered into submission and the Republicans surrendered the remain-

der of their central Dublin posts by 6 July. On 5 July, following the surrender of his garrison in the Granville Hotel, Cathal
Brugha emerged alone from the smoke, carrying a revolver in
each hand, and faced a line of Free State troops. In 1916 he
had stayed behind alone in the invested South Dublin Union,
his bullet-riddled frame propped up against a wall, bawling
out patriotic songs; he was austere, ascetic, an ecclesiastical
candlemaker by profession, and by temperament an espouser,
like Pearse, of the dark romance of heroic death. He was
brought down under Free State bullets fired from British guns,
and died in hospital two days later, thus reinforcing the twisted
analogy with 1916. Once again gutted and collapsed buildings
lay under rising smoke along both sides of O'Connell Street.
The Four Courts, gaping shell-holes scattered along its walls,
was a mess of blackened, twisted pipes and smouldering documents. Meanwhile, Churchill, in the House of Commons,
indicated the government's 'interest and sympathy' but piously
pronounced that it was 'not our business at all'.

The Civil War had by now spread to the country, as opposing troops were shaken by the shelling of the Four Courts
out of the long period of uneasy hostility which had followed
the signing of the Treaty.

JOSEPH SWEENEY: The first I heard of the opening of hostilities in the Civil War was when Sean MacEoin was visiting
Donegal. He was a senior officer in the Free State Army at
this time. He had recently been married and was spending
his honeymoon in Donegal and he'd met an accident. His
car had gone off the road down into a ravine and he sent a
telegram to me to help him out. So we got his car out for
him and repaired it and they gave him a civic reception in
Letterkenny. We were marching down the main street behind the principals when a despatch rider came up to me
from my headquarters and handed me a despatch to the
effect that the Four Courts had been attacked that morning.
So we escorted MacEoin out of our area and we then began
the task of taking back bases that the anti-Treaty forces

were occupying. That evening we took Finner Camp, and after that we took Ballyshannon Barracks to leave the way clear to the south. We attacked a barracks in Buncrana and another place down near the border, Bridgend, and we proceeded to dislodge them wherever they went until they retreated to the very heart of the county, where they set up their headquarters. I cornered a couple of their fellows who had become separated from their main body and were in a house down near the border. I spoke to them then, and they said they were very sorry that hostilities had started between us, and asked if they could be given safe conduct so they could meet with their superior officers. So that was done and I also arranged to meet them the next day to discuss things. So I went down with another fellow completely unarmed, and instead of meeting Charlie Daly, who was the opposition OC, I met his whole column, about thirty men, and we had a debate there. I think we must have talked for about three and a half hours, but we didn't get anywhere and in the end I just had to say, 'It looks as though we're going to have to regard one another as enemies from now on.'

Republicans who fled Dublin consolidated their forces under Liam Lynch in the south and west, where they were most strong. De Valera, his political base entirely eroded, had enlisted as a private in Dublin and now hastened to Clonmel to join Lynch. Republican troops were deployed throughout Munster to hold a line from Waterford to Limerick. But the Free State regime was solidifying, their regrets and conciliatory efforts fading, and Collins was persuaded by Mulcahy to leave his desk and go into uniform. The Republican line would not hold, though there was no joy in breaking it.

JOHN L. O'SULLIVAN: Feelings ran very high here in Cork and when the split appeared in the IRA it got bigger and deeper as time went on. One of the worst features of it was that it meant a second recruiting by both sides of forces that weren't engaged before in the struggle, and that made it even more bitter. A lot of us here who were in favour of the Treaty had to go on the run, because the general body of the Volunteers around Cork were anti-Treaty, and they had taken over barracks and given us a pretty rough time. But their strategy was badly based, because once they left the headquarters of the country, Dublin, they might as well have accepted defeat. When they took the war to the country they thought they could hold Munster, and they had a line from Waterford to Limerick where they concentrated all their forces to meet the advancing pro-Treaty forces coming down. But their commanders hadn't the military situation summed up right, because the National Army came around the coast and back behind their line and landed forces at different places along the coast – at Union Hall, at Tralee, at Passage West and Kenmare and Fenit – and, wherever they landed, people that supported the Provisional Government, Michael Collins and Arthur Griffith, flocked to their assistance.

I joined them and I had the great privilege of serving under Sean Hales. He was a wonderful man. I remember he had a meeting with us when we were grouping and organizing in Skibbereen, and he said, 'I'll pick my own officers now for our column tomorrow,' and he said to me, 'John L.,' he said, 'you take charge of our advance guard.' That was my job, I was the first into the towns we took from the anti-Treaty forces. Hales was a truly great man. I keep his picture here in the house. Next to Collins I think he is the best organizer I have ever met. We left Skibbereen on foot, and I remember he marched with me at the head of the column as we went to Clonakilty. We took Clonakilty and marched on to Courtmacsherry, and from a boat there we got in an 18-pound gun and four gunners and a Lancia armoured car and we hit off straight to Bandon.

The other side had us under observation all day and they brought all their forces between Bandon and us. When we came to within about three or four miles of Bandon, I was out in front and it was getting hard to advance, and Hales sent for me and he said, 'What's the position?' I told him, 'There's a wood over there,' I said, 'and there's very heavy fire coming from it. We've tried to outflank it but we can't because they seem to be extending in front of us.' So he said, 'Bring up the gun.'

And the 18-pounder was brought up. 'Put it in position,' he said. 'Now, do you see that wood? That's our target,' he said. The gunners were there, ready, obeying orders. He said, 'Now load it with a blank shell.' And someone said, 'Are you mad? A blank shell?' 'I'm not mad,' he said. 'A blank shell will do. I don't want to kill any of the poor devils.' They're the words he used. I'll never forget it. He had two brothers fighting on the other side. So the blank shell was fired, and it was the first time that artillery was used in County Cork, and it had the desired effect on the others because they retreated. It did just as much good as if it had been a live shell.

Now that will give you an idea – although a lot has been written and spoken about atrocities and about high feelings and about assaults and executions of prisoners, here at least was a man who had vision. He had no wish to annihilate anybody; he was a man of peace. He was only doing the job he was put to do, and he wanted to do it with the least loss of life on both sides. He never stopped, he kept us on the move from the time we started until we took over every town and every village and every stronghold of the others in the area. But all the time you could see that he was a man of peace.

After we took Bandon we went on for Kinsale. They had a bridge blown up there, a metal bridge, and we had no way of getting in except by boat. We had maybe a mile of river and bay to get across, and Hales said to me, 'Crowd into the boats,' he said, 'and get across and try to capture the bridgehead on the other side.' So in we got and when we were halfway across they opened fire on us from the top of the hill. And they riddled the bloody place. The fellow sitting beside me got six holes from one bullet – through his arm, through his hip and through his ankle. When the firing started the three fellows who were rowing, they were fishermen, they ducked down and let go of the oars and we were sitting ducks. The bullets were coming around us in the water just as though you'd thrown gravel onto it, and they were hitting the boat, taking chips off it. How we got out alive I don't know, but two of us grabbed the oars and pulled, and we hadn't gone two lengths of the boat before we were as safe as we are sitting here now, because their line of fire was obscured once we got in under the hill. So we landed then, and I remember taking the wounded fellow out in my arms up to a house. As a matter of fact he only died a few years ago. I was at his funeral. So anyway, we took Kinsale and headed back to Bandon.

Towns continued to fall to Free State troops in rapid succession, until Cork itself was finally taken on 10 August 1922, leaving the Republicans a more disoriented, piecemeal force. Collins made an inspection tour of the south and west, but was halted in Tralee by a message from Dublin. Arthur Griffith, exhausted from overwork and grieved at the catastrophe steadily devouring the ideal he had helped to found, had died; he had entered himself into a nursing home for a few days' rest and, washing his face on the morning of 12 August, a blood vessel had given way in his brain.

Collins returned to Dublin and, at the head of the state funeral, he helped to carry Griffith's coffin. He passed the next few days in Dublin, sullen, ill and harbouring presentiments of his own death. His friend Harry Boland had been shot dead by Free State troops in a hotel in Skerries a fortnight earlier. O'Sullivan and Dunne, in spite of his labours, had just been hanged for the shooting of Sir Henry Wilson. The ranks of his army were filling with former enemies from the RIC and British army.

He determined, however, to complete his southern tour, this time to make another attempt at peace. He sent Frank

Thornton ahead to arrange a meeting in Clonmel with Liam
Lynch; only old Volunteers on either side were to be present
at the meeting. Thornton, however, was ambushed and shot
up *en route* and, apparently delirious, was taken to hospital.

Collins nevertheless left Dublin as planned. Joseph Sweeney
visited him beforehand.

JOSEPH SWEENEY: Collins had always made it quite clear to
those of us who were more or less just playing at being
soldiers what attention to duty meant, and as time went on
his control over the fighting men became absolutely complete. Then when the split came he was all the time for
conciliation, and he was most of all anxious to unite the
fellows who were fighting men. He had a great regard for
them and he couldn't bear to see them divided. All through
the Civil War he was optimistic that he would be able to
settle with the other crowd, that he would be able to do it
by personal persuasion, which I myself thought was a very
mistaken idea.

I remember going to see him at Portobello Barracks in
Dublin, and on my way there I saw a car, a very unusual
type of car with Collins's personal driver looking after it.
That was Joe Hyland. So I went over to him and I said,
'Where did you get this yoke?' 'It belongs to the Big Fellow,'
he says. It was a Vauxhall with a long narrow body, and it
had no covering of any kind on the top. The only protection
was a windscreen in front. Then he said, 'He's going down
to west Cork.' I said, 'What?' and I immediately hared off
to headquarters where I met Mick, and I said, 'I hear you're
going to west Cork.' 'I am,' he says. I said, 'I don't know
what you're up to, but I would advise you not to go.' 'Ach,'
he said, 'nobody would shoot me in my own county.' So I
said, 'Well, Michael, I'm leaving you with the admonish-
ment that you should not go.' And that was the last time I
saw him alive.

Collins went first of all to Limerick and then on to Cork

city, where he spent the night of 20 August in the Imperial Hotel. Some time that evening he heard from a friend that a young Free State soldier named Mick Collins had died in a rush on a machine-gun post in Rochestown. Collins recorded in the notebook in which he had meticulously outlined his programme for the next two days the words: 'Michael Collins shot dead.'

Collins left the Imperial Hotel at 6.15 a.m. in a convoy under the command of Emmet Dalton. They went to Macroom, Bandon, Clonakilty and then to Sam's Cross, where Collins stopped to see his brother and other members of his family. There he bought his escort a few pints in a pub owned by a relative of his. They then moved on to Rosscarbery and Skibbereen, before turning back to Bandon, where they arrived in the early evening.

JOHN L. O'SULLIVAN: There were about a hundred of us who marched into Bandon, and we were to stay there for the night before moving on to Enniskean, Ballineen and Dunmanway. We were standing outside this hotel there – it's now the Munster Arms – and Commandant Hales was getting in touch with the military garrison there to put us up for the night. A staff officer came out and said that the general inside had sent him out for John L. O'Sullivan and Maurice Collins, who was there with me. And who was it but Michael Collins. We didn't know he was in the area at all because communications at that time were terrible. So we went in and there he was, sitting at a table, and I remember his welcome for us and how glad he was to see us and that we were making headway. Then he said, 'I'm down here to finish the Civil War.' I didn't know what he was doing at the time, but as far as I could make out from what he said and the way he said it he was down there to meet somebody from the opposing camp, that he was looking for some way of coming to terms. I've discussed it with many people since then, General Tom Barry and others, and I'm certain this is what he was there for, though I never

293

found out who he was going to meet. He asked then about which roads were open to the east, to get back to Cork, and we gave him the position and he said he was going back the Crookstown way. We left him then, and that was his last night because he was killed shortly afterwards.

The convoy then set off for Cork via the Macroom road. Dusk was falling as they entered Beal na mBlath, a largely deserted valley whose name means Mouth of the Flowers. A scout on a motorcycle up ahead had discovered an upturned dray cart on the road and had just turned around to warn the convoy when fire was opened up from the surrounding hills. Dalton shouted, 'Drive like hell!' but Collins ordered the driver to stop. He jumped out onto the road, took cover and began firing back. There was a lull as the ambush party drew back; Collins moved out from behind his cover, looked around him and took up a position further up the road. It was there that he was hit, a small bullet, perhaps a ricochet, entering his skull behind his right ear. Dalton rushed to him and took him up in his arms, blood and brain matter dripping onto the road from Collins's wound. Within a few minutes he was dead.

The news made its way throughout Ireland, reaching old friends and new enemies. Yeats wrote in a letter to a friend, 'Then again when the news came in of Michael Collins's death, one of the Ministers recited to the Cabinet . . . the entire *Adonais* of Shelley.' Fragmented and despairing as the country now was, it was briefly united in a moment of appalled grief. Nothing at that time more clearly revealed the catastrophe of the Civil War – this vivid character, the prime mover of the now truncated Irish revolution, brought down by Irishmen a few miles from his home.

JOSEPH SWEENEY: I was back in my own headquarters in Donegal when I heard he'd been killed. I was wakened up about seven o'clock in the morning and handed a despatch that had just come in on the radio, and I nearly fell on the spot because not only was he one of my commanders but he was a very old friend at that time. I felt stunned like everybody else, and I felt a sense of desolation because he was the dynamic force behind everything that happened during the period of 1919, '20, '21, and I felt terribly depressed because I couldn't see anybody who could step into his shoes and I could foresee divisions arising out of his going.

He was a most outstanding man. He had the brains not alone for military matters, but for high finance, for local government administration, for anything he turned his mind to. He always gave you an answer on the spot. There was never any quibble or delay. The side I liked about him best was the way he looked after the dependants of people who were in trouble – fellows who were arrested, who were on the run, who were in hospital or in any way couldn't help their families. There was no social welfare then, and he never forgot one of these people. When de Valera was away he used to take his life in his hands by going out to Greystones to see if Mrs de Valera was all right. That was what we called a West British suburb, full of people given over to the British way of life, and he used to go there by train amongst all these potential informers.

He could have a good night's fun too. He'd have gettogethers and singsongs in places like Vaughan's Hotel, and when a fellow like me would appear from the country he'd always make sure to take you around and introduce you to the other fellows. He'd be the life and soul of the party then. He used to get up and recite 'Kelly and Burke and Shea'. The first time I heard this thing was in Stafford prison. Everybody used to roar. He'd revert completely to his west Cork accent when he recited it. I don't think we'll ever have his like again, someone who could knit this country together into such an efficient unit as he did. Fellows would have died on the spot for him, and that went right down into the lower ranks.

MARTIN WALTON: I was ill in bed, and my mother came in. She had a 'stop press'. 'Oh my God,' she said, 'they've killed Michael Collins.' Stab. Absolute pain. I fell back in the bed. Unbelievable. Utterly unbelievable.

MAIRE COMERFORD: I was in Cork myself when Collins was killed. I had been sent there with a message for de Valera. I was all over the county looking for him, going from place to place. I came to a crossroads one morning and I could see some women standing around. To my amazement one of them said, 'Hello, Miss Comerford.' This was a young Protestant teacher, a very beautiful woman I had known in Wexford. Then she said, 'Did you know Michael Collins was shot down that road last night?' That was the first I heard of it. I didn't know enough at the time to have been sorry about it; I thought he'd given away so much. I suppose I might even have been glad, like the woman who said when she heard about it, 'Just on the ninth day of my novena.' She must have been praying for his death. But I remember hearing later that Ernie O'Malley, one of the Republican leaders, was staying at my friend Sheila Humphrey's house in Aylesbury Road in Dublin, and after she read about it in the *Irish Times* she rushed upstairs to Ernie's room and said, 'Collins has been killed in an ambush.' And Ernie said, 'That's not good news. That's very bad news.'

SEAN HARLING: I was arrested on a Sunday morning, the 3rd of September 1922, and who was it arrested me but Joe O'Reilly, Collins's ADC. I was going to Mass and this Crossley touring car came over Portobello Bridge and I heard this, 'Stop! Halt! Stop!' you see. It was Joe shouting to the driver to stop, so I went into this turning and Joe came running after me and said, 'Sean, don't pull. I'm not pulling.' He meant pulling a gun. The very next thing he said to me was, 'Wasn't it terrible about Mick?' So says I, 'Joe, it's the terriblest blow I ever got.' That's how it was. You'd be coming up against your friends all the time.

TOM BARRY: I saw a most remarkable thing. There was

1000 of us, 1000 Republican prisoners in Kilmainham Jail, and I was in one of the top cells with Oscar Traynor, the OC of the Dublin Brigade at the time. We heard a hubbub outside the cell and we came out. Now if you were ever a jailbird you'd know that there were wires stretched across to prevent poor devils of prisoners from jumping down and finishing it off quick. So I looked down through this and I saw a most remarkable sight: there were about seven or eight hundred men and they all down on their knees saying the rosary for the repose of the soul of Michael Collins. One time he was their leader against the British; then he was commander in chief of the enemy forces. It was completely illogical, but it showed a respect for the man. It was something that could only happen in a civil war.

JOHN L. O'SULLIVAN: Though we were in the area itself we never even heard about Collins's death for two days. We left Bandon for Dunmanway the morning after we met him and we were in Dunmanway for two days before we heard this terrible news. I'll never forget – the one thing I'll never forget in my life – was the feeling everybody had when they heard of his death. Everybody was stunned, everybody was speechless, everybody was shocked. People in the army and ordinary people, tears came to their eyes. It was as though life had finished for us, and the whole population of the country, city and town, felt they had lost their friend. The other side, too, they respected him and loved him, and Tom Barry was a witness to that inside Kilmainham Jail. I don't think in my time, and I've seen a fair bit of life, that I've seen the news of a death hit so hard. With all his escapes through the years, we thought he was invulnerable to any bullet. I had heard the older people say that Parnell was mourned in a very special way, but I know that in my lifetime, through the whole breadth of this country, more people grieved over the loss of Michael Collins than over any other human being since then. He was our one hope, he was the man to unify us, and now that he was dead we felt lost without a leader, and we felt the country had got the worst blow that any country ever got.

Dalton and his men went on a 'nightmare ride', as he called it, to Cork, propping up Collins's shattered head on his shoulder. The body was then put on board the SS *Classic* for the trip to Dublin. Sean Kavanagh was among the large crowd waiting at the North Wall.

SEAN KAVANAGH: The last time I saw Collins alive was when I was in Portobello Barracks to receive my orders. This was only a week or ten days before he died, and he seemed rather depressed and preoccupied. He was very anxious to bring the Civil War to an end, and I don't think his heart was ever in it. I was in Newbridge then when I heard of his death. I think I got the news of it in the morning paper. It was dreadful. I felt as though the end of the world had come to us then. I was just heartbroken. I think some of the Republican prisoners took it even harder than we did, because Mick was still the big man, they still looked up to him, and I suppose they thought he was the best person around to solve things.

I went up to Dublin right away then, along with a lot of other people. I was at the North Wall when his remains were brought in by sea. They couldn't bring him up by rail because the line was broken in so many places. They took him to St Vincent's Hospital for a post-mortem examination, and one of the men concerned in this was Oliver Gogarty. I was standing with a few other fellows from the army on the steps leading into the hospital and Gogarty came out and asked me to go down to Albert Power, the sculptor, and bring him back to do a death mask for Collins. So another fellow and myself borrowed a car and woke up Albert Power at three o'clock in the morning, and he came down to do the death mask. That was the last errand I did for poor Mick.

The two sides now faced each other with the only effective bridge between them gone, exposed in their political aimlessness and grimly preparing themselves for the final phase of the war. The Republicans had lost all political and military initiative: Lynch had ceased to listen to de Valera, and the rest simply stood resolutely by the vanishing, undefined Republic; dislodged from their bases and harried around the country by artillery and growing numbers of Free State troops, they were thrown back on a kind of anti-Black-and-Tan campaign in miniature – selective shootings, tiny flying columns and the disruption of communication. This time, however, they lacked the discreet silence and safe houses which had once allowed them to move so freely around the country. They had a measure of sympathy, but very little active support; the balladeers were among the few who kept the faith.

TOM BARRY: When I escaped from Gormanstown prison camp, where I had been transferred, I found the place in a state of chaos. I became Director of Operations, and I did my best to try and contain the Free State and take back some of the towns, which was a tough struggle given the state of morale and the terrible disorganization of our side. But I took the town of Bandon off them and I took the town of Enniskean. Then I went on to Tipperary and took Carrick-on-Suir off them and then moved over to south Tipperary and Kilkenny and some towns were handed over to us there. I brought troops into Limerick and took over hotels and surrounded the Free State troops on a Sunday morning as they were on parade and said, 'Drop your guns.' Then we got 800 rifles off the Civic Guard at the Curragh. It looked for a while that we were on the comeback militarily. De Valera said to me, 'It's a pity you weren't out earlier, Tom. You'd have made a better job of the line fighting.' I said, 'Hang it all, if I had my way there would be no line fighting. It would have been fought out in Dublin in three days and we would have shifted them.' The minute the Four Courts was attacked, anti-Treaty troops should have been brought in from the south and the west and we should have taken them on in Dublin city. Dublin might have been left in a shambles, but at least it would have been over. As it was, we hadn't a hope.

Another thing that made our position impossible was the build-up of the Free State Army from Irish regiments of the British army. They had been disbanded as part of the Treaty arrangements and sent back to Ireland. The Munster Fusiliers, the Leinsters, the Dublins, the Connaught Rangers, all these regiments were disbanded at Oswestry in Wales, they were put into civvies and sent across from Holyhead to Ireland, where they were met by Free State lorries and brought to Beggar's Bush barracks and put into green uniforms. Now some of these were probably decent men driven by hardship to join the British army. But others were violently anti-Irish and some had left Ireland in very unfavourable conditions – they were driven out because of their having done things against the Republican movement. We might well have been able to defeat the Free State until this lot came over, but after that it was impossible.

Following the deaths of Griffith and Collins, the Free State constituted itself politically under W. T. Cosgrave, with Kevin O'Higgins as Minister of Home Affairs; Mulcahy took over the army. The new regime lacked all sense of equivocation about the Civil War and hardened itself for the single task of suppressing the Republican opposition and restoring order. A Special Powers Act moved with little resistance through the lopsided Dail: amnesty was to be offered in return for a surrender, but after 15 October 1922 unauthorized possession of a weapon was punishable by death. The ghostly parallels with the earlier struggle against the British were becoming complete: the besieged Four Courts was a mock-GPO of Easter Week, the guerrilla campaign a pale derivation of 1920–21 and the draconian measures of the Free State were reminiscent of Maxwell, French and Macready.

Erskine Childers was one of the first to be arrested under

the new dispensation. Childers, author of the highly regarded
novel *The Riddle of the Sands*, had undergone a long metamorphosis from service in the British army and civil service,
through cautious espousal of Home Rule for Ireland and into
the most inveterate hatred of British imperialism and incor-
ruptible devotion to the Irish Republic. As the Republican
Director of Propaganda he had been an unrelenting critic of
the Free State regime, whose ministers – O'Higgins in particular – had conceived the deepest distaste for him. He was
arrested on 10 November in the house of his cousin, Robert
Barton.

MAIRE COMERFORD: I often used to stay out at Robert
Barton's house. This was Glendalough House, a big mansion
associated in the past with the Plantation of Ireland by
non-Irish people but which had become as much Republican
territory as any cottage belonging to people who had helped
during the revolution. Robert Barton was interned by the
Free State government and his sister was involved with the
Republican courts and the processes of government which
were being overturned by the counter-revolution. This one
cold, bleak autumn night Erskine Childers arrived there.
He was twice the Bartons' cousin, because both their parents
were cousins. He was a very tired and sick man, and he was
given a hot bath and fed and put to bed. I was driving a
Republican staff car at the time, and I went back to Dublin.
When I got back there de Valera was very anxious about
Erskine Childers's health, and he asked me to try and keep
him safe and find a place where he could rest. I had some
errands to do around the country and by the time I got back
I found he'd been arrested about an hour or two before.
Normally it would have been very hard to surprise Dulci-
nella Barton because she had very acute hearing and she
could always hear people moving about on the gravel path
outside. But the Free State troops who came to raid the
place that night were led by a man who had been a guest in
the house himself when he was on the run in the war against

the British. So he knew all about this and he brought his men around to the side of the house where there wasn't any gravel path. He also knew that the dairy maid would go out early in the morning, and when she did he just brought his men in through the open door. They surprised Childers in his bedroom. They took him down to Portobello Barracks.

During Erskine Childers's trial four Republicans were executed for possession of arms. Childers too had a gun when arrested – a small revolver given to him as a souvenir by Michael Collins. He was shot at dawn in Beggar's Bush barracks on 24 November 1922.

Reprisals of increasing horror were now taken up. On 30 November Liam Lynch issued an order that all Free State TDs who had voted for the emergency legislation under which Childers was executed were to be shot on sight. Accordingly, on 7 December 1922, Sean Hales and Padraic O Maille, both TDs on their way in an open car to the Dail, were ambushed in the street and shot. Hales died and O Maille was seriously wounded.

JOSEPH SWEENEY: All of the pro-Treaty TDs were served with notices that we were under sentence of death, and it was proved that they meant business when Sean Hales and Padraic O Maille were fired on. Hales was killed and O Maille was very badly wounded. I remember being in the government buildings, which were in the same place as they are now, and the whole place was surrounded with barbed wire. The whole government and headquarters of the army were there. W. T. Cosgrave was there and I remember on the Sunday morning we had Mass on the premises, and W.T. was a very pious man, he was going around with a rosary in his hands and getting everybody out of bed to go to Mass. I got fed up with the place that night. I said, 'I don't want to stay here any more, I had enough of jail in my time.'

So I cleared out and went to a hotel in O'Connell Street

where a number of TDs were staying. I was sharing the room with another fellow from Donegal, and I came late into the room and the first thing I did was to pull out my gun and stick it under the pillow. 'What's that?' he says. I said, 'That's a gun.' 'What do you want that for?' 'I want it to defend my life if anybody attacks me.' He got up then without saying another word, put on his clothes and went down to the manageress to get changed to another room. That was the kind of set-up we had at the time.

The Free State government's reprisals for the slaying of Hales came swift and stern. The Cabinet went into consultation and selected four prominent Republicans, one from each of Ireland's provinces, for execution. They were Rory O'Connor, Liam Mellows, Joe McKelvey and Dick Barrett, all of them taken prisoner after the surrender of the Four Courts. Mellows was a leader of great promise, praised by Connolly in 1916 for his political perspicacity. O'Connor had been best man at the wedding of Kevin O'Higgins,* the last Cabinet minister to give his reluctant consent to the executions. They were shot at dawn on 8 December in the yard of Mountjoy Prison.

JOHN L. O'SULLIVAN: The killing of poor Hales brought on the executions of the four men from the other side. One of them was Dick Barrett, and he was one of the finest fellows you could meet, a grand man. He was one of those that escaped from Spike Island when I was there. It was very hard on all of us to think that he had been executed, and I can assure you that we all regretted it. But war is war and these things are happening and have happened and will

---

*O'Higgins – a friend of Yeats called by Churchill, 'a figure from the antique cast in bronze' – was the architect of the Free State's ruthless measures. He himself said, 'No man can expect to live long who has done what I have done.' He lasted until 1927, when he was shot dead in a Dublin street.

happen again. I don't think anybody among us wanted the Civil War. It was probably forced on us a bit. But I thought that once we made the decision we had to carry on after that. We thought we were right, and I still think we were right, and I still think we had the majority of the people as the polls proved at the time. But it was a tragic war. And it was brother against brother. I remember I had one fellow with me in my column and his brother was on the other side and he was arrested in Bandon. Three or four of us went up with this fellow to Bandon to get his brother released, because as terrible as it was, brotherly love is really above civil war.

Internment had also been introduced, and there were massive arrests, far more than the prisons could accommodate. Several internment camps had been set up. Sean Kavanagh became military governor at one of them at the Curragh. Sean Harling was held in one. Tom Barry, who had nearly made his way out of Mountjoy in a Free State Army coat, was later transferred to Gormanstown camp and, on his first day there, crawled out beneath some barbed wire to freedom. Maire Comerford, Director of Propaganda for Cumann na mBan, had been arrested following a failed attempt to kidnap Cosgrave, and was put into another makeshift compound at the North Dublin Union, where she too escaped.

MAIRE COMERFORD: I escaped from the North Dublin Union. We had been moved there from Mountjoy, and I only had to take one look at the place to see that I could get out. The Free State didn't know how to make barbed-wire entanglements at that time. They were beginners at the machinery of oppression. They had put poles, strong poles into the ground at a distance out from the wall. And then from the top of the wall they stretched rigid barbed wire down to the poles, and they had other poles which had wires all around them. The result of it all was that they had constructed a kind of ladder for us. I couldn't climb the wall without this barbed wire thing to help me. It was so obvious and so tempting that I took a long time to do anything about it because I thought there must be a snare or a trap somewhere. But there wasn't; as far as they were concerned they had a barbed-wire entanglement. City people were very reclutant to do anything about it, to escape. But I was country bred, in the sense of having been brought up free, and when we were kids if you couldn't climb a fence someone threw your hat over it. Then we had to climb it because if you didn't come home with your hat there would have been a terrible row. So my childhood was very good training for escaping from this thing. I got over it quite easily.

But many more were successfully held: some 13,000 by the time hostilities dwindled into a kind of false peace. Throughout the winter the Free State government increased its efforts to wipe out Republican resistance. In the single month of January 1923, there were thirty-four executions. Morale, never very high, ebbed away as the old sobriety and discipline gave way to drunkenness and ghoulish killings. In Kerry nine Republican prisoners were tied in a circle and blown up with a land mine. Beatings in prisons became habitual. Life was at its cheapest.

There were, however, many former Volunteers in the Free State army appalled at the breaches in discipline and depressed by the executions. One of these was Joseph Sweeney.

JOSEPH SWEENEY: We captured Charlie Daly, who was OC of the Republicans up in my area in Donegal, and I remember there wasn't a shot fired in this operation. We heard that his column was up near Muckish Pass in some houses up there and we got them just as they were going to bed.

The terrible thing then was that Daly had to be executed. We had received word from Dublin that anyone captured carrying arms was to be court-martialled and sentenced to death. I had to do the job myself, to order a firing party for the execution, and it was particularly difficult because Daly and I had been very friendly when we were students, and it is an awful thing to kill a man you know in cold blood, if you're on level terms with him. Trading shots with a man in a battle is one thing, but an execution is something else altogether. I wasn't present at the execution myself, but to make sure there was no foul-up the firing party were all picked men, and they were told that they were to put them out of pain as quickly as possible. At that time you had this barbarous system that the Provo-Marshal had to go along afterwards to deliver the *coup de grâce* through the heart. I didn't agree with it, but they were orders and you had to do it.

I suppose by that stage we'd all acquired a certain amount of hardness. Personally I'd stayed alive through Easter Week and the Anglo-Irish War, and during the Civil War I drove about all over the country in an open car and walked about openly in Dublin, where I might have been assassinated at any time. By that stage of the proceedings, during the Civil War, you didn't know where you were from one day to the next and you developed this attitude where you didn't care tuppence. It sort of heightened your perception. You were all the time on guard, you didn't take anything at its face value at all in those days – you simply made sure you were in a position to fight back at any time. I suppose that did induce a certain amount of hardness.

It's very hard to describe a war among brothers. It was fierce and it was atrocious. You had family against family and brother against brother, and I've tried to wipe it out of my mind as much as possible because it is not pleasant to think about.

By May, the total of official executions had reached seventy-seven and de Valera, the last remaining principal player of the 1916–23 period, issued an order to Republican soldiers to dump arms.

6

Following the suspension of hostilities, Ireland passed, perhaps with some relief, into a kind of dreamless, if sporadically troubled, sleep. Politics steadily lost its tension, its access to higher ideals as the two regimes, North and South, solidified themselves into the most inward-looking parochialism. The Catholic Church, with all its social conservatism, went into the ascendant as the guardian of education and public morals in the South, while the North, through public pronouncement and sectarian legislation, celebrated itself as a one-party Protestant state. All over Ireland the administration, legislation and judiciary – down to the wigs on the judges' heads – grew into the image of their British counterparts. Art, particularly literary art, which had shaped the national movement in the years between the turn of the century and the Easter Rising, diverged from politics and ceased to bear malice to the established order, or else was suppressed. The IRA continued to pursue their old methods in desultory fashion, but they now lacked all context; the people, who had lived too long with the strains of revolution, had given their assent to peace, if not wholly to the Free State, and politically the IRA had little to offer that could not be found in the campaign promises of the more constitutionally minded parties.

1932, a decade after the ratification of the Treaty, was a telling year in this process of atrophication, and was marked by four significant events: the re-emergence of Eamon de Valera as head of government, a massive display of national Catholic piety in Dublin called the Eucharistic Congress, an outbreak of rioting in the North which astonished everybody by uniting Catholics and Protestants – perhaps for the first time since 1798 – over the issue of unemployment, and, finally, the unveiling of Northern Ireland's government buildings at

Stormont. Each of these, and all they implied, worked out their separate destinies. The rapprochement between Northern Catholics and Protestants had the briefest life of all: it was rent apart by pressure on the one hand from the Catholic Church, who said the riots were Marxist-inspired, and on the other by the Orange Order, who said they were a republican plot, and rioting in the North relapsed into bleak sectarianism by 1935. Stormont, on the other hand – with its imposing neo-classical frontage, its elevated setting, its wide tree-lined approach at the beginning of which stood, as a kind of sentry, a life-sized statue of Carson raising an admonitory finger in the air – conveyed, if anything, *permanence*, and it safely housed a grimly humourless and inflexible regime until its suspension by the British government in 1972. The Catholic triumphalism on display at the Eucharistic Congress realized itself in 1937, when the Free State's new constitution officially acknowledged the 'special position' of the Catholic Church in Ireland (a clause which was finally removed by referendum in 1972).

De Valera's political resurrection was the most complex of the four events of that year. In 1923 he had found himself adrift amidst the decimated republican movement, subject to arrest on sight by Free State troops and debarred from the Dail by his refusal to take the necessary oath. In 1926 he formed a new political party of reconstructed but unrepentant republicans called Fianna Fail; in 1927, through a casuistic sleight-of-hand, he finally entered the Dail, signing the oath book but declaring this an empty formality which implied no allegiance on his part to the Crown; in 1932, with the help of the IRA and a worldwide depression, this most tenacious of all Irish politicians won the election and remained in power for sixteen years.

De Valera entered government with promises of an Ireland united, free, Gaelic and self-reliant, and he immediately released all IRA prisoners. He carried out a kind of paper revolution which effectively dismantled the Treaty by abolishing the Oath, neutralizing the role of Governor–General by appointing an unsuccessful Fianna Fail candidate as a cipher, claiming jurisdiction over all thirty-two counties of Ireland and, by the passage of an External Relations Act, making the Twenty-six Counties a republic in fact if not in name. He withheld from the British Exchequer the land annuities – the mortgage payments made by Irish farmers as a result of the Land Purchase Acts which made them owners of their own land – precipitating an 'economic war' with Britain in which each country imposed tariffs on the other's exports. Irish industry grew rapidly behind these tariffs. In 1938, de Valera also secured the return of the ports in Cork and Donegal which Britain had retained under the Treaty, and thus managed to keep Ireland neutral throughout the Second World War.

But none of this brought Ireland any nearer to the imaginary land of Pearse and Connolly. Partition became ever more intractable with, in 1949, a republic finally declared in the South and the Northern Ireland government receiving a guarantee from the British that its constitutional status would not be altered without its consent; the use of the Irish language declined and the young continued to leave the country; the social order, with all its inadequacies and impoverishment, remained intact. The Ireland of the mind, defined in the Proclamation and Democratic Programme and apparently once so tangible and near at hand, now became ever more incorporeal – trivialized in campaign speeches, vanishing and reappearing like a mirage, unreachable behind the wall constructed across history by the Civil War. It nevertheless remained the most compelling presence in Irish politics.

Epilogue

1

All of the nine men and women whose lives are the subject of this book have continued to play a part in Irish public affairs, and each has achieved a certain eminence. They have advised governments, written memoirs and been guests of honour at national commemorations. Some have become pillars of the establishment and others have remained distinguished members of the republican opposition, but all have been accorded great respect in their communities.

But they have not yet been able to make peace with their eventful pasts: history has simply not allowed it. The unfulfilled promises of Easter Week and the residual bitterness of the Civil War have left the country unsettled and politically stagnant; allegiance has been in large measure withheld from the two states, North and South, and granted instead to an idealized conception of the Irish nation. Much of the political thought and rhetoric in the country has been predicated on the very *impermanence* of its two sets of political institutions; this has made Ireland compelling to observe but virtually impossible to manage. Its political history since the Civil War has been regularly disturbed by a subtext of threatened coups, private armies and hyperactive political branches of the police force.

The lives of these nine individuals, which have extended through the century from the revolutionary period of 1916–23, have been shaped and defined by this disturbing pattern of events. In this the nine have been magnified by the inherent tragedy of Irish history, and the stories of their lives read as allegories. The purpose of this final chapter is to bring their stories up to date.

★

Maire Comerford travelled to America in the latter stages of the Civil War. She had been sent to raise funds and support for the Republicans and for the purpose procured a forged passport. She returned after nine months with a few thousand pounds and her suitcase stuffed with unwanted guns – unwanted because by this time arms had been dumped and Sinn Fein was trying to reconstitute itself politically – and tried to carve out a life for herself in the despoiled and embittered Free State. It was a bleak time for Republicans; many remained in jail, others were blacklisted from all aspects of public service, including teaching and medicine, and thousands emigrated to America. Maire Comerford hung on, maintaining a tenuous link with Sinn Fein and retreating to a hilltop in County Wexford, where she ran a poultry farm.

MAIRE COMERFORD: I was one of the few who managed to stay in Ireland when thousands left. The Republicans were in abject distress and poverty. I had left Dublin and was living on a hill in Wexford. I didn't have any money, but I had credit in the shops because I had belonged to people who were able to run bills in shops. The shopkeepers wouldn't believe I had no money. It was very useful to me because only for that I wouldn't have survived. I had less and less contact with anybody else because every Republican had a very long period of being boycotted. You couldn't get any employment associated with the state at all without signing an oath of allegiance, and we wouldn't sign that. It was a terrible, dreary spell.

The boycott on Republicans was relieved when de Valera came to power in 1932; many were given jobs and the right to pensions, which drew them into the evolving political machinery of the state and away from doctrinaire republicanism. Maire Comerford declined to participate in de Valera's new political party, a decision she had made some years before.

MAIRE COMERFORD: At one stage de Valera wanted to see

me. I was to come to a place in Mount Street. My mother and Dorothy MacArdle* thought I would be followed going to see him and that he would be caught, so they spent a long time disguising me, painting my face and giving me different clothes. So I hared out in a fury and got to Mount Street and Dev was there. As soon as he saw me he fell back on the sofa with his legs in the air and howled with laughter. We sat down on either side of a table and he couldn't look at me without laughing, so he put a vase of flowers in between us so he couldn't see me. With this in place then he got to the point and he told me he wanted somebody to make a link between the various departments. This would have been a very important job if he had been in power. I was to handle documents and give out reports to the press and so on. So I told him that if I did this I wouldn't hold anything back, that if I thought something should be let out that I would let it out. He changed the subject then, and that was the end of my involvement. If you have a job like that, you have to sell yourself body and soul.

But when de Valera founded the daily newspaper the *Irish Press* as his sole point of access to the national media, she joined its staff and remained there for some thirty years. Shortly after she joined the paper she bought a small house in Sandyford outside of Dublin and began to amass the republican archive which continues to absorb her attentions. She has remained a resolute republican – marching, speaking on platforms and writing books, articles and an endless stream of letters to the press on this single theme. In the late forties and fifties she was one of the most prominent figures in the Anti-Partition League. In 1969, when de Valera was organizing the fiftieth anniversary celebrations for Dail Eireann, she drew on her archive to write a short book on the First Dail in order to highlight what she regards as its betrayal by the successive Twenty-six County governments which have followed in its

*The author of *The Irish Republic*.

wake. She has carried on a kind of cold war with all Irish governments since the establishment of the Free State, withholding from them her allegiance, denouncing their lack of principles and receiving in turn a measure of official opprobrium. In 1976, shortly before we interviewed her for the film 'Curious Journey', she was convicted in a Dublin court for her participation in a banned march commemorating the Easter Rising. She refused to pay the fine, but the authorities could not bring themselves to send her, at the age of eighty-three, to prison once again. She, as much as anyone alive today in Ireland, personifies the Irish government's troubled relationship with its own founding fathers.

John L. O'Sullivan likewise remained, at least for a time, on the militant fringe of Irish politics, where politics was at its most ambivalent: the turbulent world of undercover police and armed quasi-legal bodies which underpinned the conventional parties. He stayed in the Free State army for a few years, reaching the rank of first lieutenant, but, as he says himself, 'I hadn't any love for a peacetime army, to tell you the truth. I gave it up and went back on the farming.' He remained restive, however, and when Kevin O'Higgins advertised for ex-army officers to join the Special Branch, Mr O'Sullivan became one of the sixty detectives recruited at this time. When serving in West Meath he was given the distasteful task of arresting his old friend Moss Twomey, the officer in charge of the firing party back in 1920 when Mr O'Sullivan initially prevented the execution of the two British deserters (see page 191).

JOHN L. O'SULLIVAN: I arrested Moss Twomey in Crooked Wood, outside Mullingar. He was Chief of Staff of the IRA at the time and I was in the Special Branch. He was sitting in a car and I went up to it and opened the door. He spoke before I did and he said, 'Christ, John, I thought you were on the other side.' 'Unfortunately I am,' I said, 'and I'll have to pick you up.' 'No better bloody man,' he said. That's a fact now, that was the conversation.

Later on, then, when I had him inside the barracks in Mullingar I was shaving him, do you see, with an open razor. The chief superintendent put his head inside the door and he said, 'Christ, Twomey, aren't you a bit afraid that he'll cut your throat?' There was a lot of ill feeling in the country then, you see, from the Civil War. 'I'm not,' says Twomey. 'He'd cut yours a lot quicker.' He was right too.

The political fortunes of those who had supported the Free State underwent a disastrous reversal when de Valera came to power in 1932. There was a purge of the army, police and government departments, and many of the newly jobless re-constituted themselves as the militant opposition. An organization called the Army Comrades' Association composed of Free State army men nervous about their status in the event of a change of government emerged in late 1932 as the Blue-shirts, a more overtly political and perhaps somewhat sinister group. Eoin O'Duffy, who had been Commissioner of Police under Cosgrave but was now dismissed by de Valera, became the leader of the Blueshirts and under his hand it became Ireland's unrealized and somewhat amateurish contribution to the European fascism of the thirties. The ostensible purpose of the Blueshirts was to prevent the spread of communism and preserve free speech. In the latter capacity they did protect speakers of Cumann na nGael (the pro-Treaty party later to be called Fine Gael) from harassment by the IRA and unruly elements in Fianna Fail. O'Duffy, however, had ambitions beyond the formation of a security guard. He was a creature of the Civil War and was not entirely averse to the idea of a *coup d'état*. He was, however, effectively neutralized by Cos-grave and the more constitutionally minded members of Fine Gael. The Blueshirts underwent a number of name-changes as they dwindled in numbers and significance, finally bowing out as a contingent of adventurers who sailed to Spain to assist Franco during the Spanish Civil War.

John L. O'Sullivan was one of the founder members of the Army Comrades Association and when the Blueshirts supplanted it he became an enthusiastic participant. He believes that the Blueshirts were a purely defensive body, a check on the vengeance of Fianna Fail resulting from its own persecution by the Free State during the years of political exile.

JOHN L. O'SULLIVAN: The reason for the Blueshirts was that the right to hold political meetings or to speak from a public platform was nearly denied to everybody, unless you were in Fianna Fail. When O'Duffy left the Guards he became leader of the Blueshirts and he often sent for me to travel with him. We got up a very powerful organization, and we were able to ensure that every speaker from every party enjoyed freedom of speech. Intimidation was rife throughout the country, and if you weren't of one thinking with de Valera's people you weren't given the right to live or carry on your business.

De Valera was soon arresting members of both the Blueshirts and the IRA – which became an illegal organization in 1936 – since these two factions were threatening Ireland's fragile democracy with their wars against each other and against the state itself. Mr O'Sullivan was arrested with Eoin O'Duffy for Blueshirt activity in Westport, County Mayo, in 1933 but was quickly released. Shortly afterwards he became involved in resistance to the 'economic war' which de Valera was waging against Britain. The prohibitive tariffs were depriving large farmers of their principal export markets, and some revolted with reprisals against prominent members of Fianna Fail. Mr O'Sullivan was again arrested and was sentenced to thirteen years' imprisonment, of which he served only three and a half years before being released in September 1937. At one stage during his incarceration, in a prison where Republicans were separated from Blueshirts by barbed wire, he again met his old comrade Moss Twomey.

318

JOHN L. O'SULLIVAN: There was a big barbed-wire barrier between the Blueshirt prisoners and the Republicans. The minute Moss was brought into the prison – it was Arbour Hill – he came up to the barbed wire and he called out, 'Is John L. there?' The reply came back that I was. 'Send him out to me,' he said. So I went up and we shook hands across the barbed wire. He said that it was 'bad war' between the Blueshirts and the Republicans.

In the same year that he was arrested with O'Duffy – 1933 – Mr O'Sullivan became the Fine Gael candidate for the Dail in west Cork. The year before, Fianna Fail TDs had taken their seats in the Dail carrying pistols in their pockets, so great was their fear of a coup. Indeed, the line of demarcation between parliamentary politics and armed militancy remained vague and easily bridgeable until after the Second World War, when the Civil War at last ceased to be the guiding force in Irish politics. In post-war Ireland, John L. O'Sullivan settled down to a busy and conventional political career, and never again saw the inside of a prison. In 1950, he was elected to the Cork County Council, and he has remained a member of that body ever since. He was a member of the Seanad, the upper house of Dail Eireann, from 1954–61, and became a TD in 1969; during that year he became the Fine Gael front-bench spokesman on agriculture and was elected chairman of the Fine Gael parliamentary party.

Mr O'Sullivan lives with his family on the farm near Clonakilty on which he was raised, though his active political life keeps him travelling all over Ireland and even to Europe. When we last visited him he had recently returned from Paris on government business, and among the memorabilia of his public life he had the chains of office which he then held as chairman of the General County Councils of Ireland.

Dr Brighid Lyons Thornton has stood at a safer distance from the political tumult of the Ireland that emerged from the Civil War. She served for a time as a medical officer in the Free

State army, attaining the rank of first lieutenant and thereby becoming the first Irish woman to receive a commission in her own armed forces. At that time – the Civil War and its immediate aftermath – the King George V Hospital, where Dr Thornton had visited Sean MacEoin after his capture by the British, was being transformed into St Briccin's, and she was given an office there to help conceive its new administrative direction and form a nursing corps and team of medical orderlies. But she soon relapsed into an illness which had plagued her since childhood: tuberculosis. She became very ill and underwent a serious operation which left her almost totally incapacitated. She was advised to travel to Nice for the purity of its air and for a complete rest. There she walked along the promenade with friends from Ireland and did what she could to help other ailing patients. She also met Edward Thornton, a Free State army captain who had been invalided out and sent to Nice to take a cure, and she fell in love with him. After a time, he was sent for further treatment to Vence, where Picasso had a studio, and she to Leysin, in Switzerland. When she felt well enough she returned to Ireland, as did Edward Thornton, and they married in 1926.

For some years the Free State government under Cosgrave had been trying to recover from the desolation left by the British and the Civil War, and had been doing what it could to bring into being a well-managed society. Cosgrave was particularly concerned with implementing an effective health service, and Dr Thornton involved herself in building it up. While her husband was qualifying to be a barrister, she studied social and preventative medicine and took a degree in public health. She has since devoted her working life to the Irish health service, running clinics, working as a medical inspector and in child care and, after her retirement, at Trinity College in research. She is now, at the time of writing, nearly blind and has lost most of the use of her legs. In 1976, though, when we first met her, she was living alone in her elegant flat near Fitzwilliam Square in Dublin (her husband having died in 1946), and was still travelling across town on foot to do voluntary work at the Rotunda Hospital.

When Martin Walton was interned at Ballykinlar camp late in 1920, he found the other prisoners there teaching each other the skills and areas of knowledge in which they themselves had personal expertise. Mr Walton, who had played in cinema orchestras and taught at a college of music, and had also acted as a secretary to Martin Fitzgerald at the *Freeman's Journal*, was placed in charge of classes in the violin and in shorthand.

MARTIN WALTON: At Ballykinlar we tried to make the camp as much of a university as possible. Anybody who could teach anything helped out. I taught the violin and short-hand. Music was thought to be very important. Peadar Kearney, the author of the 'Soldier's Song',★ was in Bally-kinlar with me, and we talked things over, inside out and upside down, about founding an Irish College of Music. Peadar told me that he had a pledge from Collins that he would send three of us away to the Continent. He didn't think we knew enough to found a proper college of music, and thought it was important that we study European methods.

Mr Walton's class in the violin was very popular and his most pressing problem was to acquire enough instruments. The British officer in charge of the camp, a Colonel Innes, was agreeable to the importation of the violins, and money to buy them was provided by the American White Cross. Mr Walton then wrote to Boosey & Hawkes, a large musical-instrument dealer in London; they were not averse to selling to IRA internees and quoted a price of £2 per violin and case. An order was placed, the violins arrived and were distributed and, as there was no sign of an end to the conflict, a new

★The Irish national anthem.

321

consignment was sent for. But then the truce came, followed by the Treaty, and as the internees were returning home Mr Walton found that he was left with a large number of unwanted instruments.

MARTIN WALTON: The father of the camp, Henry Dixon, came to me and he said, 'Martin, I want to clear up the funds. Can you do anything about selling these violins?' Well, it's not etiquette to sell an instrument to a pupil. It is done, but it's not etiquette. So I asked old Quinn at the music shop in Abbey Street if he could help me, as I couldn't sell them to the internees. He said he couldn't sell violins, but 'I'll tell you what you'll do,' he said, and I can still hear his voice. 'Put an ad in the paper, it'll cost you two quid: "BEAUTIFUL VIOLIN, BOW AND CASE . . . GENUINE BARGAIN." ' So I was working for Fitzgerald in the daytime and teaching in the School of Music from half-five to half-nine six nights a week, and I asked my father to look after the replies. But he was opposed to business of any sort. Businessmen were just capitalists in his eyes. But I persuaded him that I was only trying to clear up the accounts. When I came back from work the night after placing the ad, all the fiddles were gone. And everybody paid three quid, and delighted to get them.

Mr Walton then simply followed his instincts. Like many of the revolutionaries of 1919–21 who had used their experience in the Sinn Fein Bank and other such organizations to become the leading capitalists of the new state, Mr Walton turned his period of internment to good account. He traced Boosey & Hawkes's own supplier to an address on the Continent – it was a Mr Karl Braun of Saxony – and wrote away to ask for a quote on violins. The reply came back that they were on sale for nine shillings each plus duty. Mr Walton, then an ex-prisoner in his early twenties lacking both credit and a name in the music business, decided he had nothing to lose and sent off a large order to Saxony. Mr Braun, as it happened, was a spiritualist. Where other manufacturers might have balked at such an unlikely business prospect as Mr Walton, Mr Braun gathered his board together and held a seance. Many years later, when the two men met, Mr Walton was told how he received his credit rating.

MARTIN WALTON: Karl Braun was a spiritualist. Now I don't know whether you believe in spiritualism or not – I don't know whether I believe in it myself – but that's what he said he was, anyway. He told me that one night he gathered his people together around a table and they had this thing with a wine glass in the centre. They opened the window then and they held hands and they got in touch with Aunt Sally or whoever. The wine glass went this way and that way, and according to Karl Braun it told them a lot about me and that I was worthy of credit. The violins were shipped off to Dublin then and I put a small ad in the paper bringing the price down to thirty-five bob. I was soon selling the bloody things by the hundred. Then he started sending along mandolins and pianos and God knows what else and the whole thing just took off from there.

Mr Walton began his business by trading from home, but in 1924 he took over a shop in North Frederick Street, near Parnell Square. Around that time he also opened the Dublin College of Music. His music business grew in size, scope and prosperity, diverging into instrument manufacture, publishing and recording. He even sponsored a famous music programme on Irish radio – 'The Walton Programme: your weekly reminder of the grace and beauty that lie in the heritage of Irish songs, the songs our fathers loved'. Walton's Musical Instrument Galleries, now run by Mr Walton's son Paddy, is the largest general musical-instrument shop in Europe.

Mr Walton now lives in a large house called Ashtown Lodge in Castleknock, near one of the north gates of the Phoenix Park. The house was once owned by a Colonel Dugdale, a grandfather of the present-day Republican activist Rose Dugdale. Colonel Dugdale, a British army officer, died in 1912, and his daughters turned the house into a convalescent home for injured soldiers. A Colonel Sandbach lived there during the First World War, and during the Easter Rising he was visited by General Maxwell. Mr Walton moved there in 1933. He is, like Maire Comerford, an archivist, though on a grander scale, and like her he is moved to collect out of a painful sense of historical continuity. The house has become a kind of nationalist library and museum, the many rooms in its upper floor filled to the ceiling with neat chronological piles of nationalist and revolutionary newspapers, political pamphlets, theatre bills and documents. Hundreds of leather-bound historical works line the walls and in Mr Walton's study is a small stack of republican rifles. In the front hallway are the death masks of Fintan Lalor, the nineteenth-century nationalist and anti-landlord campaigner much admired by Connolly and Pearse, and Peadar Kearney, Mr Walton's friend and the author of Ireland's national anthem. Through a rear window can be seen an experimental vineyard and in the dining-room is a priceless Bossi mantelpiece of inlaid Italian marble. Off the hallway is an old ballroom, with a short sweeping staircase and an Adam mantelpiece; when we were first shown this room it was knee-deep in old violins. Outside the house is a kennel, for Mr Walton's daughter raises Kerry Blues and Irish wolfhounds. The Irish wolfhound is one of the symbolic fixtures – along with the harp, the round tower, the shamrock and mournful, dark-haired Caitlin ni Houlihan – of nineteenth-century Irish nationalism, and these massive grey dogs, whose ancestors are said to have run with the ancient Fenians, move freely in and out of the house.

Sean Kavanagh first saw the inside of Mountjoy prison when he was brought there by the British, handcuffed to Rory O'Connor, in 1921. In 1924, at the behest of Kevin O'Higgins, he returned to that prison as deputy governor, having served two years in the Free State army as military governor of Hare Park internment camp at the Curragh. Four years later he became the governor, and remained in that post for nearly forty years.

It is difficult to imagine this courteous and soft-spoken man in such a role. Indeed it was perhaps only his lack of personal harshness in dealing with prison strikes and riots by incarcerated Republicans, on behalf of a government half in sympathy with their aims, that made the prison manageable at all. Unlike many who held jobs with explosive political implications, he survived several changes of government and – having looked after virtually every prominent Republican of the post-Civil War period, from senior men like Sean MacBride to the flamboyant and wayward Volunteer, Brendan Behan – he retired peacefully in the early 1960s. Afterwards, he worked for a time as the sales administrator of Telecommunications Limited and, following the death of his wife in 1978, he moved from his home in Rathmines to live with his married daughter.

The late Major-General Joseph Sweeney was the only career soldier among our nine veterans, and he survived the political turbulence of the twenties and thirties, maintaining a detached professionalism until his retirement in 1940. He served out the Civil War – a particularly disturbing time for him because of the execution of his friend Charlie Daly and others at Drumboe – as OC of the Donegal Command, and he remained a member of the Dail until 1923.

During the latter part of March 1924, General Sweeney briefly served as Acting Chief of Staff during an incident which came to be known as the Army Mutiny. This bizarre and complex episode, which had its origins in a disillusionment with the Free State from within the ranks of its own army, began when senior army men despatched an ultimatum to W. T. Cosgrave: he must either make an immediate and discernible move on the promises of Collins about the Republic or else face a mutiny. Arms were grabbed and hoarded and there was an implicit hope that old comrades, since split by the Civil War, would be reunited in a march against the British in the North.

The ultimatum was withdrawn pending negotiations. In the midst of these, on St Patrick's Day, 17 March 1924, another errant faction within the Free State army, led by Richard Mulcahy, surrounded one of Collins's old meeting places, Devlin's pub in Parnell Street. Following an open gun battle, ten of the mutineers were arrested. Kevin O'Higgins, meanwhile, wanted the army purged of all its politicized and revolutionary remnants and, with several of the mutineers behind bars, he forced the resignation of Mulcahy as Minister of Defence and fired a number of his cohorts.

However, the mutiny had not yet fully played itself out. Some of the mutineers contacted leading Republicans and between them they conceived a desperate plan which they hoped would provoke retaliation from Britain and renew the old fight. Four men dressed in Free State army uniforms drove a long, yellow Rolls Royce to the landing dock at Cobh, which the British used as the point of embarkation for the base on Spike Island which they had retained under the Treaty; when a number of British soldiers appeared on the dock, two Thompson machine-guns appeared through the windows of the limousine and their magazines were emptied into the crowd, wounding five civilians, a British officer and eighteen soldiers, and killing one private. This event occurred on 21 March 1924. General Sweeney, who was the first to discover documents relating to the plans of the mutineers, had been appointed Acting Chief of Staff the day before and he now had to contend with the nervous anticipation which ran through the army. But 'saner counsels', as they might have been called at the time, prevailed and the Army Mutiny was quickly buried in history. The Free State government apologized and paid compensation, the British accepted and the incident was closed.

General Sweeney ascended steadily in rank – becoming Quartermaster-General in February 1929 and Chief of Staff in June 1929 – and took up a succession of the most important commands in Ireland. When de Valera came dramatically to power in 1932, General Sweeney was General Officer Commanding at the Curragh, the largest camp in Ireland and the site of the famous mutiny in 1914. Rumours of coups and mutinies again moved subterraneously through the country in 1932, and General Sweeney was himself asked by members of the army what he intended to do about de Valera. He was committed to democracy, and he replied that he intended to keep the peace, even to the point of defending de Valera's government against any threat of force.

Eight years later, shortly after the beginning of the Second World War, General Sweeney became General Officer Commanding of the Western Command, based at Athlone. At this time the return of the ports and Irish neutrality had left Britain's western flank exposed to German attack. Senior British civil servants and politicians tried to rectify this through a conciliatory manoeuvre which demonstrated an amazing equivocation about the fate of the Northern six counties: they promised de Valera Irish unity in return for his participation in the war. It was a display of British expediency which the Northern Protestants have not forgotten. De Valera, perhaps sensing a trap and perhaps too well aware of the popularity of neutrality, refused, and Churchill relapsed into the old style of dire stentorian threats of a punitive invasion. At one stage the Irish army was placed on alert and General Sweeney deployed some of his troops north to the border. There was no invasion, however, and Churchill reluctantly restricted himself to derisory remarks. In a victory broadcast at the end of the war he announced, 'Had it not been for the loyalty and friendship of Northern Ireland . . . we should have been forced to come to close quarters with Mr de Valera or perish from the earth. However, with a restraint and poise with which I say history will find few parallels, His Majesty's Government never laid a violent hand upon them, though at times it would have been quite easy and quite natural. And we left Mr de Valera's government to frolic with the German and later with the Japanese representatives to their hearts' content.' De Valera replied with a dignified and classic exposition of the role of small, neutral nations and was clearly the moral victor in the exchange. He and his country survived intact what the Irish blithely referred to as 'the Emergency', his personal political base more firmly established than ever.

General Sweeney retired from active service at the end of 1940 and took up a job as an insurance inspector for the Canada Life Assurance Company, a post which he held for ten years. In 1950 he became an area officer for the Irish Red Cross Society and in 1956 was made its general secretary; in that capacity he travelled to Hungary in the aftermath of the uprising there to help bring refugees to Ireland. He finally retired in 1963.

General Sweeney died in a Dublin nursing home in late November 1980. Shortly before that, he had completed a tape-recording for us giving his answers to a few important questions which we had been unable to ask him personally; he was, even then, highly articulate, his impeccable memory full of details. At the time of his death he was one of the most eminent of the survivors of Ireland's revolutionary past: he had been a student of Patrick Pearse and an early member of the Volunteers; he had served in the GPO during Easter Week and was the youngest member to be elected to the First Dail; he was a senior officer in the IRA during the Anglo-Irish War and had a long and distinguished career in the Irish army. The state thus appropriately responded to his death with a military funeral, the body being transported by artillery gun carriage to a Dublin church, and thence by hearse to Donegal. The cortege stopped *en route* at the barracks in Athlone, where it was met by a line of troops with reversed arms. It then travelled north by the long route, via Sligo, as it could not cross the border. Dusk had fallen by the time it passed into Donegal, and at the crossroads of each small town and village, cars were waiting with their headlights on to join in the procession. By the time it arrived at Burtonport, where General Sweeney was born in 1897, the cavalcade was two miles long. The funeral Mass took place the following morning, and afterwards the cortege, preceded by a military band, drove to Dungloe. The coffin, covered in a tricolour and with the

Major-General's sword and cap laid out on top, moved slowly through the town on a gun carriage and on to the old churchyard. There the final rituals were enacted, the Last Post was sounded and three volleys were fired over the coffin as it was lowered into the grave.

Colonel David Neligan continued to live dangerously as an intelligence officer, first for the army and then for the police, until he became a victim of the great political reshuffle in 1932 – when de Valera unceremoniously placed him in one of the safest sinecures of all: the Land Commission. He had served out the Civil War as a Free State intelligence officer in Kerry, and in its aftermath became one of the principal architects of the new state police force. The army intelligence department, run by Professor Hogan out of Oriel House in Dublin, had lost its purpose after the Civil War, and Professor Hogan asked Colonel Neligan to write a report on what might be done with it. He suggested that it should be entirely disbanded, but that those of its officers who were willing should be transferred to the police as detectives. Kevin O'Higgins, who was anxious that all political red herrings like Oriel House should be removed from the army, took up the suggestion and appointed Colonel Neligan to take charge of Dublin's detective branch. When the two police departments in the country – the old Royal Irish Constabulary and the Dublin Metropolitan Police – were amalgamated into one force, the Garda Siochana, in 1925, David Neligan became head of the Special Branch for the entire Free State. It was a sensitive, even unnerving job, its principal brief being to hunt down what remained of the IRA. Many of his prime targets were comrades from the pre-Treaty days, though old loyalties did nothing to decrease the enmity between the Free State and the Republican opposition; this, if anything, grew more bitter in the fifteen years which followed de Valera's 'dump arms' order.

Eoin O'Duffy, as Commissioner of Police, was one of the most active forces in the Free State in pressing the hard line against the IRA, and when de Valera came to power with what O'Duffy regarded as a party of reconstructed outlaws, O'Duffy would not recognize the legitimacy of the new government. He drafted a document which was in effect a call to arms to unseat de Valera and circulated it for supporting signatures among his comrades in the army and police. When it came to Colonel Neligan he declared he wanted nothing to do with it and urged the others to do the same. Cosgrave, who believed that parliamentary democracy would be the only salvation for the fragile state, heard about O'Duffy's seditious document and anxiously summoned Colonel Neligan for a report. But by then the brief life of that particular plot had come to an end and he was able to reassure Cosgrave that he had nothing to worry about.

De Valera soon afterwards consolidated his position with a snap election and a few key dismissals. He had been escorted into power by the IRA and knew that his militant supporters would not tolerate the presence of such old enemies as O'Duffy and Neligan in senior posts; Neligan was sacked first and then O'Duffy. Colonel Eamon Broy, who like Neligan had spied for Collins from within the ranks of the G Division, had remained loyal to de Valera and was now appointed to replace O'Duffy. He recruited from the IRA and the division which he created, known as the Broy Harriers, eventually hounded Republicans with as much remorseless tenacity as had Neligan. O'Duffy passed through the permutations of home-grown fascism until his retirement. David Neligan was deposited in the Land Commission where, as he said himself, 'I stared at the wall for twelve months.' De Valera, he said, had written on his file 'Never to be promoted', and he did not emerge from his post until his retirement in 1964.

David Neligan has a fine verbal felicity as well as an eye for farce, and when he had retired he took up a suggestion by the great Irish short-story writer Frank O'Connor to write a book about his experiences with Michael Collins. O'Connor had joined the Republican side during the Civil War, but had afterwards grown increasingly attracted to the character of Collins and during the thirties he decided to write his biography, *The Big Fellow*. In the course of his researches he met David Neligan.

DAVID NELIGAN: Frank O'Connor told me a yarn one day. He said that Sean MacEntee, who later became Taoiseach, had invited him to lunch in the Dail. He went up – he wouldn't eat as much as a crow, but he went up anyway. And Sean MacEntee said to him, 'Did you see Neligan yet?' 'Oh that bastard,' says O'Connor, 'I wouldn't go next to near him.' So MacEntee said to him, 'You're making a great mistake. That man has been much maligned. He's a thoroughly decent fellow.' So O'Connor came along to see me.

But I said later to O'Connor that if MacEntee was a friend of mine he had a damned poor way of showing it. He was Fianna Fail Minister of Finance at the time and his boss had dumped me in the Land Commission.

One winter some thirty years after that meeting David Neligan sat down to write his book, which he called *The Spy in the Castle*. He then began to hunt around for a publisher. By this time he had become acquainted with the poet Patrick Kavanagh. 'I knew him very well. He used to come in and see me when I was in the Land Commission. He never asked me for anything, but I used to give him a few bob when he was skint. He was a very nice decent fellow, but he never had any luck, only bad luck.' Kavanagh read the book in manuscript and suggested it to his friend Timothy O'Keefe, then an editor at the London publisher MacGibbon & Kee, with the result that the book was finally published in 1968. It is a lively and largely jocular account, but it concludes with a lament for his slain friends, Michael Collins and Kevin O'Higgins, and the assertion that if he were offered the choice of living life over again he would avoid politics. 'It was well said,' he remarks, 'revolution devours her own children.'

Colonel Neligan now lives with his wife in Booterstown, a suburb to the south of Dublin where he can still be seen cycling along the shore of Dublin Bay. His son of the same name, a dentist, has followed him into public life, though in a different direction: he is a frequent speaker at socialist gatherings and is an active member of the Socialist Labour Party. He has yet, according to his father, to be deterred by the inevitable disillusionment which attends public life.

General Tom Barry died in Cork on 2 July 1980, the day after his eighty-third birthday. Though his military talents remained unexploited after the Civil War, he was nevertheless one of the legendary figures of recent Irish history: a folk hero in his early twenties because of his resourcefulness, his bravery and his brilliant tactical innovations; a voice of clarity and decisiveness amid the agonized meanderings of the post-Civil War IRA; and in later years the patriarchal advocate and adviser of the Republican movement. He personified an unbroken republican line, speaking in recent years at commemoration ceremonies at Kilmichael and Crossbarry in support of the IRA and the need to drive British soldiers from the North of Ireland. His death brought forward tributes from all quarters of the establishment, but, like Shaw's Saint Joan, his common sense and self-confident, unwavering faith had disturbed their equanimity often enough for them not to wish to see him resurrected.

It pained him that his generation had waged the hardest and most successful fight against the British in all of Irish history, only to see it washed away in the Civil War. His life thereafter thus became a pursuit of the moment when the country was united, when fighting was the only momentum, and when the victory of the Republic still seemed possible. He married Leslie Price, a leading figure in Cumann na mBan, in 1921, and they both endured the privations suffered by all Republicans in the immediate aftermath of the Civil War. They thought of emigrating to America but managed to hold on until General Barry was appointed General Superintendent of Cork Harbour in 1927, a job he held until his retirement in 1965. In the meantime he remained in the IRA, holding his command in

Cork, sitting on the executive and straining, along with everyone else, to find a way by which the organization might once
again assert itself effectively in Irish affairs. But throughout
the twenties and thirties the IRA was being picked apart:
Cosgrave and O'Higgins hounded it and de Valera, having
used it, isolated the organization before moving in to finish it
off. Tom Barry was himself arrested several times by de Valera's government during the thirties on such charges as sedition, unlawful association, refusal to answer questions, and
contempt. He returned each time to active participation in the
leadership, though others were less tenacious: many grew bored with the inactivity and internal dissension and either emigrated or simply dropped out; the left tried to politicize the
organization and, having failed, reformed itself into splinter
groups; others joined Fianna Fail in search of jobs or even
purposeful political activity. The IRA was becoming a spent
and rather abstract force.

Two events in 1936 disturbed even further the IRA's vain
attempts to hold itself together. The first was a dispute between two of its leading officers, Sean MacBride and Sean
Russell, over attitude and policy. MacBride, who was later
awarded a Nobel Peace Prize, was the son of the executed
leader of Easter Week, John MacBride, and the quixotic
beauty and impassioned republican Maud Gonne. He had been
raised by his mother in sophisticated Paris; he was a politician,
having formed the IRA offshoot party Cumann Poblachta na
h-Eireann; he was an extremely clever lawyer with a passion
for detail and he spoke with the precision and even the accent
of a French intellectual. Russell, on the other hand, was an
old-style militaristic Fenian; he had scant patience for either
politics or intellectuals, and he believed that the sole business
of the IRA was to collect arms and recruits and to strike hard
at England. His single policy at this time was to mount a
ruthless and concerted bombing campaign in England, using
Ireland as a base.

This policy had a divisive effect on the IRA, and while its
members were preoccupied with debating it, the organization

was further disturbed by the compelling fight in Spain between Franco's fascists and the socialist republicans of Madrid. The war which Camus saw as everyone's 'personal tragedy' had a galvanizing effect on Ireland: just as Eoin O'Duffy and his right-wing nationalists, denied a power base at home, sailed there to take up the frontline defence of Catholicism and hierarchical order against the dark communist threat, so those in the left wing of the IRA, enchanted by the republican stand, went there also as the James Connolly Battalion of the Abraham Lincoln Brigade.

The IRA held an Army Convention in this atmosphere, divided over the lure of Spain and Russell's idea for a campaign in England. In the midst of it Tom Barry stood up and called for an immediate move against the British in the North – something the Northern Volunteers had been vehemently advocating for years. He was, as ever, one of the IRA's most popular and respected leaders, and his proposal swept a delegation anxious to do anything that would unite it in effective action. With this resolution plus the flight to Spain and the MacBride/Russell split over their heads, the Army Council appointed General Barry Chief of Staff, and he immediately began to formulate plans for a Northern campaign. He also forbade participation in the Spanish adventure, declaring that enough Irishmen had died in foreign wars.

In neither initiative, however, was he successful. The flow of recruits to Spain did not stop and the Northern campaign, centred on the seizure of the Armagh military barracks, was called off at the last moment. There had been a massive leak – all of Dublin and Belfast appeared to be privy to the plan. The only option was to cancel and the IRA was left with yet another anti-climax.

General Barry resigned his command the following year. Russell, in the meantime, had not been inactive: he had travelled to America and gained support for his English campaign; his men were now in control of the IRA structure in England and others were well placed in the hierarchy at home. At the Army Convention in 1938, Russell became Chief of Staff and

334

his proposals for a bombing campaign in England were made the single most important priority. Barry led the opposition to the idea, seeing it as a fruitless and squalid exercise, and when it became clear that it was to be implemented, he, along with MacBride and many other senior men, left the IRA. The intellectuals, the heroes from the glory days of the fight against the British, and the most able and disciplined of the rank and file were now virtually all gone.

The English campaign went ahead in the spring of 1939 and was at times spectacular, but it wound down over the summer and autumn through police pressure and its own aimlessness. The IRA then entered into a period of hibernation, in which the old command structure disappeared and virtually everyone still interested in the movement was behind bars. Nevertheless, periods of quiet in the IRA were also periods of ferment and reorganization, and the organization emerged again in a stunning series of arms raids in the early fifties. One of these – at Armagh in 1953 – was apparently based on the plan which General Barry had devised in 1936. With this momentum, a Northern campaign was finally launched in 1956, but it too dwindled to an inconclusive end some five years later. The border remained solid, machine politics continued to prevail in the Twenty-six Counties and the North was as wretchedly Unionist as ever; the IRA, meanwhile, appeared to be atrophying.

When General Barry formally parted with the IRA in 1938, he returned to a quieter life in Cork. When the war broke out in Europe and de Valera declared Ireland's intention to remain neutral, he fully approved and offered his services to the Irish army in the event that that neutrality might need to be defended in the course of a British invasion. But the army merely put him in uniform and marched him with everyone else around the barracks yard, a pointless exercise which quickly bored him. He returned home again. In 1948, acting on a dare from his wife, he wrote a book about his involvement in the Anglo-Irish War which was published the following year under the title *Guerrilla Days in Ireland*. It is extremely well written, and it stands above other memoirs of the period in its lucidity, its commitment and above all in the practical shrewdness for guerrilla warfare which it displays. It has become a handbook not only for later generations of the IRA but also for aspiring revolutionaries in emerging nations throughout the world. It led General Barry into contact with the Israeli revolutionary army, the Irgun Zvai Leumi, who sought his advice in their battle against the British. It also became one of the standard texts at the American West Point military academy and even, to the delight of its author, at Sandhurst.

Tom Barry bore his legendary status well. He neither traded on it nor looked forever backwards to its source. His face had none of the vagueness or disgruntlement associated with those engrossed in or embittered by the past. He was, rather, clear and incisive about the present, giving the impression of easy competence in all things, and his eyes, though rheumy and half blind, were so penetrating that it would seem impossible to lie or equivocate in his presence. He was also gracious, he enjoyed the company of witty and alert minds and, for a man who calmly accepted violence as human, he was highly sensitive and sympathetic. He realized more than others of his generation that the Civil War was the greatest disaster of his time, and made every effort to counteract the antagonisms between Irishmen that emanated from it. In 1965 he unveiled a memorial to Michael Collins near Collins's birthplace at Sam's Cross, Clonakilty, and said to the mixed gathering of Republicans and Free Staters, 'Let us bury the dead past of dissensions. Let us leave it that each of us, like I did myself, believed in the correctness of their choice. I concede that those on the opposite side believed that their decision was the right one too.'

But he also remained hardheaded and unambiguous in his commitment to republicanism – the republicanism of the IRA – right to the end of his life. Though he had been outside the command structure of the IRA since the late thirties he scrutinized all its transformations with intense interest, and when the young Volunteers took to the streets in the North in the early seventies he gave them all the support he could. It was, to his mind, the same fight that he and his column had waged fifty years earlier in west Cork.

We last visited General Barry at his small flat in Patrick Street in Cork on a Saturday evening in mid-June 1980, just over a fortnight before his death. He would, he said, like to make it into his eighty-fourth year, just a couple of weeks away – which he did by a single day. He then spoke in fine detail of his own funeral, as though he were planning a tactical operation. His body, he said, would be brought quietly to a nearby church for a private funeral. After the burial a brief, dispassionate obituary would be phoned in to the *Cork Examiner* for publication the following day. There was to be in no case a large military funeral. He spoke with great conviction and even relish on the matter, and later his instructions were carefully adhered to. The church service and graveside ritual over the tricolour-covered coffin were attended only by close friends and relatives. But by then all of Ireland knew about it; within hours of his death, the news had been broadcast and printed in all the national media and tributes and messages of condolence were arriving at St Finbar's Hospital where Mrs Barry has been confined for some years. At the cemetery, ringed around the few mourners were photographers, journalists and policemen, and a police helicopter passed overhead. It was, in spite of General Barry's directive, a national occasion, with appropriate levels of official apprehensiveness.

The life of the late Sean Harling, the last of the participants in this book to be accounted for, was perhaps even more disturbingly allegorical than any of the others. He had been an ambivalent Republican in the Civil War – he had left the question of his allegiance to an instinctive turning in the Phibsborough Road on the morning of the shelling of the Four Courts (see page 285) – but he had nevertheless spent most of it in an internment camp at the Curragh. In the days of penury which followed the Civil War he lived with his wife and children in a small gate lodge on the Dartry Road in Dublin. Like all Republicans, he had no prospects of a job. He had worked in the First Dail, had been an assistant to both de Valera and Collins and served in various of the underground government departments during the Anglo-Irish War; but although he knew many of those who held senior posts in the Free State civil service, no one was going to risk giving a job to a known Republican. Survival for himself and his small family became increasingly difficult.

Then one evening in the mid-twenties Mr Harling discovered that his mantelpiece clock, a wedding present, had been stolen, and he took the audacious step, for one who was outside the law, of personally reporting the matter to the police. There was an inspector on duty, an expert on the IRA, who recognized Mr Harling and reported the astonishing fact of his presence to his superior. Hasty arrangements were made and Mr Harling was taken under guard to Dublin Castle. Questioning and discussions went on for hours and in the end Mr Harling left some time after midnight with a firm offer of a job as an agent for the Special Branch. He dreaded taking it – less because of the danger than because of the stigma of betrayal which it carried – and he made final efforts to find another way out of his poverty. But none was forthcoming and, having clearly stated that he would not betray confidences about Republican men and materials gained *before* he took the new job, he reluctantly embarked on his brief career as an undercover police agent for the Free State. His boss, of course, was David Neligan, then head of the Special Branch.

Some time later a dump of 50,000 rounds of IRA ammunition was seized in a raid by Free State police. Mr Harling was suspected as having provided the tip-off. The IRA, then enduring one of the lowest periods in its history, ordered a court martial, which Mr Harling understandably did not attend. He began instead to associate more openly with the Free State police. Then one winter night, 28 January 1928, he was ambushed on his way home from work by two IRA men.

DAVID NELIGAN: It was poverty drove Harling into working

with us. I felt sorry for the poor wretch. He was a very tiny little man as you know, and he used to be brought home in a squad car. From where he was dropped off he had to walk about 400 yards. There was a seat on the road, put up by the tram company, and there were two men sitting on the seat one night when Harling came home. He was afraid they had designs on him, poor devil, he had the wind up. So he crossed the road to get away from them and they ran after him and opened fire. There were two big pillars by the gate lodge where Harling was living, and he stood behind one of them. There was a shoot-out then and Harling fired and blew half of one of their heads off. What would you say the other man did? Well, there was a great man in the Olympics that year, and he wouldn't have stood a dog's chance with the man on the Dartry Road. He did seventy around the corner.

After this harrowing event, Mr Harling became a marked man and David Neligan thought that he would be safer out of the country for a time. Tickets to America for himself and his family were purchased at government expense, a few hundred pounds' subsistence money was provided and David Neligan personally arranged with the American consul in Dublin for the necessary travelling papers. But Mr Harling and his family had no wish to stay in America and they returned home after a few months. He was again without a job and began the tedious routine of knocking on doors in the civil service. His pressure was incessant and this time the government relented. Mr Harling was made a clerical officer in the Revenue Commissioners' office. But he had played both sides in the Civil War feud and would have to pay a price; like David Neligan, he served in an unwanted sinecure without promotion until his retirement in 1966.

When we travelled to Dublin in the autumn of 1979 to show the film 'Curious Journey' to the old people who were in it, we had not seen them for three years. They were very old at the time and we always feared that one of them would die before we could see them again. Mrs Harling, meeting us at the door to her house, confirmed that this had in fact happened, that her husband had died that August after an illness. She then invited us in and told us an extraordinary story about his death.

The story began during the height of the fighting in central Dublin at the start of the Civil War, when Mr Harling was a senior brigade officer in the Fianna, the republican boy-scout movement which he had joined at the age of eleven in 1913. A detachment of these young boys, fighting with the Republicans, had a post at 35 North Great George's Street, just a few hundred yards away from O'Connell Street, where the fighting was still intense. Mr Harling was at this time busy taking over premises in central Dublin on behalf of the Republicans, and at one stage he visited the North Great George's Street post to check on the boys under his command. Mrs Harling, who was then Nora Radigan, was serving there as a Red Cross nurse. Her husband-to-be, whom she did not know well at the time, asked her if everyone was all right. He was told that there had been a single, terrible casualty – a young boy named Clark, who had been shot dead by a Free State sniper. His body was still there in North Great George's Street.

Mr Harling despatched one of the Fianna to notify young Clark's family and to make arrangements for the funeral. The report came back that Clark had lived with his aunt in one of the poorest parts of Dublin and that her only wish was that he be given a decent burial. Above all, could he be spared the ignominy of a quicklime grave? she asked. Mr Harling was determined that her request should be met. He placed the body in the back of a small commercial van and instructed Nora Radigan to get into the front seat beside him. He gave her his gun to hold on her lap and told her to watch out for Free State troops. They then took off at high speed across Dublin for Glasnevin cemetery, where Emmet, Parnell, Collins and many other of Ireland's heroes are buried. Young Clark was to have a patriot's grave.

It was a hair-raising trip. Mr Harling took the corners on

two wheels and they were fired on by Free State snipers from the roof of Mountjoy prison. But they arrived intact and Mr Harling went directly to the gravekeeper to commandeer a grave. As was customary, he signed a receipt and said that the grave would be paid for 'when the Republic came into being'.

He did not wait that long, however. When the Civil War was over, at a time when he himself was destitute, he went to a number of prominent Republicans, including Eamon de Valera, to raise money for the young boy's grave. When he had done so he paid for it and the grave was officially registered in Mr Harling's name. Throughout his life he made regular pilgrimages to Glasnevin cemetery and on each occasion that we saw him he spoke at considerable length about the death of young Clark and the strange circumstances of his burial. It was a paternal affection, as though the fatherless young boy had been adopted after his death.

Years later, as Mr Harling lay dying in his hospital bed in 1979, he was at times delirious. His children had travelled from their homes in Chicago to be at his bedside, but he had difficulty in recognizing them. The past appeared to be overtaking his mind. One evening, very shortly before he died, he was visited as usual by his wife. It was summertime, just as it had been when he had driven young Clark's body through the war-wracked Dublin streets to Glasnevin cemetery. When he saw his wife, his eyes, she told us, took on a sudden alertness. His mind seemed to return to that moment fifty-seven years earlier, still so vividly remembered. To him she appeared as Nora Radigan, the Red Cross nurse whom he would later marry, and the hospital room became the besieged Republican post, filled with frightened young boys, at 35 North Great George's Street. Mr Harling seemed to emerge from the imposed inertia of his delirium and illness, and became precise and commanding. The van, he told his wife, was to be ordered around to the front door, where he would meet her. They were to set out immediately across Dublin. *They must get to Glasnevin*. It was an isolated moment of stunning clarity: he was again the Fianna brigade leader in charge of a

341

group of boys; but, sensing the imminence of his own death, he was also young Clark. His final act would be to transport himself to his own grave.

Mr Harling died not long afterwards. His funeral was a dignified affair attended by a number of public officials. Messages of condolence were sent from members of the government and civil service. Having left the church, the funeral procession moved on to Glasnevin cemetery for the burial. The choice of a grave had long been made: it had been held in Mr Harling's name for over half a century. The past – or rather a precise moment of the past during the Civil War – had lived with Mr Harling throughout his life and was now realizing itself in his death. After the prayers and eulogies, his coffin was lowered into the grave which had long contained young Clark. They were buried together and above them now is a large stone Celtic cross bearing their two names.

2

I have arranged . . . to increase the animosity between the Orangemen and the United Irish. Upon that animosity depends the safety of the centre counties of the North.

General Charles Edmund Knox, 1798

Meanwhile, the Northern state was setting out on its own bleak journey of official bigotry and one-party rule. It could not take its first secure steps until the Boundary Commission promised in the Treaty collapsed unceremoniously in 1925, for up until then the Northern state's very existence had been a live question. The Boundary Commission, it will be remembered, was to readjust the border in accordance with the wishes of the people, and many nationalists thus expected that Fermanagh, Tyrone and large portions of Derry, Armagh and Down would be transferred to the jurisdiction of the Free State, leaving the rest too small to be viably governed.

The story of the Boundary Commission's demise is embarrassingly brief. It was to be composed of three representatives: one from the British government and one each from the two governments within Ireland. The majority view within the whole of Ireland – the anti-partition view – was thus placed in a fixed minority of one to two. The British government's nominee, Mr Justice Feetham, was a South African judge well disposed to the Imperial outlook. Sir James Craig boycotted the Boundary Commission, but a close friend and equally ardent Unionist named Fisher – appointed by the British – went along in his place. The Free State government's nominee was the gentle Gaelic scholar Eoin MacNeill – an Ulsterman by birth, a moderate by disposition, and, it turned out, a singularly timid negotiator.

The Boundary Commission pondered for a year until the news was leaked to the press that only the most minor adjustments to the border were being contemplated. This, of course, was what Feetham and Fisher wanted and MacNeill, permanently outnumbered, was apparently trailing dutifully, if a little reluctantly, behind them.

When these sorry facts were revealed MacNeill resigned and Free State ministers Cosgrave, O'Higgins and Ernest Blythe hastened to London to bring the matter of the Boundary Commission to a conclusion. Where Redmond had fretted and stalled and Collins had argued and subverted, these three Free State ministers made an apparently effortless capitulation. They agreed with the British government to a revoking of the Boundary Commission clause of the Treaty – in effect a final assent to partition – in exchange for a writing-off of certain outstanding financial obligations set out in the Treaty. Cosgrave, apparently blissfully unaware of the awful irony, told the Dail that he had got precisely what he wanted from the British government – 'a huge O'.

Partition – a virtually unheard-of concept at the turn of the century – thus became a reality, with the border as we know it firmly and unequivocally established. The new, adjusted border meandered its meaningless way through the Ulster countryside, dismembering its topographical features and even, it is said, bisecting an old man's cottage. It separated families, bred suspicion and cut off the town of Derry from its traditional Donegal hinterland. With its jagged edges, its loops, its inlets and its swirls, it looked more like a battered and pockmarked coastline than a border.

Behind it, to the north, grew one of the great neglected monsters of modern Europe: the Northern state. The Unionist majority there took on the familiar characteristics of ruling classes in other colonial outposts – a fanatical loyalty to the Imperial Crown and an air of inherited superiority. They were, in this respect, like nineteenth-century Mexican Creoles or twentieth-century white Rhodesians. They were also desperately insecure. One third of their fellow citizens within the enclave were Catholics who invariably voted Nationalist or Republican and who did not acknowledge the legitimacy of the state. To the south and west was the twenty-six-county Free State, which wished to incorporate the remaining six counties of Ireland under its jurisdiction. To the Unionist leaders, the border – ideally a kind of Chinese Wall – was seen as a leaky dyke tenuously holding at bay the rest of Ireland, and they peered over it southwards with narrow-eyed apprehensiveness. Their slogan was 'What we have, we hold' – and they held what they had until the abolition of Stormont in 1972.

The most vivid historical memory for Northern Unionists is the siege of Derry in 1688–9, when thirteen Protestant apprentice boys shut the gates of the walled city on advancing Catholic troops loyal to King James II. Some 30,000 Protestants were gathered within the walls and heroically endured weeks of starvation and mortar attacks until James II's army was finally driven off. Throughout the centuries which followed, Northern Protestants – believing themselves surrounded and infiltrated by Catholics – conceived of themselves in terms of these siege conditions, and they laid their defences accordingly. A Special Powers Act which sanctioned virtually *anything* in the name of order was passed in 1922; it was renewed yearly until it was made a permanent feature of the state in 1933. The Special Constabulary grew out of the notion that the entire adult male Protestant population in the North should be made into an armed garrison. Many of Carson's old Ulster Volunteers were dressed up in B Special uniforms and given guns and thereafter proceeded to lead pogroms against Catholics. The B Specials were finally disbanded under pressure from the British government – itself under pressure from world opinion – in the early seventies, but many simply changed uniforms and became members of the new Ulster Defence Regiment. The Orange Order – an oath-bound secret society designed to preserve at all costs the Protestant ascendancy – became after partition an invisible government which guided the established one at Stormont. Their influence over the state was complete, for they not only determined government policy, but also shaped Loyalist culture, dictated employment and gave a political direction to religion. All but three of the Northern state's cabinet ministers between 1920 and 1972 were members of the Orange Order. In 1934, Sir James Craig, Grand Master of the Orange Institution of County Down and Prime Minister of the Northern state, announced to his parliament: 'I have always said I am an Orangeman first and a politician and a member of this Parliament afterwards. . . . All I boast is that we are a Protestant Parliament and a Protestant state.' Orangemen had achieved an ascendancy over the body politic that would have been envied by another secret society – the Ku Klux Klan.

In such a context, the machinery of government became a patronage system given over to the preservation of Protestant dominance – a system that was maintained by a set of iniquitous voting procedures. Proportional representation, designed to help Catholics into a share of the government, was abolished, and the system of confining the vote in local elections to tenants or owners of houses was preserved long after it had been abandoned elsewhere in Britain. Certain monied citizens were entitled to up to six votes under this system, according to the value of their property, while many of the poor were entirely disenfranchised. This naturally favoured Protestants, who had a disproportionate share of the wealth, but also encouraged Unionists in charge of council housing to allocate better houses to Protestants, who would gratefully respond with their votes.

Perhaps the most blatant feature of institutionalized bigotry in the Northern state was the gerrymandering of constituency boundaries there. Areas with Catholic majorities were carved up in such a way that they would return a majority of Unionist candidates. The most notorious case of all was Derry city: here Catholics counted for over 60 per cent of the total population yet the Unionists invariably held a majority of twelve seats to eight on the city corporation. This was accomplished by dividing the city into three wards, into one of which was crammed 87 per cent of the Catholic population while the same proportion of the Protestant population was spread over two wards. The first ward returned a total of eight seats while the other two returned a total of twelve, and Derry Unionists thus had things their own way in a city in which they were considerably outnumbered.

Such sordid politics were enacted and endlessly re-enacted against an even more sordid social and economic background. Wage levels were 60 per cent of the British average and unemployment, which stood at 40 per cent in the first years of the new state's existence, settled down to an intolerable average of about 25 per cent. In the 1930s families were still being crammed into tiny rooms and 87 per cent of the houses in the countryside lacked running water. Tuberculosis was rampant and each year large numbers of children died in workhouses. Protestants suffered from the general malaise along with Catholics – though in lesser proportions – but nevertheless could not be persuaded to rebel against their prescribed role as protectors of the state. All attempts to organize politics along class lines rather than religious ones failed over the pervasive question of the right of the state to exist.

This aberrant little society was sustained not only in the name of Britain, but also with its active connivance. Britain equipped and kitted out the B Specials, maintained a permanent garrison of troops to back up the local police, and subsidized the state's unbalanced budget. Britain was always there with its funds, its army and its legal expertise and powers to buttress the Orange ascendancy. Yet when questions were raised in the British Parliament about the North's inequitable st ucture, they were sanctimoniously ruled out of order; the North of Ireland was said to have its own parliament to deal with such matters.

To be a Catholic trapped within this forgotten enclave was to endure a kind of misery unknown in Britain in this century. Catholics were despised and feared by their Protestant neighbours, structurally excluded from political representation and largely abandoned by the rest of the world. Each summer they were subjected to crude displays of Orange triumphalism when the siege of Derry and the Protestant victory at the Battle of the Boyne in 1690 were commemorated in marches and mock battles. On these occasions the Orangemen set out along their route wearing bowler hats in memory of Carson's Volunteers and sashes bearing the arcane symbols of the Orange Order. They beat their Lambeg drums and shouted 'No surrender!' In Derry, on the march commemorating the relief of the siege in 1689, the modern-day Apprentice Boys paused on the high ground of the walled city where it overlooks the Catholic ghetto of the Bogside and rained down pennies on its inhabitants. The Orange strategy was abundantly clear: they would simply starve the Catholics out. They would exclude them from politics and employment and create a culture so loaded with Reformation zeal that Catholics could simply not bear to live in it.

But resentment against such a regime could not be indefinitely contained. In 1968 – that vintage year for revolt when Czechoslovak dissidents, Parisian students and American anti-war activists took to the streets – the political minority in the North of Ireland at last began to assert itself. The generation of Catholics then coming of age was the first to attend university in significant numbers; many passed from the slums into the middle class. They would no longer tolerate second-class citizenship. They saw the irresistible parallels between their own plight and that of the blacks in the southern states of America, and like them formed civil rights organizations based on marching and civil disobedience. The Northern Ireland Civil Rights Association was formed in 1967 around a programme of reforms and their campaign got under way in a series of marches the following year. The issues at stake were spectacularly internationalized on 5 October 1968 when a civil rights march in Derry was surrounded by the RUC, who then closed in with water cannons and truncheons; the appalling images of this police riot were broadcast via television all over the world.

The Orangemen looked at the civil rights movement and

thought they saw in it the old republican threat. The B Specials, the RUC, paramilitary groups like the Ulster Volunteer Force and unruly Orange mobs goaded and brutalized the civil rights marchers at every opportunity. On 4 January 1969 a great civil rights trek across Ulster from Belfast to Derry was halted by the RUC at Burntollet Bridge and then set upon by an Orange mob (including off-duty police) who descended from the surrounding hills armed with stones and planks of wood. The marchers pushed on into Derry and were that night besieged in the Bogside by the RUC. Barricades were erected by local Catholics and the area in effect seceded from the Northern state.

As had happened before in Ireland, events on the street quickly acquired a momentum which elected officials could not contain. Riotous battles between Catholics and Protestants engulfed Derry and Belfast in August 1969 and, ominously, British troops were brought in to keep the peace. Catholics, who had been terrorized all their lives by B Specials and Orange mobs, at first welcomed the troops for the respite which they offered. But it did not take long for the British army to indicate its traditional allegiances: it was there to preserve the status quo – the Unionist hegemony. When the IRA finally awoke from its slumbers to assume its normal role in the North of protecting Catholics from pogroms, the British army moved into the Catholic ghettoes in a series of brutally executed arms raids – though there was little in the way of arms in Ireland at that time. The IRA responded with a bombing campaign against commercial targets. Later, when the small Catholic enclave in Belfast called the Short Strand was invaded by the Ulster Volunteer Force, a small detachment of the IRA emerged from the dilapidated tenements and beat them off. They were thereafter virtually the sole defenders and representatives of a large section of the Catholic populace. They soon established military and civil control over several nationalist areas.

The civil disturbance gradually became a war as the IRA took the offensive against British troops. The first shooting of a British soldier by the IRA occurred in February 1971 and as the IRA's confidence and expertise grew, British casualties quickly escalated. In August 1971 the British government responded by using the Special Powers Act to introduce internment without trial. In the early hours of 9 August, British troops descended upon selected areas and carried off 342 men suspected of republican sympathies. Women in these areas rattled their dustbin lids on the pavement as a warning against the raids and, with additional help from tip-offs, the IRA escaped the net and emerged virtually intact. Those who were held later reported an assortment of brutal treatments: some were thrown backwards from helicopters they thought were high in the air; others had to run the gauntlet of truncheon-wielding soldiers, barefoot over broken glass or barbed wire. A smaller group were used to test a refined, futuristic interrogation method known as 'sensory deprivation'. As various international commissions were later to report, these had their heads covered with hoods and were forced to lean against a wall supported by their outstretched arms. If they moved, they were beaten or kicked. They were not allowed to sleep or eat and they endured a continuous high-pitched background noise. The object was to induce a temporary insanity which would make information more easily forthcoming; in many cases its effects were permanent.

Catholics responded to internment with a massive programme of civil disobedience. Barricades were erected in virtually all the Catholic ghettoes; a rent-and-rate strike was instituted and Catholic politicians and officials withdrew from the state apparatus; an alternative assembly was convened which denied the authority of Stormont. A series of protest marches was also held, despite a ban. One such march took place in Derry on a Sunday afternoon, 30 January 1972; it was quickly to achieve an awful notoriety as 'Bloody Sunday' – the second so-named slaughter of innocent Irish civilians by British troops in recent Irish history (see page 171). This one occurred when the march was halted at a British army barricade in the Bogside. As troops moved in to make arrests, members of the Parachute Regiment opened fire and shot dead thirteen unarmed civilians. The Derry City Coroner returned a verdict of wilful murder.

The British government at last began to stir itself from its policy of benign neglect. On 22 March 1972 the Tory Government under Edward Heath summoned the Northern state's Prime Minister, Brian Faulkner, to Downing Street. He was told that security was thenceforth to be the responsibility of Westminster; internment would be phased out and referenda would have to be taken on the question of the border. Faulkner and his Cabinet refused to accept these proposals and resigned. The result was the end of Stormont. From 24 March 1972, the British government in London assumed full control of the Northern state.

Within a year the colonial imaginations of the British politicians and civil servants had produced a scheme for a solution. It was designed to include something for everybody: the Unionists were to get a further guarantee of the constitutional status of their state as well as their own assembly; nationalists were granted a share in the power of this assembly through the provision of a fixed number of seats on an executive coalition; and Dublin was allowed a nod towards unity through Lloyd George's old device of a Council of Ireland to be composed of representatives from both the Northern and the Southern states. In December 1973 representatives from London, Dublin and Belfast came together at Sunningdale in Berkshire to give their assent to this arrangement. However, by striving to be all things to all men it pleased none of those who held the true power on the streets of the North. The IRA regarded it as an irrelevancy and hardline Unionists proclaimed it a great betrayal of their cause. The latter group took matters into their own hands by organizing a general strike among Protestant workers. Within two weeks the Six Counties were effectively paralysed and the Sunningdale agreement was quietly abandoned. Politics passed back into the void.

Since then 'proposals for solutions' have emitted from successive British governments. These have quickly expired against a background of static Unionist resistance and a seemingly interminable guerrilla war between the IRA and the British army.

At the time of writing, the three principals in the struggle – the IRA, the Unionists and the British government – are deployed in varying degrees of strength and purpose. The IRA, despite the monotonous predictions of their imminent demise, seem as strong as ever. Their campaign to win political status for their imprisoned members has won the attention and sympathy of the world. In particular, the extraordinary series of hunger strikes carried out in 1981 has revealed like nothing else in living memory the brutishness and barrenness of Britain's presence in Ireland. Further, they still appear to be capable of sustaining enormous popular support and of inflicting considerable damage on the British forces.

The Unionists, on the other hand, have grown increasingly insecure. They see the end of their old ascendancy and are terrified of the abyss. Some know that the old order has passed and are trying to think of new ways forward, but most would prefer to return to that comfortable world where their authority was at least grudgingly tolerated. They want Stormont and the B Specials back. They want the Croppies – the Catholics – to lie down again. Ian Paisley has sworn himself to try to make this delusion a reality. He has quite deliberately cast himself as a latterday Carson, the saviour of Ulster. He has signed his own Covenant and has displayed to the press his own private army. He has even been dressing like Carson. But the comparison is otherwise imprecise – disastrously so for Paisley, who has none of the suave aristocratic deportment of the Dublin barrister, nor his highly placed connections in the English Tory hierarchy. Unionism in the face of a disinterested England is a spent force and Paisley, with his Biblical wrath, is perhaps its final figurehead.

For its part, the British government, as ever, is entangled in politics and has adopted equivocation as a policy. A hard line against the IRA and a constitutional guarantee to the

Unionists are policies both traditional and apparently necessary for political survival. Yet the war in Ireland is costing the government dearly, both in funds and international embarrassment. The British public is no longer emotionally attached to Irish Unionism. The British government would appear to be cautiously aspiring to the thing which Unionists fear most – a graceful disengagement from Ireland. Yet the politicians are treading extremely warily. They remember how the issue of Ireland overshadowed all others in the Westminster Parliament from the heyday of Parnell to the onset of the First World War, and they do not wish a return to that state of affairs. Ireland, if not handled with sufficient finesse, can still bring down a government: the issue must simply be made to disappear quietly.

There is about all of this a ghastly familiarity. Once again Ireland is disfigured by bombed-out buildings and hideous deaths. Funeral processions for the battle casualties continue to snake their way through the streets. There are hunger strikes, assassination squads and incidents of torture and intimidation. A whole generation will be forever haunted by a close and regular proximity to violent death. It is, as ever, a war of nerves, and of endurance, in which the British army and the local nationalist population see who can best outlast the strain. Over the whole conflict, and over the whole set of relationships between Britain and Ireland, Unionists still hold their veto, and British politicians in remote committee rooms in London continue to strive for yet another formula that will satisfy everybody and put an end to the war. The issue at stake remains the same as it has been for centuries: the British presence in Ireland.

Republicanism and Orangeism are irreconcilable. There can be no political compromise which would allow them to coexist, because any single tenet of the one excludes by definition the entire set of beliefs of the other. The idea of Orangeism is sectarian, retrogressive and oligarchical. It is fanatically loyal to the British monarchy, but suspicious of the British Parliament. It draws its sustenance from the historical moment when the consolidation of the English conquest of Ireland coincided with the Reformation: it thus endlessly celebrates the Protestant victory over the Catholics. It has no other purpose except to preserve this dominance.

The idea of republicanism, on the other hand, is secular, progressive and democratic. It grew from an ancient and popular resistance in Ireland to British rule adapted to the ideas of the French Revolution. Wolfe Tone and the failed rebellion of 1798 were the products of this adaptation. It was two years before that, in 1796, that the principles of Irish republicanism were first articulated by Wolfe Tone: '. . . to break the connection with England . . . to assert the independence of my country, to unite the whole people of Ireland and to substitute the common name of Irishman in the place of the denomination of Protestant, Catholic and Dissenter'. These ideals underwent a further evolutionary refinement in 1916, when the Celtic nationalism of Patrick Pearse was fused with the revolutionary socialism of James Connolly in the Easter Proclamation.

Orangeism has remained static since the Battle of the Boyne in 1690; republicanism has renewed itself with the most vital political ideas of each age. Orangeism trades in the exclusion of people; republicanism aspires to unity. Orangeism has presented its case to the world in over half a century of disastrous government and offers nothing more than an endless perpetuation of the same monotonous image. Republicanism is not yet realized.

The choice between them is open only to the British government, which holds all legislative power in the matter. If the British choose to maintain their rule in Ireland, either through the Orange Order or, as at present, directly from Westminster, they will serve only to perpetuate the repetitive sequence of insurrections which has characterized Ireland's history. The British cannot govern Ireland by consensus, only by force, and as Edmund Burke has said, 'The use of force is but *temporary*. It may subdue for a moment; but it does not

354

remove the necessity of subduing again: and a nation is not governed which is perpetually to be conquered.'

As long as the British remain in Ireland, what is known as the National Question will remain paramount in Irish affairs. It supersedes all other matters – economic, social and political. It brings down governments. It also, in effect, stops time, for all hope for progress is abandoned pending a final answer to this vital question. George Bernard Shaw, writing in 1904, described it thus: 'A healthy nation is as unconscious of its nationality as a healthy man of his bones. But if you break a nation's nationality it will think of nothing else but getting it set again. It will listen to no reformer, to no philosopher, to no preacher, until the demand of the Nationalist is granted. It will attend to no business, however vital, except the business of unification and liberation.'

The historian Croce wrote of the years which followed Italy's achievement of unification in 1870: 'Prose had succeeded to poetry.' 'Poetry' here refers to the romance of the struggle which had just ended and 'prose' to the anti-climactic business of government to which Italians had to apply themselves after 1870. The same has been said of Ireland in the aftermath of the Treaty. But the Treaty was a makeshift political compromise that no one saw as a final solution; its unfinished business was sufficiently intrusive in Irish affairs to keep alive the 'poetry' at the expense of the 'prose'. Poetry, in this particular sense, is timeless, outraged and singleminded. It refers to a pre-Conquest past as a pretext for a Utopian future. It celebrates in exalted phrases heroic endeavour and suffering for the sake of the cause. It is still the dominant genre in Ireland.

Prose, to pursue the crude analogy, is less rarefied and pure; it is supposed to be more complex and mundane. It can only 'succeed to poetry' in Ireland when Britain has departed and the National Question is answered. This will in effect mark the beginning of modern history in Ireland, when Irish people are at last left alone with the problem of how to live together. Prose is a far more suitable mode of discourse for this than poetry. It finds its meaning *in* time rather than, like poetry, trying to transcend time. Its form is more elastic, less bound by convention and, above all, more accessible to the process of synthesis than poetry. Ireland's post-colonial prose, if it is to be effective, must be an amalgam of traditions: it must have the tenacity of the Ulster planters along with the elegance of the Georgian gentry; the spontaneous intricacy of the medieval scribes along with the earthy sensuality of the bards. It should, in true Protestant style, celebrate the individual conscience and, like such laughting patriots as Tone and Collins, it should never take itself too seriously. It should look to the past for its richness rather than for a political theology and, like all good prose, it should never be overly eager to please. Only through such prose can Ireland at last make peace with its past.

3

In Maire Comerford's reply to our request to interview her for the film 'Curious Journey', she wrote, 'I would not be at all happy if the burden of the message you seek to put across was limited to what are called "old historical wrongs" or exclusively to the past in a sentimental way. To explain what you call England's guilt in the terrible story cannot be done without explaining her present guilt in failing to bring it to a proper conclusion. Much of England's hypocrisy consists of acknowledging "past wrongs" while keeping the present ones going.' The purpose of this book has been to somehow find the present through the past. Our nine veterans feel the present disaster in Ireland most acutely because in their pasts they were unable, despite monumental efforts, to bring about a 'proper conclusion' to the story of England's conquest of Ireland. We asked each of them to explain to us where they hoped their efforts would eventually lead Ireland and how they might relate to their Protestant countrymen in the North. The following are some of their replies:

MAIRE COMERFORD: People refer to the emancipation of Ireland as though freedom has already been won. But if a man is handcuffed or tied by the foot to another man or to something else, is he a free man? Can Ireland be held to be free while a portion of her territory is held? The partitioned area includes Armagh, the ecclesiastical capital of Ireland. It includes the crowning place of the O'Neills, the kings of Ireland, and it includes areas inhabited by people with the most ancient Gaelic traditions. And they're all abused, treated as inferiors. They have been deprived of houses and of votes. They've been gerrymandered and every crime in the calendar of civil rights has been committed against them.

Partition has made it impossible for the nation to develop, impossible to have democracy and impossible to have anything in the country but civil war. This evil has been persistent for many years. It came to the surface in 1968 and 1969 with the demand for civil rights, and the consequent attack on the nationalist population has meant that men have again had to take up arms to defend their people. It is a defensive war and – I love to hear this repeated as often as possible – it is generally admitted that the guerrilla cannot be defeated. So quite obviously I would like to see Britain withdraw her troops and partition end.

There has been a lot of thought about the role of Protestants in a united Ireland, and the federal idea is well advanced, where people could control their own destinies on a more local level. The election system would have to be revised so that Protestants had more representation. After the Treaty we made peace with the Protestant Ascendancy here and I see no reason why we cannot do the same with the Northern Protestants. And in any case the Protestants – the Northern Protestants in particular – were the beginning of our democracy, the beginning of our peace movement and of the republican tradition. You had Wolfe Tone and the United Irishmen. Wolfe Tone was a Protestant; he was the first Protestant who sat down among Catholics to work towards emancipation. We can never forget these men. We have a debt towards Protestants and they towards us and I am confident that if the British withdrew there would be no bloodbath. It's the presence of the British and their intrigues which make sure that this evil continues.

JOSEPH SWEENEY: Being an Ulsterman from Donegal, I don't feel there's all that much difference between the Northern Protestant and the Northern Catholic, because from my own boyhood days I have had many contacts with both groups and still have many friends there. I personally don't think the present campaign of violence is doing any good to bring them together, but I think it must be said that the British government is responsible for the divisions which do exist. They have perpetrated division from the time Lord Randolph Churchill referred to playing the Orange card, and Westminster have always backed up the Orange Order as against the nationalist organizations. They wanted a firm base for themselves in the North.

My hope is that there will be a final reconciliation between all our people. I think we have a lot to offer one another. The North has been traditionally industrial and the rest of Ireland has been agricultural and these should be complementary rather than kept apart. The Northerners I know are great businessmen, and I would say that a lot of businessmen here wouldn't be long in business once they were able to extend through the whole country. I would certainly welcome the Protestants. I never make any distinction about what a man's religion is. I meet them on their own terms. I like to judge a man as I meet him and religion never enters into it. In these days when religious attitudes all around are changing I don't think there's any great difference between us all.

MARTIN WALTON: All you can do is hope that the country will be united, and that we'll all have the sense enough to build a nation from it, along with the courage and determination and all the other requisites. I think that's the only hope. It's utter nonsense to talk about 'bombing a million Protestants in'. That's certainly not what the IRA is trying to do. There's no reason why we cannot all live together, and in fact Protestants have been the most progressive of all in the movement for independence from Britain. If you go through our history for the past 200 years, you have Wolfe Tone, Thomas Davis, William Shaw (a completely forgotten man), Isaac Butt, the founder of the Home Rule business, Parnell of course. Coming down further you have Roger Casement, Erskine Childers and a lot of others. I think in our little company in 1916 there were four Protestants who went out with us.

JOHN L. O'SULLIVAN: There is only one thing that I hope for Ireland, and that is that some agreement will be made between our people in the North and ourselves. And I hope the British government, who have more power than anyone else in the matter, will come out as soon as possible and try to bridge the gap that is there. I think it's their duty, they inflicted this on the country and I believe there is good will enough among the British people to do this. I know that the great majority of the Irish people want peace and prosperity and there is no such thing as an anti-British feeling here. The only feeling we have is that the leaders of British public opinion can still learn the lesson that history should have taught them by now.

TOM BARRY: Well, I'm an old man. I'm in my eightieth year, and I don't like pontificating. I believe that old men should stand aside and leave it to people who are responsible. But I'm as sure as I'm sitting here facing you that you'll never have peace amongst the Six County people, or between Britain and Ireland, until the British army of occupation is removed from our island. I'm positive of that. This thing that's going on now, it may fail, it may fizzle out, it may be patched up – I don't know because I have nothing to do with things there now. But I'm as positive as day follows night and night follows day and that rivers flow that you'll never have peace in this country until the British army and the British administration in the Six Counties is shifted. That is only a surmise of mine of course, but it is a surmise based on the facts of Irish history. There is always another generation who will grow up and try to drive the British out. Now I see the danger there of sectarian warfare, but I have never met an Irishman of any creed who thought it was a wrong thing for a man to be a Jew or a Muslim or anything else. I know that here in Cork the medium-sized farmers – Protestant and Catholic – get together to help each other out at harvest time. The *meitheall* they call it in Irish, the potato-digging, and Protestants and Catholics come together to help get the crop up, and afterwards they go out and have a night together. This thing has been exaggerated out of its context, this hatred between Protestants and Catholics. But unfortunately this division has been fostered by the British, who have long been the masters of divide-and-rule. Now I know that if the British left you may have isolated incidents of madmen still going around killing one another, as you will always have, but I have sufficient faith in my fellow countrymen in the North that they will settle down and end this sectarian killing once the British are out of the way. You may have some of it, but in the long run it is the one hope for the Irish people.

Bibliography

Barry, Tom: *Guerrilla Days in Ireland*, Anvil Books, Tralee, Co. Kerry, 1968.

Beaslai, Piaras: *Michael Collins and the Making of a New Ireland*, Vols. I and II, Phoenix Publishing Company, Dublin, 1930.

Beaslai, Piaras, and O Dubhghusa, Sean (eds.): *An tOglach*, Old IRA Publications, Dublin, 1971.

Bell, Geoffrey: *The Protestants of Ulster*, Pluto Press, London, 1976.

Bell, J. Bowyer: *The Secret Army: A History of the IRA, 1916–1970*, Sphere Books, London, 1972.

Beloff, Max: *Imperial Sunset: Britain's Liberal Empire, 1897–1921*, Vol. I, Alfred A. Knopf, New York, 1970.

Boyce, D. G.: *Englishmen and Irish Troubles: British Public Opinion and the Making of Irish Policy, 1918–22*, Jonathan Cape, London, 1972.

Broad, Richard, et al.: *The Troubles*, Macdonald-Futura, London, 1980.

Butler, Ewan: *Barry's Flying Column*, Leo Cooper, London, 1971.

Capuchin Annual, 1966–72, Church Street, Dublin.

Caulfield, Max: *The Easter Rebellion*, Frederick Muller, London, 1964.

Clarke, Thomas J.: *Glimpses of an Irish Felon's Prison Life*, National Publications Committee, Cork, 1970.

Coffey, Thomas M.: *Agony at Easter: The 1916 Irish Uprising*, Penguin Books, Harmondsworth, 1971.

Coogan, Tim Pat: *The IRA*, Fontana, London, 1971.

Cronin, Sean: *The Revolutionaries: The Story of Twelve Great Irishmen*, Republican Publications, Dublin, 1971.

Dail Eireann: *Minutes of Proceedings of the First Parliament of the Republic of Ireland*, 1919–21, The Stationery Office, Dublin.

Dail Eireann: *Debate on the Treaty between Great Britain and Ireland*, 1922, The Stationery Office, Dublin.

Dalton, Charles: *With the Dublin Brigade 1917–1921*, Peter Davies, London, 1929.

D'Alton, Revd E. A.: *History of Ireland*, Vols. VI–VIII, Gresham Publishing Company, London, 1925.

Dangerfield, George: *The Damnable Question: A Study in Anglo-Irish Relations*, Quartet Books, London, 1979.

Duff, Charles: *Six Days to Shake an Empire*, J. M. Dent, London, 1966.

Dunraven, Earl of: *The Legacy of Past Years: A Study of Irish History*, John Murray, London, 1912.

Easter Commemoration Digest, Graphic Publications, Dublin, 1966.

Edwards, Owen Dudley and Pyle, Fergus (eds.): *1916: The Easter Rising*, MacGibbon and Kee, London, 1968.

Ellis, P. Beresford: *A History of the Irish Working Class*, Victor Gollancz, London, 1972.

Farrell, Michael: *Northern Ireland: The Orange State*, Pluto Press, London, 1976.

Figgis, Darrel: *Recollections of the Irish War*, Ernest Benn, London, 1927.

Fitzgerald, Redmond: *Cry Blood, Cry Erin*, Barrie and Rockliff, London, 1966.

Fitzgerald, William G.: *The Voice of Ireland*, Virtue and Co., Dublin, 1924.

Fitzgibbon, Constantine: *Out of the Lion's Paw*, Macdonald, London, 1969.

Forester, Margery: *Michael Collins – The Lost Leader*, Sidgwick and Jackson, London, 1971.

Fox, R. M.: *Green Banners: The Story of the Irish Struggle*, Secker and Warburg, London, 1938.

Greaves, C. Desmond: *The Life and Times of James Connolly*, Lawrence and Wishart, London, 1961.

Greaves, C. Desmond: *Liam Mellows and the Irish Revolution*, Lawrence and Wishart, London, 1971.

Hewitt, James (ed.): *Eye-Witnesses to Ireland in Revolt*, Osprey Publishing, Reading, 1974.

Inglis, Brian: *Roger Casement*, Hodder and Stoughton, London, 1973.

Inglis, Brian: *The Story of Ireland*, Faber and Faber, London, 1970.

'IO': *The Administration of Ireland, 1920*, Philip Allan and Co., London, 1921.

Irish Uprising 1916–1922, The, A CBS Legacy Collection Book, New York, 1966.

Jackson, T. A., *Ireland Her Own*, Cobbett Press, London, 1947.

Jones, Thomas: *Whitehall Diary; Vol. III, Ireland, 1918–25*, Keith Middlemas (ed.), Oxford University Press, London, 1971.

Kee, Robert: *The Green Flag: A History of Irish Nationalism*, Weidenfeld and Nicolson, London, 1972.

Kee, Robert: *Ireland: A History*, Weidenfeld and Nicolson, London, 1980.

Levenson, Samuel: *Maud Gonne*, Cassell, London, 1976.

Longford, Lord (Frank Pakenham): *Peace by Ordeal*, Sidgwick and Jackson, London, 1972.

Longford, Lord and O'Neill, Thomas P.: *Eamon de Valera*, Hutchinson, London, 1970.

Lyons, F. S. L.: *The Fall of Parnell*, Routledge and Kegan Paul, London, 1960.

Lyons, F. S. L.: *Culture and Anarchy in Ireland 1890–1939*, Oxford University Press, Oxford, 1979.

Macardle, Dorothy: *The Irish Republic*, Victor Gollancz, London, 1937.

McCann, Eamon: *War in an Irish Town*, Penguin Books, Harmondsworth, 1974.

Mac Eoin, Uinseann (ed.): *Survivors*, Argenta Publications, Dublin, 1980.

McHugh, Roger (ed.): *Dublin 1916*, Arlington Books, London, 1966.

MacLochlainn, Piaras F. (ed.): *Last Words: Letters and Statements of the Leaders Executed after the Rising at Easter 1916*, Kilmainham Jail Restoration Society, Dublin, 1971.

MacLysaght, Edward: *Changing Times: Ireland since 1898*, Colin Smyth, Gerrards Cross, Bucks, 1978.

Macready, Sir Nevil: *Annals of an Active Life*, Vol. II, Hutchinson, London, 1924.

Mansergh, Nicholas: *The Irish Question 1840–1921*, George Allen and Unwin, London, 1975.

Martin, F. X., OSA (ed.): *Leaders and Men of the Easter Rising: Dublin 1916*, Methuen, London, 1967.

Morris, James: *Pax Britannica: The Climax of an Empire*, Faber and Faber, London, 1968.

Neeson, Eoin: *The Civil War in Ireland*, The Mercier Press, Cork, 1966.

Neeson, Eoin: *The Life and Death of Michael Collins*, The Mercier Press, Cork, 1968.

Neill, Kenneth: *An Illustrated History of the Irish People*, Gill and Macmillan, Dublin, 1979.

Neligan, David: *The Spy in the Castle*, MacGibbon and Kee, London, 1968.

O'Brien, Conor Cruise: *States of Ireland*, Hutchinson, London, 1972.

O'Brien, Conor Cruise: 'Passion and Cunning: The Politics of W. B. Yeats' in *Literature in Revolution, TriQuarterly 23/24*, Newman, Charles, and White, George (eds.): Northwestern University, Evanston, Ill., 1972.

O'Brien, Nora Connolly: *Portrait of a Rebel Father*, Talbot Press, Dublin, 1935.

O'Casey, Sean: *Autobiography*, Vols. II–IV, Pan Books, London, 1972.

O'Connor, Batt: *With Michael Collins in the Fight for Irish Independence*, Peter Davies, London, 1929.

O'Connor, Frank: *The Big Fellow: Michael Collins and the Irish Revolution*, Clonmore and Reynolds, Dublin, 1965.

O'Connor, Frank: 'Guests of the Nation', in *Tears of the Shamrock: An Anthology of Contemporary Short Stories on the Theme of Ireland's Struggle for Nationhood*, Marcus, David (ed.), Wolfe Publishing, London, 1972.

O'Connor, Rt Hon. Sir James: *History of Ireland 1798–1924*, Vols. I and II, Edward Arnold, London, 1925.

O'Connor, Ulick: *The Troubles: Ireland 1912–22*, Bobbs-Merril, New York, 1975.

O Dubhghaill, M. (ed.): *Insurrection Fires at Eastertide*, The Mercier Press, Cork, 1966.

O'Faolain, Sean: *The Irish*, Penguin Books, West Drayton, 1947.

O'Malley, Ernie: *The Singing Flame*, Anvil Books, Dublin, 1978.

Pearse, Padraic H.: *Collected Works: Political Writings and Speeches*, Phoenix Publishing, Dublin, 1924.

Ranelagh, John: *Ireland: An Illustrated History*, Collins, London, 1981.

Rebel Cork's Fighting Story, Anvil Books, Tralee, Co. Kerry.

Riddell, Lord: *Lord Riddell's War Diary 1914–1918*, Ivor Nicholson and Watson, London, 1933.

Ryan, Desmond: *James Connolly*, Talbot Press, Dublin, 1924.

Ryan, Desmond: *The Rising: The Complete Story of Easter Week*, Golden Eagle Books, Dublin, 1949.

Scott, C. P.: *The Political Diaries of C. P. Scott 1911–1928*, Wilson, Trevor (ed.), Collins, London, 1970.

Shaw, George Bernard: 'Preface for Politicians', *John Bull's Other Island*, Constable, London, 1930.

Shaw, George Bernard: *The Matter with Ireland*, Greene, David H., and Lawrence, Dan H. (eds.), Rupert Hart-Davis, London, 1962.

Stephens, James: *The Insurrection in Dublin*, Maunsel and Co., Dublin, 1916.

Stevenson, Frances: *Lloyd George: A Diary by Frances Stevenson*, Taylor, A. J. P. (ed.), Hutchinson, London, 1971.

Sworn to be Free: The Complete Book of IRA Jailbreaks 1918–1921, Anvil Books, Tralee, Co. Kerry, 1971.

Talbot, Hayden, *Michael Collins' Own Story*, Hutchinson, London, 1923.

Taylor, Rex: *Michael Collins*, Four Square, London, 1961.

Thompson, Paul: *Voice of the Past: Oral History*, Oxford University Press, Oxford, 1978.

Thornley, David: 'De Valera Between the Wars' in *Empire to Commonwealth*, No. 46 of *History of the 20th Century*, Taylor, A. J. P. (ed.), BPC Publishing, London.

Weekly Irish Times: *Sinn Fein Rebellion Handbook*, Irish Times, Dublin, 1917.

Williams, Desmond (ed.): *The Irish Struggle*, Routledge and Kegan Paul, London, 1966.

Yeats, W. B.: *Selected Poetry*, Jeffares, A. Norman (ed.), Pan Books, London, 1965.

Yeats, W. B.: *Selected Prose*, Jeffares, A. Norman (ed.), Pan Books, London, 1976.

Younger, Calton: *Ireland's Civil War*, Fontana, London, 1970.

Younger, Calton: *A State of Disunion*, Frederick Muller, London, 1972.

Index

Page numbers in italics refer to interviews with the nine contributors.

Irish National Aid Association, 95,
102
Irish Parliamentary Party, 15, 18,
106, 109, 114, 117, 123
Irish Red Cross, 328
Irish Republican Army, 26, 53, 74,
133, 135, 140–43, 146, 154–9,
163, 167, 172, 174, 177, 179,
181, 185, 187–8, 193, 197, 208–9,
218, 228–9, 232–3, 238–43,
246–7, 252, 261, 263, 268, 272–5,
277, 281–2, 288, 307–8, 316–19,
321, 328–30, 332–8, 349–53, 359
Irish Republican Brotherhood, 7,
11, 21–3, 27, 30, 36, 41, 47–9,
53, 100–102, 110–13, 134, 193,
264–5
Irish Times, 4, 98, 148
Irish Trades Union Congress, 162
Irish Transport and General
Workers' Union, 25
Irish Volunteers, 24, 26–8, 30,
32–4, 39, 47, 49–50, 52–8, 64,
67, 70, 74, 76–7, 84, 95–6,
101–2, 107, 110–11, 115, 118,
121, 125, 131, 328
Irish Volunteers' Dependants'
Fund, 95
Irish White Cross, 209
Iveagh, Lord, 24

Jacob's biscuit factory, 55, 58–9
James II, King, 345
Johnstone, Colonel Edgeworth, 139,
141–2
John the Divine, Saint, 49
Jones, Tom, 224, 257

Kavanagh, Joe, 118, 136, 217
Kavanagh, Patrick, 331
Kavanagh, Sean, *34–5*, 53, *56–7,
125–6, 135–8, 173–5, 177–8*, 200,
201–5, 210–11, 214–16, 234, 298,
304, *324–5*
Kearney, Peadar, 22, 321, 324

Kelly, Nicholas, 232–3
Kennedy, Tim, 140, 155–6
Kent, Thomas, 82
Keogh, Tom, 217
Keynes, John Maynard, 104
Kiernan, Helen, 108
Kiernan, Kitty, 281
Kildare Street Club, 139
Kilmainham Jail, 77–8, 203–4,
210–11, 297
Kilmichael (Co. Cork), 181–2, 196,
285, 332
King George V Hospital (now St
Briccin's), 178, 212–13, 320
King, Major, 202, 204
Kingsbridge Station, 63, 86, 157,
168, 201–2
King's Liverpool, 220
King's Shropshire Light Infantry,
146
Kipling, Rudyard, 75
Kitchener, Lord, 32, 97–8
Knox, General Charles Edmund,
343

Labour Party (British), 31, 224
Lalor, Fintan, 324
Lancers, 55, 57
Land Commission (Free State),
329–31
Land League, 12, 25, 155
Land Purchase Acts, 309
Larkin, Jim, 25, 26
League of Nations, 270
Leinster Fusiliers, 300
Lemass, Sean, 111
Lenin, Vladimir, 20
Lennon, Jimmy, 201
Leonard, Joe, 216–17
Lewes Jail, 108
Liberal Party, 7, 18–19, 30–31
Liberty Hall (Dublin), 50, 52, 69,
140
Lincoln Jail, 123, 150
Lindsay, Lieutenant, 77